The **PACIFIC COAST** *of* **MEXICO**

The PACIFIC COAST of MEXICO

From Mazatlán to Ixtapa-Zihuatanejo

A Traveler's Guide by Memo Barroso

Harmony Books/New York

A mi madre Consuelo y a mi padre Guillermo
con todo mi corazón

Copyright © 1986 by Guillermo Barroso
All rights reserved. No part of this book may be repro-
duced or transmitted in any form or by any means,
electronic or mechanical, including photocopying, re-
cording, or by any information storage and retrieval
system, without permission in writing from the pub-
lisher.

Published by Harmony Books, a division of Crown Pub-
lishers, Inc., 225 Park Avenue South, New York, New
York 10003, and represented in Canada by the Cana-
dian MANDA Group
HARMONY and colophon are trademarks of Crown
Publishers, Inc.
Manufactured in the United States of America

Cartography by True Sims

Library of Congress Cataloging-in-Publication Data

Barroso, Memo.
   The Pacific coast of Mexico from Mazatlán to Ixtapa-
Zihuatanejo.

   1. Mexico—Description and travel—1987–Guide
books. 2. Pacific Coast (Mexico)—Description and travel—
Guide-books.   3. Beaches—Mexico—Pacific Coast—
Guide-books.   I. Title.
F1209.B37   1986   917.2'04834   86-19467
ISBN 0-517-55860-2 (pbk.)
10 9 8 7 6 5 4 3 2
FIRST EDITION

Contents

The
PACIFIC
COAST of
MEXICO

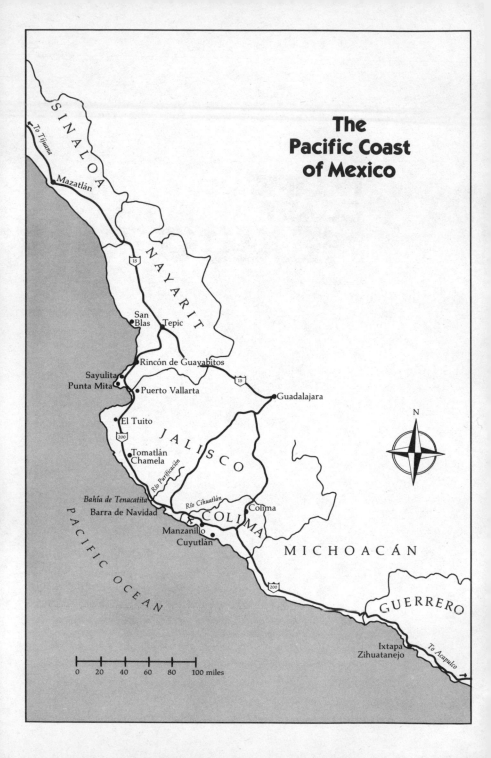

The
Pacific Coast
of Mexico

INTRODUCTION

THE REGION

This book covers an 800-mile-long stretch of Mexico's beautiful Pacific coast. Included in this area are the popular beach resorts of Mazatlán, Puerto Vallarta, Manzanillo, and Ixtapa-Zihuatanejo, as well as the smaller beach towns of San Blas, Guayabitos, and Barra de Navidad, and a large number of tiny beach villages and beautiful, desolate beaches.

For the most part, this region of Mexico's Pacific coast is edged by towering mountain chains that are offshoots of the western Sierra Madre. Cradled between the mountains and the sea are numerous valleys. Some are tiny, a mere rest on the curving, steep road before another set of hills and mountain ranges; others are huge valleys that can take an hour or longer to cross by car. With the fertile soils formed over the eons from mountain sediments brought down by the rains, valleys such as Puerto Vallarta's Valle de Banderas are important centers for cattle breeding and agriculture.

As you travel south from Mazatlán to Puerto Vallarta, Manzanillo, and finally to Ixtapa-Zihuatanejo, the highway unrolls a travelogue of farmers tilling the land and planting or harvesting crops, boys tending herds of cattle and goats, and women washing clothes in the rivers.

Being a snowbird, you may not know that you are passing thousands of acres of coconut, mango, lime, and banana plantations. Or that the white birds sitting on the humped backs of grazing Brahma cattle are cattle egrets picking off parasites.

Throughout the whole region, a menu unfolds of choice beaches to suit every taste. The selection is varied, from Mazatlán's and

Puerto Vallarta's bustling beaches to the more low-key beach towns of San Blas and Barra de Navidad, to the desolate beaches of Punta Mita and Chamela. Compare the beaches to your favorite, delectable dessert and you'll find you can never get enough of that sweet, sweet stuff.

CLIMATE

In the region's coastal areas, temperatures range from a low of 60°F. on a few cool winter nights from December to February to highs of 100°F. in the sizzling month of May. During the rainy season, mid-June to mid-October, daytime temperatures range between 80° and 95°F., but the high humidity makes it feel even hotter. During the rest of the year the average daytime temperature is 85°F.

Unlike the constant drizzling rains that are so common in North American winters, intermittent tropical downpours usually occur in the afternoons and may pour as much as 6 inches in half an hour. A typical rainy-season day begins with a clear, bright sunny morning filled with the scent of damp soil and greenery. Toward noon, a few fleecy white clouds appear in the sky and grow in number and size as the hours pass. The first downpour of the day occurs around 4:00 P.M. and others may follow during the evening and night. During the winter season, a few days of cloudy, rainy weather can be expected as the aftermath of large cold-weather fronts making their way down from the United States and Canada.

Remember, in the tropical areas of Mexico, there are basically two seasons—the hot one and the very hot one.

VEGETATION

A generous amount of sunshine and the seasonal rains make the region's vegetation among the most varied and rich in the country.

In the lowlands adjacent to the coast, the vegetation is of the savannah type: tall grass and scattered trees such as *cuastecomate*, *huanacaxtle*, and other indigenous trees that still carry the names given them by the Indians who once inhabited these lands.

The region's mountain area, climbing to an altitude of 2,000 feet, is covered with tropical forest or jungle vegetation. Much like a greenhouse effect, the tall jungle trees—pochote, brazil, and rosewoods such as *barcino* and *tampinziran*—mesh together to create a canopy preventing the sun's rays from penetrating to the ground to dry up its reserves of moisture. The heat that reflects off the treetops causes high humidity beneath the tree canopy, providing moisture to ferns, philodendrons, and other undergrowth. At night, when the temperatures drop, the humidity forms condensation on the leaves which drops to the ground, and the cycle begins again.

Ironically, although the vegetation is rich, the ground is often made up of clay, sand, and rock with only about a foot of fertile topsoil.

WILDLIFE

It's only natural that a region of such rich and varied vegetation would have the accompanying wildlife. The region teems with small species such as armadillos, opossums, skunks, badgers, squirrels, etc. In some remote and inaccessible areas, jaguar, deer, and wild boar are common. Forever elusive but always present are snakes and numerous species of iguanas and lizards.

The region is also a paradise for bird watchers as there are dozens of tropical and water bird species. Check the bird watching, beachcombing, fishing, snorkeling, and scuba-diving sections of this guide for more detailed information on particular birds, fish, and shells found in the region.

THE PEOPLE

The Mexican people of today are the result of over 450 years of blending of Spanish and Indian ethnic groups. *Mestizo* is the name given to the people of this ethnic blend. But the family origins of most Mexicans are lost in the chromosomes of history, and to indicate their origin, Mexicans will proudly mention their city and the state where they were born rather than their ethnic backgrounds.

GETTING THERE

Airplane Aeromexico, Mexicana, and Western are the main airlines serving the international airports of Mazatlán, Puerto Vallarta, Manzanillo, and Ixtapa-Zihuatanejo with direct flights from many United States cities. Canadian travelers have to change.planes at a connecting American city.

Before buying your ticket from an airline, check with travel agents for the best deal on excursions, off-season promotions, and vacation packages. In some cases, airfare and 6 nights at one of the better hotels will not cost much more than regular airfare.

If you are planning to visit the Pacific coast during the high tourist season—December through March—make airline reservations about 6 months in advance.

Bus Mexico has an extensive bus system connecting every city in the country with even the smallest and remotest village. Mexican buses are inexpensive and some first-class lines have buses as comfortable as those in the United States and Canada.

Tres Estrellas bus line has daily departures from Tijuana at the United States border to Mazatlán and continuing on to Puerto Vallarta and Manzanillo. From there, to reach Ixtapa-Zihuatanejo you must change buses at the city of Lázaro Cárdenas. Numerous bus routes from Tijuana to Guadalajara pass through Mazatlán and Tepic where connections can be made to Puerto Vallarta and San Blas. Direct bus lines connect Guadalajara to Manzanillo.

Here a few pointers for bus travelers:

1. Mexican bus tickets are not open-dated; they are valid for a specific hour and day. If you miss the bus, you lose your money.

2. In first-class and on most second-class bus lines, you will get a numbered bus seat. You may pick the seat of your choice: *ventanilla* (window) or *pasillo* (aisle).

3. First-class buses are slightly more expensive than second-class and generally faster and more comfortable.

4. There is a lot of passenger traffic on weekends and at long holiday periods such as Christmas and Easter. Buy your bus ticket at least one or two days in advance during these periods.

5. Do not drink a lot of liquids before a long trip unless you are sure your bus has a toilet or makes frequent stops.

Car The most pleasant way to see the region is by car. A car gives you the freedom to reach remote villages and hidden beaches; to stop when and where you want; and best of all, to carry camping, diving, and fishing equipment that will make your vacation more enjoyable. However, driving in Mexico requires extra caution, attention, and patience. You will have to contend with narrow, two-lane roads filled with potholes, inadequate road signs, animals grazing on the road's edge, and of course, careless drivers.

Road traffic is heavy on the main roads from the United States border to Guadalajara, but thins down considerably from Tepic to Puerto Vallarta and even more from Puerto Vallarta to Manzanillo and Ixtapa-Zihuatanejo. For safer driving, keep in mind the following hints:

1. Avoid driving at night and never park your vehicle for the night alongside the highway.

2. Keep your speed under 50 mph (75 km per hour) on two-way highways. The speed limit in cities is 40 mph (60 kph) unless otherwise posted.

3. Keep a constant eye on your rearview mirror, especially before passing a slow vehicle.

4. Always slow down when approaching a narrow bridge (*puente angosto*). The rule, supposedly, is that the vehicle closest to the bridge has the right of way. Don't trust this rule.

5. *Topes* are concrete or asphalt bumps designed to slow down traffic through towns. Keep an eye out for them as they are not always marked.

6. In many cities one-way streets are not always marked. If in doubt as to what direction the traffic flows, check to see which direction the cars are parked. When approaching intersections, stop and check traffic to your right and left.

Car Insurance American and Canadian insurance policies are not valid in Mexico, but you can buy short-term insurance at border towns as you cross into Mexico. If you are a member of the American Automobile Association (AAA), or its Canadian counterparts, you can buy Mexican car insurance in advance. These automobile associations are also a valuable source of good maps and tourist information.

Fuel Pemex (Petróleos Mexicanos) is the only oil company throughout Mexico and is government owned and controlled. Gas stations are found everywhere and generally there is no problem buying gas, but during heavy vacation periods, some stations may run out. Diesel is available at all gas stations. There are two types of gas in Mexico—Nova (81-octane leaded gasoline), selling for about 17¢ a liter, and Extra (94-octane unleaded gasoline) at around 22¢ a liter. There are 3.8 liters in a gallon. In the Pacific coast area it is difficult to find Extra (unleaded gasoline), so it is advisable to drive a car that uses leaded gas.

Your Car's Mechanical Condition The best way to avoid mechanical problems is to have your car in top shape before leaving on your trip. If you know how to make minor car repairs, pack your own tools and some spare parts, such as a fan belt, condenser, points, spark plugs, etc. Some car brands are not sold in Mexico (Volvo, Mazda, Honda, Fiat, Cadillac, Pontiac, and Oldsmobile are among them) and you could run into serious complications getting parts in the event of a breakdown.

Green Angels Easily recognizable by the green pickup trucks they drive, the Green Angels are mechanics sponsored by the Department of Tourism who offer free mechanical assistance to tourists. They cruise the highways and their frequency depends on how heavily traveled the highway is. There is no Green Angel service between Manzanillo and Ixtapa-Zihuatanejo. Tipping is recommended.

Train Two trains depart daily from Nogales at the United States border to Guadalajara. They stop at Mazatlán and Tepic, where you can transfer to a bus to reach Puerto Vallarta and points south.

Ferry Check the "Getting There" sections of Mazatlán and Puerto Vallarta for ferry information.

ENTRY REQUIREMENTS AND CUSTOMS

American and Canadian visitors to Mexico need a tourist card. To obtain one you must have proof of citizenship. Birth certificate, valid passport, voter's registration card, naturalization papers, or armed-services discharge papers are acceptable. A driver's license is not valid for this purpose.

Tourist cards can be obtained at the following places:

1. Mexican consulates in major American and Canadian cities.

2. Offices of the Mexican National Tourist Council in major American and Canadian cities.

3. Authorized airline offices.

4. Mexican immigration offices at point of entry.

Tourist cards are issued free of charge and are valid for up to 6 months. When you obtain your tourist card, it is advisable to ask for more time than you need as a precaution against delayed or lost flights, illness, car problems, etc.

It is usually difficult to obtain extension permits unless you can prove that you are in an emergency situation. Often the easiest way to obtain additional time in Mexico is to leave the country and visit the nearest border point and obtain a new tourist card as you return.

When traveling with their parents, children under 15 can be included on one parent's tourist card. But take note: a parent cannot leave the country alone if children are included on his or her tourist card. To avoid any complications in case of separate departures, request individual tourist cards for each member of the family.

To travel alone in Mexico, minors under 18 need a notarized affidavit in duplicate, certifying that the parents or legal guardians authorize their trip. Birth certificates or naturalization papers will also be necessary to obtain the tourist card.

All visitors must turn in their tourist cards to the authorities when leaving Mexico. If your tourist card is lost or stolen, contact the nearest immigration office. There are Mexican immigration offices in Mazatlán, Puerto Vallarta, Manzanillo, and Ixtapa-Zihuatanejo.

Both Canadian and American authorities suggest that if you are planning an extended visit, you might want to register with the consulate representative of your country so that you can be reached in case of emergency.

Visitors may take into Mexico the following items duty free: up to 110 pounds of clothing and personal articles; one camera, one movie camera, and 12 rolls of film for each; used sporting equipment; 200 cigarettes, 50 cigars, or 9 ounces of loose tobacco (adults only); and professional equipment or instruments for personal use.

To take vehicles, trailers, and boats into Mexico you must obtain a Temporary Importation Permit at the border entry point. To obtain this permit you will need proof of ownership, state, registration card, valid license plates, and valid driver's license. Temporary Importation Permits are issued free of charge and are

MEXICAN HOLIDAYS AND *PUENTES*

Millions of Mexicans live and work in urban areas such as Mexico City, with its twelve or thirteen or who knows how many million inhabitants.

The tensions and pressures of city life are like a great storm that builds up and finally unchains itself during the holiday periods. Then huge waves of vacationers from the storm's centers—Mexico City, Guadalajara, Puebla—hit beach resorts all over Mexico, flooding buses, trains, airplanes, hotels, and restaurants. These human storms are very predictable and occur during Semana Santa (Easter Week) and Navidad (Christmas).

Foreign vacationers planning to visit Mexico during these holiday periods are advised to make transportation and hotel reservations 3 to 4 months before their visit.

Puentes, literally meaning "bridges," have become a tradition among bureaucrats and white- and blue-collar workers. Let's assume, for example, that a Thursday happens to be a legal holiday. This day automatically becomes a pillar of the bridge, with Saturday and Sunday being the other pillars. The temptation to leave the bridge unfinished is too great and thousands of workers will add the missing span by getting Friday off, thus becoming architects of their vacation bridges.

The legal Mexican holidays are the following:

January 1, New Year's Day
February 5, Flag Day
March 21, Nationalization of the Oil Industry
May 1, Labor Day
May 5, Battle of Puebla
September 16, Independence Day
October 12, Columbus Day
November 20, Anniversary of the Revolution
December 12, Our Lady of Guadalupe (not a legal holiday, but nevertheless celebrated throughout the country)
December 25, Christmas Day

Puentes, however, will rarely affect your traveling plans.

valid for the same period of time as the vehicle owner's tourist card. The temporary importation of a vehicle into Mexico is noted on your tourist card, and you cannot leave the country without it. In the event that you should need to leave Mexico without your vehicle, you must leave it in the custody of customs and you will be charged a storage fee.

Boat owners must pay a small monthly fee for boats under 22 feet in length and must place a customs bond on boats over 22 feet.

BRINGING PETS TO MEXICO

If you wish to bring your dog or cat to Mexico a vaccination certificate is required signed by a licensed veterinarian and must include the date of vaccination, type of vaccine used, and a description of the pet. A rabies shot for dogs over 3 months of age is necessary 30 days prior to departure. This does not apply to cats. All pets must be free of disease upon inspection at the port of entry. For additional information in the United States write to Office of Veterinarian Public Health Services, Center for Disease Control, Atlanta, Georgia 30333. In Canada contact the nearest customs office. As a precaution, contact the nearest Mexican consulate to ensure your pet meets the necessary entry requirements.

DON'T BE A DOPE

Whereas Mexico has a very liberal attitude toward alcohol (you could actually send a 10-year-old to the nearest liquor store to buy you a bottle of tequila), it is totally intolerant of drugs. A single joint could easily land you in jail for months before your case came up for trial. In Mexico you are guilty until proven innocent and bond is denied to foreigners on the basis that you could leave the country before being tried.

Be wary of local strangers who invite you to smoke a joint. Pot smoking is not a Mexican custom. It's a serious social taboo, not a symbol of camaraderie and is not done with the same casualness as in North America.

RETURNING HOME

UNITED STATES CITIZENS

Personal duty-free exemption on articles acquired abroad is $400 U.S. if the articles are for personal use or gifts; you have not claimed the exemption within the preceding 30 days, and the articles accompany you.

You may include in this duty-free exemption 100 cigars and 200 cigarettes and 1 liter (33.8 fl. oz.) wine, beer, or liquor if you are 21 or over. Customs enforces the laws of the state in which you arrive. Some states do not allow individuals to import more liquor than listed even if they are willing to pay the duty.

Articles imported in excess of your exemption will be subject to duty. Articles purchased in duty-free shops are subject to duty and restrictions but may be included in your personal exemption.

Some items must meet certain requirements, require a license or permit, or may be prohibited entry. Among restricted or prohibited articles are: firearms and ammunition; fruits, plants, vegetables, and their products; hazardous articles (e.g., fireworks); lottery tickets; meats, poultry, and products; narcotics and dangerous drugs including medicine containing same; switchblade knives; wildlife; pets.

CANADIAN CITIZENS

Personal duty-free exemption on articles acquired abroad is $300 Canadian once every calendar year if articles are for personal use or gifts and articles accompany you. Included in the duty-free exemption are 50 cigars, 200 cigarettes, and 2 lbs. of tobacco, and 1.1 liters (40 oz.) of wine or liquor or twenty-four 12 oz. cans or bottles or the equivalent—8.2 liters (288 fl. oz.) of beer or ale if you meet the age requirements set by the province or territory you're entering. Goods exceeding this amount are subject to duty.

You may not bring firearms that can be easily concealed without a permit from your local police authorities. Automatic weapons and fireworks are prohibited.

For specific information on livestock, pets, meat and meat products, plants, fresh fruit and vegetables, contact: Agriculture Canada, Ottawa, Ontario K1A 0C5.

There are a large number of animals, birds, reptiles, fish, insects, and certain forms of plant life that are on the endangered species list and are prohibited, including their by-products. To find out what you can bring back, write: Convention Administrator, Canadian Wildlife Service, Environment Canada, Ottawa, Ontario K1A 0E7.

The pamphlet "I Declare" is available at travel agencies, passport offices, or by writing Public Relations Branch, Revenue Canada, Customs and Excise, Connaught Building, Ottawa, Ontario, K1A 0L5.

WHAT TO BRING

The weather in this region is ideal for wearing nothing but a big smile, but it is nevertheless advisable to wear some clothes to match it. Here are a few tips to help you choose your wardrobe.

1. Wear lightweight, light-colored fabrics—dark colors soak up the sun.

2. Wear cotton and cotton-blend fabrics. Clothes made entirely of synthetic fibers do not "breathe" and are hot and sticky.

3. Wear loose pants. Tight designer jeans will make you look sexy, but as you sweat you will feel like a wet banana in its skin.

4. Take a sweater for cool nights in the winter months.

5. Take lightweight rain gear for the rainy season (mid-June through mid-October) and the occasional rainy days in the winter months (December through March).

TAX

Impuesto is the Spanish word for tax, and it's interesting to note that it comes from the Spanish verb *imponer*, "to impose." In Mexico, there is a steep 15 percent sales tax that is levied on most items and services. This tax is called added value tax (I.V.A.) and is either included in the price or added at the time of sale. The I.V.A. is not charged on unprocessed food items (vegetables, fruits, meat, etc.), at market food stands, and should not be charged by street and beach vendors. Whenever you are charged the 15 percent in boutiques, shops, etc., ask for a receipt (*nota*). If they have no receipts, then you have the leverage to purchase the item without paying the tax.

6. A hat and sandals are advisable for the beach as well as a pair of comfortable walking shoes.

7. Bring personal items such as hearing-aid batteries, contact lens solution and cleaner, sunscreen, suntan lotion, and polarized sunglasses.

Feel free to bring your own fishing, snorkeling equipment, etc., as it is expensive and hard to get.

WHERE TO STAY

The hotels, motels, bungalows, and condo-hotels listed are a selection of the best values for your money. For quick reference they are grouped into five price ranges (for a double room) and all prices quoted are in U.S. dollars.

Cheap: up to $15
Budget: up to $25
Moderate: up to $50
Plush: up to $80
Deluxe: from $81 upward

Inflation makes it impractical to quote actual rates. For dollar bearers, however, the constant devaluation of the peso is nothing but good news. In fact, in the great majority of the hotels in the

---

THE NAKED TRUTH

The closer you get to the equator, the hotter you'll be and the more you'll want to shed your clothes. On most Mexican public beaches, any time you totally expose yourself below your own equator, you run the risk of creating a hot situation.

For liberated women wishing to sunbathe topless at public beaches, the problem usually is not offending morals, but rather attracting morons.

Avoid nude sunbathing around Mexican families, drunks, and in crowds made up mostly of Mexicans. Confine nude sunbathing to desolate beaches and keep your clothes close at hand.

first three categories, room prices were lower by two or more dollars in December 1985 than in December 1984.

Reservations It is recommended that reservations be made 6 months in advance for busy holiday periods—Christmas season, December 20 to January 5, and Easter week. Reservations can be made by phone or telex to major hotels by writing to the address given for each hotel, or by contacting your travel agent. Most hotels in the cheap range do not accept reservations.

European vs. American Plan Briefly, the European Plan is a room without meals and the American Plan is a room with meals. The European Plan gives you the freedom to eat what you want, when you want, and where you want. The American Plan can save you money, but limits you to eating what you are served (there are often specific dining hours) and always in the same restaurant. Also, under this plan there is usually no refund or credit for meals not taken. However, very few hotels in this region offer rooms with meals.

RESTAURANTS

Restaurants in this book are a cross section of the better restaurants in various budget categories. For each restaurant listed I have included the name, address, and telephone number (when available), types of food served, and some personal observations.

In restaurants selected for this guide, I have estimated the cost of a meal consisting of a main course with a soup or salad and a couple of beers or glasses of wine.

Luxury and hotel restaurants are not included in this guide. The food guide beginning on page 190 gives you a detailed description of the most common Mexican dishes in the region.

BEACHES AND ACTIVITIES

BEACH AND JUNGLE HIKES

The beaches chosen for hiking are uninhabited, easily accessible, private, and offer a number of activities, such as snorkeling, fishing, beachcombing, and bird watching.

The hiking distances are between 2 and 4 miles round trip over flat, sandy terrain or rocky shoreline depending on the beach. In some cases it is necessary to bring food and water.

When not writing books, I take individuals and groups on beach and jungle hikes and camping trips or a combination of all three. On request, I will take nature photographers, bird watchers, and butterfly and shell collectors to areas that suit their interests. Write to: Memo Barroso, Basilio Badillo 237, Puerto Vallarta, Jal., Mexico. Telephone messages: Tel. 20836.

CEILING FANS

Throughout the tropical regions of Mexico, budget-priced hotels are usually equipped with ceiling fans instead of air conditioning. The advantages of ceiling fans are obvious. They cool you, provide air circulation, and make you feel as if you were sleeping outdoors, simply by adjusting the fan's speed to your favorite setting: gentle breeze, rude breeze, gale, whale of gale, or hurricane.

But if you are 6 feet tall or more, ceiling fans can sometimes be a cause for concern. Here is a list of precautions to take when you check into a hotel room equipped with a ceiling fan and you feel like a helpless carrot inside a gigantic Cuisinart.

1. The tallest person in your party should check to make sure that the fan cannot be touched with arms outstretched. (Make sure the fan is off first.)
2. If the fan is low enough to make you worry, put suitcases, backpacks, table, chairs, beach bums, or anything that will prevent you from stepping into the area below it.
3. Be careful when handling long objects such as fishing rods, spear guns, or when shaking clothes.
4. If the fan is over your bed, make a mental note of it, and when you wake up in the morning, *do not stand on the bed* to stretch. Under the circumstances, it is better to go unstretched all day.

If your height excludes you from this problem, you need only remember not to invite basketball players to your room.

BEACHCOMBING

Beachcombing is a relaxing pastime that can be practiced by anyone taking a walk on the beach and requires no special skills, credentials, or memberships. Good beachcombing areas can be found throughout the region's coastline.

When beachcombing, wear polarized sunglasses to protect your eyes from the sun reflecting off the sand.

BIRD WATCHING

The rich vegetation of this region provides an ideal habitat for numerous species of tropical birds. As an amateur bird watcher, I am always amazed at the variety and number of birds I spot, but am often unable to identify. Beautiful, brightly colored humming-birds, for instance, are a fleeting source of pleasure and a lasting reason for frustration. They appear from nowhere and disappear just as quickly. It takes a photographic memory set at 1000th of a second to remember any of their features to be able to identify

TANNING TIPS

Every day hundreds of pale sun worshipers converge upon Mexico's beaches to make offerings of peeled skin to the great sun god. Use the following guidelines to keep yourself from looking like a shedding snake:

1. The longer it has been since you last were in the sun, the more likely you are to burn.
2. The lighter and drier your skin is, the faster you can burn.
3. The sun's burning rays are more intense between 10:00 A.M. and 3:00 P.M.
4. Sunscreens allow you to stay in the sun for a longer period of time than your skin type would normally tolerate. For instance, a sunscreen with a "1" protection factor means that you can stay in the sun twice as long.
5. Suntan products help to promote a tan, but may not contain a protective sunscreen.
6. Be careful not to fall asleep in the sun.
7. If possible, start your tan before arriving.
8. The sun's burning rays penetrate through the ocean's surface. Wear a T-shirt when swimming or snorkeling.

COCONUT BOMBS

I don't know how coconuts climb up to the top of coconut trees, but I know for a fact that ever since the law of gravity went into effect, they use it to crash down to the ground with the force of a crate of apples.

In a city, you don't cross a street before looking for oncoming traffic. Where there are coconut trees, there are sure to be coconuts, so don't walk, stand, camp, or park your car directly under their path.

them. But never mind their identifying features or their intriguing names—long-tailed hermits, plain-capped starthroats, etc.—what counts is the memory of a pleasant sight. Who knows, years from now, when you are contemplating a flower, the same hummingbird may appear out of the foliage of your mind and inject you with the nectar of a sweet memory.

If you are serious about bird watching and wish to identify the species you see, equip yourself with one of the field guides to Mexican birds available in bookstores in the United States and Canada. I used *A Field Guide to Mexican Birds* by Roger Tory Peterson and Edward Chalif and the *Audubon Water Bird Guide* by Richard H. Pough to identify the birds mentioned in this book.

I often regretted not having a field guide with me to identify the countless migratory birds from the north that winter in the area.

CAMPING

The trailer park/campgrounds covered in this guide are all clean and offer basic facilities (restrooms, showers, and barbecue pits) and the more complete ones offer full hook-ups, swimming pools, shade, etc. Do not camp on roadsides or public beaches. Use your discretion when camping in areas other than designated campgrounds. Other campers are often a good source of campground information.

FISHING

The Pacific coast's fishing is as varied and abundant as it is legendary. Jacks, groupers, perch, and other species can be caught from the shore, while off-shore barrilete, toro, bonito, dorado, and bill fish are plentiful.

Fishing equipment is available in the region's major beach resorts but the variety is limited and the cost is much higher than in the United States and Canada. For shore fishing, come prepared with an assortment of spoons, feather jigs, hooks, sinkers, wire leader, rods, and reels. I have found a surf-casting rod to be invaluable in many areas.

Large fishing-tackle stores in the United States and Canada are usually well acquainted with the fishing equipment you will need in Mexico. I recommend that you pay one a visit before leaving home.

Deep-sea fishing boats are available in Mazatlán, Puerto Vallarta, Manzanillo, and Ixtapa-Zihuatanejo. Arrangements for deep-sea fishing can be made for a half day or a full day, and the boat operators will furnish all the tackle and bait needed for sailfish, marlins, dorado, and other deep-sea species.

COMMON SPANISH FISH NAMES

The following is a list of the most common Spanish fish names. Commercial species such as red snapper (*huachinango*) usually have one name throughout the entire country. Lesser-known species such as triggerfish often have as many different names as there are regions in the country.

Albacore *Albacore*	Parrotfish *Perico, pez loro*
Ballyhoo, Baloa *Escribano*	Pompano *Palometa*
Barracuda *Barracuda*	Porgy *Mojarra*
Bass *Cabrilla*	Red snapper *Huachinango*
Bonefish *Macabí*	Roosterfish *Pez gallo*
Catfish *Bagre*	Sailfish *Pez vela*
Dorado *Dorado*	Sardine *Sardina*
Grouper *Cherna*	Sea bass *Mero*
Jack *Jurel*	Snapper *Pargo*
Mackerel *Sierra*	Snook *Robálo*
Marlin *Marlín*	Swordfish *Pez espada*
Mojarra *Mojarra*	Tarpon *Sábalo*
Mullet *Lisa*	Triggerfish *Pez puerco, bota*
Needlefish *Picuda*	Tuna *Atún*

SCUBA DIVING

Scuba-diving conditions vary greatly throughout the region. Except for Manzanillo, dive shops can be found in the main beach resorts and at the Hotel Plaza Careyes, south of Puerto Vallarta.

From my research and interviews with first-time divers, the consensus is that the resort course given at the main resorts is for the most part too brief and inadequate to prepare for an emergency. When you dive for the first time, make sure to pair up with an experienced diver. In my opinion, the most professional dive shop in the region is at the Hotel Plaza Careyes.

SNORKELING

If exploring the underwater world appeals to you, then you will find plenty of opportunities to do so along the region's rocky shoreline. I recommend that you bring along your mask and snorkel. Often the rental snorkeling equipment available in many places is barely adequate to find a bar of soap lost in the depths of your bathtub.

A TO Z

Each chapter in this book has an A to Z section with specific information on airports, airlines, bank locations and their business hours, tourist information, important telephone numbers and addresses, postal and communications offices.

BANKS AND MONEY

Banking hours throughout Mexico are from 9:00 A.M. to 1:30 P.M., Monday through Friday. Most banks will readily exchange American currency and traveler's checks, but some will not exchange Canadian currency and traveler's checks. Banks give the best rate of exchange for your money or traveler's checks. Exchange booths, hotels, and restaurants usually give less than the official exchange rate.

Traveler's checks are readily accepted in tourist areas throughout Mexico. Make sure the company you are buying from has refund offices in the cities or region that you are going to visit.

Major credit cards are accepted in the better restaurants, hotels, and shops. With some credit cards it is possible to make cash withdrawals from major Mexican banks.

The peso is the Mexican currency unit and is divided into 100 centavos (which have virtually disappeared from circulation). At present coins are minted in 5, 10, 20, 50, 100, and 200 pesos denominations. Peso bills are printed in the following denominations and colors: 500 (green), 1,000 (brown), 2,000 (green), 5,000 (red and green), 10,000 (light green) and 20,000 (light blue).

At present the peso is floating and its value varies depending on supply and demand and on the rate of inflation (the higher the rate of inflation the likelier the peso will undergo other major devaluations). For your reference, the exchange rate on December 31, 1984, was 209 pesos for $1. Exactly a year later, it was 450 pesos for $1. These rates, and the prices given throughout this book, refer to U.S. dollars.

CAR RENTALS

Cars can be rented in Puerto Vallarta, Manzanillo, Ixtapa, and Mazatlán from American and Mexican companies. The rates are competitive, so it is wise to shop around for the best deals. Compare prices for a given vehicle and ask what year model it is. If a vehicle of a given brand is cheaper but older in one rental than in another, then go for the newer one. It's worth paying a

---

IT'S A STEAL

One way to find out if a dog will eat meat is to leave unguarded a ham leg, a few steaks, and, why not, a few hot dogs too. Likewise, one way to find out if thieves will steal is to leave unguarded your camera, money, and other valuables where a well-trained retriever can make them change owners in a fraction of a second.

1. Traveler's checks are a fantastic invention. Use them. Keep the traveler's checks separate from the sales receipts and numbers. They are essential for refunds.
2. On busy beaches, always keep your possessions within sight when you go for a swim or buy a drink. Keep cameras and other valuables out of sight so you won't target yourself as someone worth robbing.

higher price as rental vehicles get a lot of wear and tear and they don't always get the proper maintenance.

When renting a car, do not assume that it is in good shape simply because you are renting from a well-known company. Before you accept the car, check with a clerk for any damage so you are not charged for it later. Make sure all tires are in good shape and remember that a spare is only spare until you need it. Make sure it has air. Check the jack, windshield wipers, door locks and hand brake, headlights and taillights. Pretend that you are buying the car rather than renting.

Most rental agencies have branches at the airports, major hotels, and in the downtown areas of the major resorts. The jeep model is the favorite of most tourists, though many other types are available. Open-top VW Safaris are available at a few places, but they are a discontinued model, the last of which were made in 1980.

Your American or Canadian driver's license is valid when driving in Mexico. To rent a vehicle you must have your license, and a major credit card. Persons under 25 years of age may be required to pay a cash deposit and pay a higher deductible. In any event, regardless of your age, get full details of your liabilities before renting, and inquire whether the rate you are quoted includes collision insurance, medical insurance, and tax (15 percent of the total bill).

DEPARTURE TAX

Don't forget that there is an airport departure tax for all international destinations. At present writing it is approximately $10.

POST OFFICE, TELEGRAPH, AND
TELEPHONE SERVICES

Post and telegraph offices are located in the downtown areas of towns and cities.

Airmail rates to the United States and Canada are the equivalent of less than 15¢ for letters and postcards. Telegrams with a maximum of ten words cost about 25¢ within Mexico and about $5 to the States for 15 words. To Canada there is a per-word charge, no charge for the address.

To receive mail through general delivery, mail should be addressed to Your Name; Lista de Correos; City, State, Mexico. Telegrams and money orders should be addressed to Your Name;

Lista de Telegrafos; City, State, Mexico. Letters, telegrams, and money orders are held for 10 days before they are returned to sender. Of course, mail and telegrams can be addressed to your hotel.

Most hotels offer international phone service. You may also place international calls through some long-distance offices (*larga distancia*) authorized by the Mexican telephone company. Depending on their size, towns and cities have one or more *larga distancia* office.

The "Useful Spanish Expressions" section of this book will help you communicate with Spanish-speaking clerks who will process your call.

Listed are the telephone area code numbers for the main cities: Barra de Navidad, 333; Ixtapa-Zihuatanejo, 743; Manzanillo, 333; Mazatlán, 678; San Blas, 321; Puerto Vallarta, 322.

Money may be sent to you in Mexico in the following ways:

1. Via telex from a bank in the United States or Canada to a major bank in Mexico. Banamex and Bancomer are the largest. You must include the following information: Your Name, name of bank in Mexico (Banamex or Bancomer), City and State of receiving bank (e.g., Puerto Vallarta, Jalisco or Manzanillo, Colima), Mexico. This service normally takes 3 to 5 working days.

2. Through a telegraph office in the United States (this service is not available for Canada) addressed to either Your Name; Lista de Telegrafos; City, State, Mexico; *or* to Your Name; name of hotel; street address, City, State, Mexico. This service may take 3 to 7 days.

3. A money order via registered mail. This service is the slowest of the three.

Any amount sent to you is payable only in pesos.

Readers are advised to cross-reference to other areas throughout this guide for additional information on a given subject. For example, if you are planning to shore fish or shop in Mazatlán, by simply cross-checking these topics in the Puerto Vallarta section, you can gain extra hints to help you with your traveling concerns.

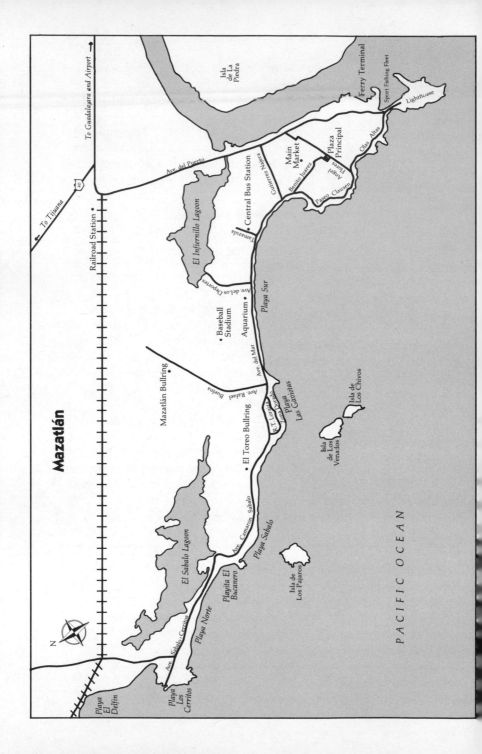

MAZATLÁN

Mazatlán was settled in 1531, by a handful of Spanish soldiers who established a small lookout post there. As with other ports along Mexico's Pacific coast, centuries went by before Mazatlán gained importance, but by the early nineteenth century it became the main port of the Pacific coast. Its economic importance has placed Mazatlán on the stage of some of Mexico's historical highlights. In 1847, Mazatlán was blockaded by American warships, during what is known north of the border as the Mexican War, and south of it as the American Invasion. A few years later, in 1864, Mazatlán was blockaded again, this time by French warships. The city, bombarded and unable to defend itself, surrendered. To conclude its warlike past, Mazatlán was the first city on the American continent to be bombed from the air. This incident took place in 1914. It was during the Mexican Revolution, when an airplane from Venustiano Carranza's forces dropped a crudely built bomb on the city.

Mazatlán today, with its half-million inhabitants, is Mexico's main Pacific Ocean port, and home of the largest Pacific shrimp fleet. The major industries are fishing, boat building, and packing plants.

Apart from its importance as an industrial city, Mazatlán is also one of Mexico's main tourist centers. Although both industry and tourism are vital to the city's economy, they are totally separate. The pungent smells of the fish- and shrimp-packing plants are miles away from the fresh, salty ocean air at the tourist area.

GETTING THERE

Airplane Aeromexico, Mexicano, and Western airlines service Mazatlán with direct flights from several West Coast cities. Residents of the Los Angeles and San Diego area can save money by going by land to Tijuana and then taking the plane to Mazatlán from there.

Bus Several bus lines run 24-hour-a-day service between the border cities of Tijuana and Nogales and Mazatlán. When you arrive at the bus station in either border city, you can be bound for Mazatlán within 2 hours. Expect delays during peak vacation periods and on weekends. Tres Estrellas, a first class bus line, has the most comfortable buses. The trip takes approximately 20 hours from Tijuana to Mazatlán.

Car The most direct route to Mazatlán from the United States is via Mexico's Highway 15, which starts at Nogales, Sonora (across from Nogales, Arizona). The distance is 750 miles over fairly flat terrain, but the two-lane highway is one of the most heavily traveled in Mexico. Mazatlán can also be reached via the less traveled Baja California Mex 1 Highway. It is 915 miles from Tijuana to La Paz with daily ferry connections to Mazatlán.

Ferry The ferry leaves from La Paz every afternoon around 5:00 P.M., arriving in Mazatlán 15 hours later. For ticket information see "Ferries" in the A to Z section.

Trains See "Trains" in the "A to Z" section.

GETTING AROUND

Mazatlán is a large city with numerous avenues connecting the even more numerous neighborhoods (*colonias*) of the city. Unmarked or poorly marked, each neighborhood is a little maze of streets where even veteran taxi drivers can get lost. But visitors need not worry, as the city's tourist accommodations are located along the main artery. This artery is called the Shore Front Avenue, better known in Spanish as *El Malecón*.

Mazatlán's Malecón runs roughly on a north-to-south axis with two lanes of traffic in each direction. As Shore Front Avenue winds itself around the shoreline's contours it changes names a few times. At first this may sound confusing, but given its 16-km (10-mile) length these subdivisions make it easier to find a given address. The Malecón subdivisions are:

Sabalo-Cerritos is the northernmost stretch of the *Malecón* and the least traveled. It is about 2 miles long and houses a handful of condominium buildings. Sabalo-Cerritos runs one block parallel to the sea.

Camaron-Sabalo is a 2-mile stretch where Mazatlán's greatest concentration of hotels, restaurants, bars, and tourist shops can be found. The area between its southern end and R.T. Loaiza is the heart of the tourist area known as Zona Dorada (Golden Zone). Camaron-Sabalo is about 2 miles long and runs one to two blocks parallel to the sea.

Avenida Del Mar runs for about 2 miles right next to the beach unlike the previous stretches of the Malecón. Along its length are a number of restaurants and reasonably priced hotels.

Paseo Clausen starts where the shoreline becomes rocky, and the road twists and winds for approximately a mile. It ends at the turn-around in front of the Shrimp Bucket Restaurant-Bar, where Olas Altas begins.

Olas Altas is the southernmost and shortest stretch of the Malecón, less than a mile in length. Along it are some of Mazatlán's traditional old hotels. East of Olas Altas is the oldest, most attractive residential part of town.

Also off Olas Altas, follow Calle Angel Flores for a few short blocks and you will be right downtown. Continue on to the end and you will reach the port area. Along Ave. Emillo Barragan turn right here to get to the ferry terminal and, at the very end of this avenue, to the sports fishing fleets.

CITY TRANSPORTATION

City buses crisscross the city and serve even the most remote neighborhoods. Fares are very inexpensive, in the nickel-and-dime category. It is advisable, however, to have a rough idea of the city's bus routes and some basic Spanish to ask the bus driver "¿Pasa por _____?" (Do you go by _____?). Once you are on the bus make sure to hold on to the hand railings as most bus drivers behave as if they are driving a cattle truck back at the ranch.

Pulmonias (literally meaning pneumonia) are open-air converted VW bugs. They look like dune buggies wearing a square, beach chair umbrella. Like taxis, they cruise the city's streets and avenues, but only hold up to four passengers with hand luggage. Taxis range in size from Datsuns and Renaults to Fords, K-cars, and Chevys. They are easily found all over town cruising, or at taxi stands by the main hotels. Ask your hotel clerk for the going rate to your destination, or inquire directly to your taxi or *pulmonia* driver: "*¿Cuanto cuesta a* _____?" (How much does it cost to _____?).

WHERE TO STAY

The greatest concentration of tourist hotels in Mazatlán is found in the Zona Dorada, or Golden Zone. Hotels in this zone and north of it generally become more expensive the farther north they are. The hotel farthest north in the area is the Camino Real. Past it, the accommodations are time-share and full-ownership condominiums.

The hotels included in this list are located either right on the beach or directly across the Malecón. Those in the Zona Dorada and north of it are on the beach, those south of the Zona Dorada are on the oceanfront, across the Malacón. Most of these latter hotels become less expensive the farther south they are, as the beach beside the Malecón gradually turns from sandy beach into rocky shoreline.

While many more hotels in the cheap and budget categories can be found one or more blocks from the beach and the Malecón, they are not included here. Their rates are usually the same as those more conveniently beside the ocean.

CHEAP

Hotel Freeman *Olas Altas 200.* At one time the grand hotel of the area, since the northern zone was developed, Hotel Freeman has become one of the bargain hotels, still with a certain air of grandeur. Ceiling fans. Does not take reservations. Tel. 13484.

Hotel La Siesta *Olas Altas 11.* About 50 rooms, located on Olas Altas south of the Malecón. One of the few nice hotels in this section. For quieter rooms ask for those away from the lively Shrimp Bucket Restaurant under the hotel. Tel. 12334.

BUDGET

Posada Sante Fe *Ave. Camaron Sabalo, Zona Dorada.* Accommodations with or without kitchens, some with private terraces facing the ocean. About 20 rooms. Gardens, a barbecue *palapa*, air conditioning in all rooms. Right on the beach. Res.: P.O. Box 22. Tel. 35444.

Hotel Motel Sands *Ave. Del Mar 1910.* One of the older motels in town, it has 60 air-conditioned rooms with telephone and TV and is located right in the middle of Playa Norte across the Malecón from the beach. Swimming pool. Res.: P.O. Box 209. Tel. 20000.

Bungalows Damy's *Ave. Del Mar 1200.* Thirty new, clean bungalows equipped with kitchenettes. Air conditioning, pool, and motel-like parking. Only a block south of Zona Dorada and across the Malecón from the beach. Tel. 34700.

Hotel Belmar *Olas Altas 166.* Also one of the older hotels in town, and built in colonial style, now enlarged with a new wing. Ceiling fan or air conditioning in the rooms, pool, interesting old bar and restaurant. Tel. 20799.

Hotel Aquamarina *Ave. Del Mar 110.* Approximately 80 rooms and 20 junior suites. Air conditioning, pool, restaurant-bar, and across the Malecón from Playa Norte. Res.: P.O. Box 301. Tel. 17080.

Motel Marley *R.T. Loaiza 226.* Located right in the center of Zona Dorada, this clean new motel has an excellent beach location, all rooms air-conditioned and equipped with kitchenette, swimming pool. Under the same management as Hotel Los Arcos just down the street, which has similar accommodations. Res.: P.O. Box 214. Tel. 35533.

Hotel Las Brisas *Ave. Del Mar 900.* A modern 7-story building with air conditioning, telephones, pool, tennis court, and a restaurant-bar. Res.: P.O. Box 456. Tel. 30333.

Casa Contenta Apartments and Motel *R.T. Loaiza 224.* Right on the beach with a complex of nicely furnished apartments with fully equipped kitchens and living/dining-room areas. Tel. 39986.

Hotel de Cima *Ave. Del Mar 30.* On Playa Norte, across the beach from the Malecón. In its category it's a bargain, as it has excellent service, nicely furnished rooms and public areas, with many of the facilities usually found in more expensive hotels. Air-conditioned rooms with phone, swimming pool, tennis court, travel agencies, nightclub, restaurant-bar. Res.: P.O. Box 350. Tel. 14119. Telex 066-865.

Hotel Posada de Don Pelayo *Ave. Del Mar 1111.* Much like the De Cima, the Don Pelayo offers facilities and services that would make it twice as expensive if it was located on the Zona Dorada. Hotel rooms and suites equipped with air conditioning, telephones, refrigerator, and kitchenettes. It has a restaurant-bar, pool, and is located on the Malecón across from the beach. Res.: P.O. Box 1088. Tel. 31888. Telex 66894.

MODERATE

Hotel Puesta de Sol *Ave. Camaron Sabalo.* Large modern hotel but on the plain side. Right on the beach. Restaurant-bar, pool. Res.: P.O. Box 355. Tel. 35411. Telex 066716 TAOLNE.

Hotel Costa de Oro *Ave. Camaron Sabalo.* Large hotel with 250 comfortable, nicely furnished rooms, most with ocean view. Right on the less crowded part of the beach and a short distance from the Zona Dorada. Restaurant-bar and pool. Res.: P.O. Box 130. Tel. 35888. Telex 066-886.

Hotel Oceano Palace *Ave. Camaron Sabalo.* Another large modern hotel on the beach, with no outstanding features other than its proximity to the ocean. Res.: P.O. Box 411. Tel. 39666. Telex 66834.

Hotel Suites Las Flores *R.T. Loaiza 212.* A large hotel offering studio-apartments with fully equipped kitchenettes, air conditioning, TV, telephones, and terraces overlooking the ocean. Res.: P.O. Box 583. Tel. 35100. Telex 066-714.

PLUSH

Los Sabalos *R.T. Loaiza, Zona Dorada.* In contrast to the many plain-looking concrete masses found along the beach, Los Sabalos is an attractive, modern building with excellent ambiance and facilities. In addition to its numerous suites, it offers double rooms whose prices fall in the moderate price category. Tennis courts, Jacuzzi, mini-club, restaurants, and bars. Res.: P.O. Box 944. Tel. 35409. Telex 66750.

Hotel Playa Mazatlán *R.T. Loaiza, Zona Dorada.* In my opinion, this hotel typifies the best Mazatlán has to offer. The first hotel built in this section but still one of the nicest, with a welcoming atmosphere, where it's easy to meet and mingle with the other guests. Its 415 rooms are equipped with air conditioning, telephones, and most have balconies or terraces. Swimming pool, shops, and all the services you would expect from an excellent hotel like this. Right on the most popular beach. Res.: P.O. Box 207. Tel. 34444. Telex 66848.

Holiday Inn Hotel *Ave. Camaron Sabalo 696.* As far as Holiday Inns go, this is one of the nicer-looking ones. Two hundred rooms with sea or mountain view, air conditioning, TV. Very nice and spacious green grounds. Disco, restaurants, and bars, and located on an uncrowded stretch of the beach. Res.: P.O. Box 222. Tel. 32222. Telex 668-767.

DELUXE

El Cid Resort *Ave. Camaron Sabalo.* Mazatlán's only deluxe hotel, El Cid has 600 rooms and suites, 11 restaurants, lighted tennis courts, swimming pools, etc., and the city's best disco. In short, it is the most complete luxury resort in Mazatlán. Some moderately priced rooms available. Res.: P.O. Box 813. Tel. 33333. Telex 66712.

RESTAURANTS

Among the most pleasant experiences awaiting visitors to Mazatlán is its unusual quantity of restaurants and the quality of the food they serve. Naturally, as Mazatlán is an important fishing town, it has a large number of seafood restaurants. The restaurant prices in Mazatlán are generally lower than in the other beach resorts included in this guide. Numerous eat-in or take-out fast-food restaurants can be found around the Malecón and the Zona Dorada.

Following is a selection of good restaurants easily accessible to the hotel zones. Many more excellent restaurants can be found throughout the city.

Restaurant Joncol's *Calle Angel Flores 608, downtown.* One of the oldest restaurants in town, Joncol's meals are typical of the good food served in Mazatlán. A large, varied menu with tasty daily lunch specials (*comida corrida*). On Sundays, the lunch special is fancier and a little more expensive. Open all day. Tel. 12187.

Restaurant El Griego *Calle Angel Flores 918.* A very clean, small eatery operated by its Greek owner, Apostoli, it serves twenty different kinds of pizzas and pastas. Good food at bargain prices. Beer and wine only. Open for lunch and dinner. Tel. 23669.

Restaurant-Bar Doney *Calle Mariano Escobedo 610.* Offers a menu of delicious and unusual Mexican dishes such as green pepper soup, chicken market-style, *carne asada* Doney. All the food is home-cooked in the restaurant, even the tortillas and the time-consuming mole sauces. The elegant ambiance and carefully prepared food would lead you to expect much higher prices, but in fact Doney is one of the least expensive restaurants in Mazatlán. Lunch specials 12 noon to 4:00 P.M. Open daily for lunch and dinner. Private rooms for groups. Tel. 12651.

Restaurant Madrid *Olas Altas.* A handy sidewalk café for people staying on the Olas Altas stretch of the Malecón. It's good, inexpensive, and its ample, varied menu includes a few Spanish specialties such as *potage* and *fabada.* Open all day. Tel. 17480.

Restaurant Mamucas *Simon Bolivar 404.* One of the most popular seafood restaurants in Mazatlán. The dishes are just as good as their names are funny; for example, "Shrimp 50 Megatons," "Fish Popeye El Marino," "Oysters in Orbit," and "Squids Indian Killer," all served in authentic mess-hall ambiance. Another good inexpensive restaurant. Open 10:00 A.M. to 10:00 P.M. daily. Tel. 13490.

Restaurant Puerto Azul *Ave. Del Mar and Calle Gutierrez Najera.* A rather plain-looking restaurant, but has specials such as Pescado Sarandeado (fish in a spicy marinade, char-broiled) and char-broiled *chipotle* fish make it worth a visit. Open for lunch and dinner.

Restaurant-Bar Aha-Toro *Ave. Camaron Sabalo, Zona Dorada.* The hangout for bullfight aficionados, particularly after bullfights on Sundays. The menu consists mostly of seafoods, such as fish Almandine, Catalina, and Aha Toro. Also serve Mexican food and some meat dishes such as tenderloin tips in *chipotle* sauce. Open for lunch and dinner. Aha-Toro has one of Mazatlán's nicest bars. Tel. 36646.

Restaurant-Bar Casa de Bruno *Ave. Camaron Sabalo 214.* Plain-looking but with a good reputation for its food. Specializes in flambé dishes such as pepper steak and champagne shrimp. Offers a number of Mexican plates. Open from noon to 11:00 P.M. and the bar stays open until 1:00 A.M. Tel. 36241.

Restaurant-Bar Las Tres Islas *Ave. Camaron Sabalo 1900.* A *palapa* restaurant right on the beach serving seafood, including lobster thermidor, assorted seafood platters (*parrillada*), and several house specialties, such as *pescado Sarandeado,* a char-broiled fish which is brought to your table in its terra-cotta brazier. Served daily between noon and 6:00 P.M. The restaurant-bar is open until midnight.

Restaurant-Bar El Parador Español *Ave. Camaron Sabalo in front of Hotel El Cid.* Clean with a pleasant atmosphere and some open-air tables. Spanish cuisine featuring gazpacho and paellas. Open daily for breakfast, lunch, and dinner. Tel. 30767.

Restaurant-Bar Los Pelicanos *Ave. Del Mar 556.* This large and very elegant restaurant offers a choice of ambiance—the wood-paneled and stained-glass main dining room or the informal *palapa*-roofed section overlooking the ocean. Both have identical menus and prices. A trio moves from table to table. House specialties include their award-winning shrimp casserole, pork chops in prune sauce, oxtail soup and bouillabaisse. Open for lunch and dinner from 1:00 P.M. to midnight. Bar closes at 2:00 A.M. Tel. 26839.

Restaurant-Bar Los Arcos *Ave. Camaron Sabalo between the El Cid and the Holiday Inn.* Another popular seafood restaurant with a very original menu. Many of the dishes will require an explanation from the waiter. Shrimp and fish ceviches are also among their specialties. Open noon to 10:00 P.M. Tel. 39577.

Restaurant-Bar Tony Plaza *Calle R.T. Loaiza in front of Playa Mazatlán Hotel.* Fancy dining with specialties such as St. Germain shrimp, flambéed tequila shrimp, chicken in garlic sauce, pepper steak, and seafood chowder. A quartet plays music. After dinner visit the adjoining bar with live music and a dance floor. Open from noon to midnight, the bar from 9:00 P.M. to 3:00 A.M. Tel. 34233.

Heraclio's Steak House *Ave. Del Mar 1103.* A steak house just like you would find at home, serving prime Sonora meats such as rib eye, T-bone, and the house specialty, prime rib. Tel. 25638.

Shangri-La Restaurant *Calle R.T. Loaiza in the Zona Dorada.* The only quality Chinese restaurant in town with Mandarin, Szechuan, and Cantonese dishes on the large menu. Open 1:00 P.M. to 11:00 P.M. daily. Tel. 36746.

NIGHTLIFE

Mazatlán has a large enough local population to provide lively nightlife even in low tourist season. And when the high tourist season arrives, Mazatlán comes to life when the sun goes down.

The nightlife starts around 5:00 P.M. when exhausted tourists start to leave the suntanning shift. As everyone disbands for happy shower hour, party plotters emerge among your new-found friends and suggestions pour: "Hey let's get some *cerveza* and tequila chasers and have a party in my room tonight." "No," says another, "let's go to Mr. Frogs for drinks, dinner, and drinks." A mediator jumps in and suggests: "Let's have drinks in his room and then we'll go to Mr. Frogs." "Yeah" is the consensus. Here are a few suggestions to totally confuse future party plotters.

Assuming that back at home you live in a quiet town or neigh-borhood and you are ready to raise hell about silence, then head straight for Mazatlán's noise-pollution award-winner **Señor Frogs** on Ave. Del Mar. This superpopular restaurant-bar has equally noisy dining and drinking sections. Best of all, you usually have to stand in line for a while before you can get in. Another popular, but less noisy restaurant-bar is **El Patio**, also on Ave. Del Mar. A great favorite of people who prefer a lively atmosphere over noisy chaos is **El Shrimp Bucket** on Olas Altas. There you can go from the fun, but serious service and good food, of their restaurant to the dancing, drinking, and singing of their "La Cantina" bar. Live mariachi, marimba, or Latin groups conduct the merrymaking.

For drinking, people watching, and mingling, the following bars are among the most popular (outside of hotel bars). **Aha Toro** on Camaron Sabalo's Zona Dorada is a pleasant bar, and the place to hang out after Sunday-afternoon bullfights. If the guy sitting next to you tells you he is the most famous *matador* or *toro* in all of Mexico, just go along with it. The motto of this place is "A little bull doesn't hurt anybody." A couple of blocks behind Aha Toro on R.T. Loaiza, is the **Gringo Lingo Cantina** where they are totally bilingual when it comes to margaritas, cuba libres, piña coladas, and *cervezas*. The Gringo Lingo is a semi-open-air bar good for meeting and mingling.

Instead of fading out, Mexican discos are as popular as ever. **El Caracol Tango Palace** is a giant disco, with six music video screens, which can accommodate up to 1,000 people.

Scattered along the Malecón's Camaron-Sabalo are a few old-fashioned discos where you can bop 'til you drop. They are **Valentino, Princess,** and **Confetti.** Many of the big hotels have discos and/or a live music nightclub where you can practice your cha-cha, mambos, cumbias, and other highly contagious dance steps.

For a breath of fresh dancing air, try **Tony's Bar** (on R.T. Loaiza) featuring an excellent tropical group live from 10:00 P.M. to 2:00 A.M.

Mexican fiestas offer low-key partying and a glimpse of the Mexican folk music, dances, and food. Hotel Playa Mazatlán has Mexican fiestas four times a week, on Tuesday, Thursday, Friday, and Saturday at 7:00 P.M. They are open to nonguests. For reservations see your hotel's travel agency or call Tel. 31120 at Playa Mazatlán. Every Sunday evening at 8:00 P.M., the Playa Mazatlán offers a fireworks display with the ocean as a backdrop. You can watch the show comfortably over dinner at the Terraza Playa Restaurant, or from the beach.

SHOPPING

In Mazatlán most of the shops are concentrated within a two to three block radius in Zona Dorada. On a short two-block stretch of R.T. Loaiza (between Hotel Las Flores and Playa Mazatlán), are about half a dozen craft shopping centers, housing perhaps as many as a hundred shops. Here you should be able to find just about anything that you are not looking for, including: oversize brass animals, baskets, wood carvings, papier-mâché vegetables, fruits, and animals, along with rugs and blankets made of wool and cotton. Other tempting purchases might be the pottery from various regions of Mexico, onyx jewelry, beachwear, or silver and gold jewelry.

As a wise shopper, before purchasing, you would do well to take a survey of the items available in these shops. Oftentimes, several shops will carry the same item, in the same color and same size, with very different prices.

The following shops on R.T. Loaiza are worth mentioning. **Designer's Bazaar** is a large two-level shop. On the lower level there is a large selection of Varcelino-designed clothing, and on the upper level there is the brass and papier-mâché zoo of Sergio Bustamante. **Boutique Maya**, a new shop built in the shape of a pyramid, specializes in quality onyx articles, leather jackets, and shoes made from exotic skins. **Casa Roberto** (at Playa Mazatlán Hotel) carries original paintings, Mexican colonial wood furniture, brass chandeliers, lamps, and an assortment of tropical hardwood items such as cutting boards, boxes, and trivets.

Along Camaron-Sabalo, from Zona Dorada to El Cid Hotel, are located a number of shops. The following specialize in casual sportswear and beachwear: **Piña Colada, Polo, Capriccio, Ruben Torres,** and **Ocean Pacific.**

BEACHES AND ACTIVITIES

Mazatlán's beaches sometimes resemble a tropical hospital sun ward. Rows upon rows of impatient patients sit in their beach chairs, arms outstretched, waiting for a badly needed transfusion of Doctor Sun's invigorating cure-all golden rays. Patients who checked in with common winter ailments such as blizzard blues, snow allergies, frozen brain, and drizzle gloom report almost total recovery after just a day of treatment. The services of the local sun wards could not be complete without the numerous thirst-aid stations. They are specifically designed for the patients' full recovery. Piña coladas, margaritas, and plenty of other folk remedies are sold across the counter. The motto of the professionally staffed thirst-aid stations is: "We unconditionally guarantee that you will feel better today. If not, we'll start all over tomorrow." To complete your total recovery program the beaches of Mazatlán offer a number of activities that are sure to get your frozen blood circulating again. Fishing, snorkeling, scuba diving, and windsurfing are among the activities awaiting to make you feel good all over.

Except for El Cerrito and El Delfin, all other beaches can be reached via city buses. Mazatlán's beaches are located next to the Malecón or a couple of blocks from it. The beaches here are described from south to north.

Playa Olas Altas Located along the Olas Altas section of the Malecón, it's the southernmost and smallest of the city's beaches. Handy if you are staying on this side of town and all right for tanning, but it has a steep grade, strong waves, and rocky bottom that make it less than desirable for swimming. Frequented by the neighborhood's young surfers on weekends.

Playa Sur Located along the length of the Malecón's Ave. Del Mar and shaped like a fish hook, this narrow sandy beach is

about 3 miles long. Despite its narrowness, it is still a nice beach
to visit. The ocean here is a delightful Mazatlán blue with playful,
rolling waves which in bad weather turn naturally into rough
players. Along this golden sandy stretch are located shaded seafood restaurants.

Playa Las Gaviotas Located along Zona Dorada, Las Gaviotas
(the sea gulls) is Mazatlán's best stretch of beach. It's about a mile
long and carpeted wall-to-wall with the Pacific's finest and warmest
golden sand. The Three Islands directly across from Las Gaviotas
break the strength of the waves, but this does not mean that they
break into small, tame waves. Gaviotas stretches from Los Sabalos
Hotel, for about 1 mile north, to around the area of El Cid Hotel,
where it is then known as Playa Sabalo. Numerous "thirst aid"
stations can be found at the hotels on Las Gaviotas. For the best
hamburgers in Mazatlán go to La Playita food stand at the Hotel
Playa Mazatlán.

Playa Sabalo It runs parallel to the Camaron-Sabalo stretch of
the Malecón (between El Cid and the Camino Real hotels). It is
the continuation of Playa Las Gaviotas to the south with an
equally beautiful warm welcome mat of soft sand. The waves here
are larger and livelier than at Las Gaviotas, and in stormy weather
they can be quite rough. Restaurant-Bar Las Tres Islas (between
the Holiday Inn and the Caravelle Hotel) is the only beach restaurant along Playa Sabalo. (Try Pescado Sarandeado served at
your table on a hot charcoal brazier.) Other restaurants are at the
hotels along the beach.

Playita El Bucanero A couple of hundred yards north of the
Camino Real Hotel, which is by the bridge connecting El Sabalo
Lagoon with the sea, this *playita* (little beach) is actually the south
end of the long *playa norte*. El Bucanero has a wide sandy area,
part of which is edged by the Sabalo Lagoon and part by the
ocean. The lagoon side is smooth and calm, which makes it ideal
for children and for floating around on an air mattress. The ocean
side can be rough and should be approached with caution. A
restaurant serves the usual seafood fare. There is a parking area
right next to the beach.

Playa Norte Running parallel to the northernmost stretch of the
Malecón (called Sabalo-Cerritos), this is the last frontier of
Mazatlán's beaches, a 3-mile-long, wide, generally deserted beach
scattered with a few condominium buildings. Playa Norte's rivals
in beauty would be the neighboring beaches of Sabalo and Las

Gaviotas. They offer soft golden sand, bathed by the rolling waves of the blue Pacific. In contrast, however, Playa Norte offers an ocean of quiet and privacy. There is a good little restaurant on the southern end called El Bucanero.

The restaurant on the northern end is literally for the dogs. I sat there waiting for a fish fillet that I had ordered, surrounded by about a half a dozen drooling dogs. I took a bite of the fillet and suddenly realized why they had so many dogs. They are the only creatures that would be able to eat the food there.

Playa Los Cerritos Follow Camaron-Sabalo-Cerritos to its very end. This beach, which is located at Punta Los Cerritos, is the northernmost beach of all the beaches found along the Malecón. It is a very rocky beach and, because of its location, the waves are quite rough. This tiny beach is protected from the large ocean waves by a natural rock wall, which acts as an efficient wave breaker, allowing Playa Los Cerritos to be safe enough for you to wade.

The two restaurants here are out to lunch. Not only in service, but also in attitude and prices.

Playa El Delfin Follow the Malecón's stretch of Sabalo-Cerritos north for about 2 km (1½ miles), until you see on your left a building with a sign *Campamento Recreativo dif.* A couple of hundred yards from there is a two-lane road going east. Take this road for a short way to the railway tracks. Turn left at the tracks. About a third of a mile down you'll be able to spot the beach. El Delfin is the northernmost of the beaches found in the Mazatlán area, as well as the farthest from town. The components that make a beach ideal for most Mexicans are restaurants and shady trees. Because El Delfin does not provide these fundamentals, along with the fact that it is not served by public transportation, the number of locals that drive there on weekends are few. El Delfin, therefore, is also one of the emptiest beaches. El Delfin is a fairly narrow strip of beach edged by a steep dunelike sand ridge. The steepness of a sand ridge like this usually indicates an equally steep grade once you are in the water. Swimming is safe as long as the sea is calm. Otherwise expect a strong, undertow as the waves rush back to the sea from the sand ridge. If the sea is rough go to the lagoon behind the beach, where you can swim, frolic, float, and explore on an inflatable boat or air mattress. The edge of the quiet lagoon closest to the ocean is a tiny sandy beach. The rest of the lagoon is edged by vegetation where, if you are not careful, you may puncture your inflatable toys. Bring your own food and drink. When parking your car watch out for soft sand areas so that it will not get stuck.

Playa Isla Venados Take the *Ocean Express* amphibian from Las Flores Hotel, or its counterpart *Tiburon* from El Cid Hotel. This small beach is located on the protected (leeward) side of Isla Venados. It's a shallow, sandy beach with waves only inches high, but the beach's ends are very rocky. On the north end the rocks are very sharp so definitely stay out. On the south end, the rocks are round, smooth, and slippery. Again, definitely stay away.

Despite its busy tourist traffic, Playa Los Venados is not equipped with appropriate tourist facilities. There are no restaurants, restrooms, or beach vendors, but soft drinks, beer, and quiet are available. If you love the place, the last amphibian leaves about 4:00 P.M. If you hate it, then stay on the amphibian. It goes back to civilization right on schedule, that is, after the crew has their scheduled beer and restroom breaks.

BEACH HIKING

Mazatlán's long beaches naturally lend themselves to a leisurely hike. If you wish to combine your hike with happenings, people and body watching, then Playa Las Gaviotas is your best bet. Here you can watch in action the strolling bazaars, known as beach vendors, trying to sell their wares to one after another of the deactivated tourist bodies. Poor vendors, little do they know that these solar-powered bodies are here to recharge their batteries. These deactivated tourist bodies have been programmed to shake their heads and say "No Grashas. No Deenehro." Strangely enough, you might notice that the lazing bodies lying on the beach, sweat more than the vendors, who carry kilos and kilos of merchandise.

If you prefer to hike along the lonelier beaches with just the company of your shadow and the sound of your own footsteps on the soft sand, then here are a couple of quiet suggestions.

Playa Norte The silence and peacefulness of this long, sandy beach is greatly enhanced at sunset, when a backdrop of colors sets the stage for dreaming and maybe romancing.

Playa Isla Venados This is the most adventurous of the beach hikes available in Mazatlán. Prepare for undertaking this short, pleasant hike by finding out the times of low and high tide from

the crew of the amphibian that takes you to the island. Here is
how to ask: "¿A que hora sube/baja la marea?" (What time does the
tide go up/down?) The reason for this is that the stretch of shoreline where you take your hike is very narrow, and at high tide it's
covered by the sea. Therefore, you would want to go on your
hike when the tide is low and return before it goes up. Once you
are at Los Venados Beach, start walking south. Soon the sandy
beach ends and the shoreline turns rocky. Your path continues on
the narrow passageway between the steep hillside and the sea.
Walk carefully. The rocks are round, smooth, and slippery when
wet. If you are observant, you will discover along this part of
your hike a species of ants that seem to be true sea lovers. I have
seen ants near the sea in the dry parts of the beach, but I had
never seen ants that seemed so much at home right at the water's
edge, and, in fact, in rocks, surrounded by water. So watch your
step again. The hike is about 10 to 15 minutes long (depending on
how long you stop to watch the ants). At the end of the hike
there is a tiny sandy beach at the south end of Isla Venados. Isla
Chivos is an effortless stone's throw from here, and can be easily
reached in a short swim. It is recommended that you wear hiking
shoes. Thongs are unsafe in this kind of terrain. Bring along your
snorkeling gear and something to drink to quench your thirst.

CAMPING/TRAILER PARKS

There are no campgrounds in Mazatlán; however, if you are
traveling by car, pickup, or van, trailer parks can often accommodate your vehicle and tent, except during peak season. Trailer
homes and any vehicles requiring full hook-up facilities will find
it impossible to get a space from November to March. Regulars
with trailer home campers spend their winters at the same trailer
park year after year and reserve months ahead of time. Newcom-
ers are advised to contact trailer parks well ahead to inquire about
future openings. In Mazatlán, there are about half a dozen trailer
parks ranging from those that are without shade and are dirty to
excellent ones. The following two parks are clean, efficiently run,
centrally located, and open year-round.

Las Palmas Trailer Camp   *Camaron-Sabalo 333, P.O. Box 1032.*
Located right in the heart of Zona Dorada, two blocks from Playa
Las Gaviotas, it has 65 full hook-up, palm-shaded spaces. Facili-
ties include swimming pool, showers, and camping spaces.

Mar Rosa Trailer Park   *Camaron-Sabalo, P.O. Box 435.* Right on

Sabalo Beach, not too far from the heart of Zona Dorada, this park has 60 full hook-up, shady spaces. It can accommodate a few tent campers, with showers and restrooms. Gabriela is the Mar Rosa's manager and public-relations star. She is an invaluable source of information for guests and nonguests.

DEEP-SEA FISHING

Mazatlán has an international reputation as a great deep-sea fishing center. Two factors contribute to this reputation. The first one is, naturally, the fish. Every year an estimated 5,000 bill fish (blue and striped marlin and sailfish) are caught in the area's blue waters. That's an average of over 13 a day. Add to that thousands of mid-size species, such as dorado and yellow fin tuna, and you'll understand why hardly any fisherman comes off a cruiser without a big fish and a big smile. The second factor is the quality of fishing cruisers available here and the professional level of the crews that man them. You should see these sea hawks as they leave the port at full speed. You can tell they are not just going to take you for a ride. From the minute they are in open water they start scanning the horizon for a sign of fish. They watch for concentrations of seabirds in the distance and look for feeding dolphins. They analyze what appears to be an unusual whitecap (maybe it was a fish splash), and they watch other cruisers for signs of a catch. If they think there is a catch, they rush in that direction. The crew's fishing enthusiasm is understandable; they hope that if there is a good catch, anglers will share some of the fish with them.

There are about ten sports fishing fleets in Mazatlán, with anywhere from two to ten cruisers each. The largest and most reputable of them is the **Star Fleet** run by Bill Heimpell, who has been in the business for 32 years. The Star Fleet has ten 40- to 43-foot cruisers equipped with two-way radios, life preservers, restrooms, four lines, and two chairs. Fishing rates for a full day's trip for two to six passengers cost from $180 to $215. Departures are at 7:00 A.M., returning at 3:00 P.M. Party boats for up to four people are also available. For information and reservations: Star Fleet, Tel. 23878 and 14852. Other fleets recommended are **Bibi**, Tel. 13640, and **Faro**, Tel. 12824. Mazatlán's game fishing calendar is as follows:

> Blue and striped marlin: January to June
> Sailfish: June to December
> Dorado: All year
> Yellow fin tuna: All year

SAILING

Hobiecats can be rented at a couple of spots along Las Gaviotas and Sabalo beaches. The most complete water sports shop found here is **Aqua Sports Center**, located on the beach, right next to El Cid Hotel. They have six 16-foot and two 14-foot Hobiecats renting for about $12 an hour. Aqua Sports will provide you with a guide at no extra charge just for the asking. A cash deposit or a driver's license is usually required. Aqua Sports is open daily from 9:00 A.M. to 5:00 P.M., Tel. 33333, ext. 1341.

SCUBA DIVING

Mazatlán is blessed with miles and miles of sandy beaches, which provide endless hours of suntanning; however, for the scuba diver this amount of sand is nothing but a kick in the tanks. Within easy reach of Mazatlán there are only a few good diving spots found along the protected (leeward) side of Isla Los Chivos, Isla Los Venados, and Isla Los Pajaros, a few miles across Mazatlán's Playa Las Gaviotas. The best visibility is around the 30-foot range between the months of November to June. The most reputable dive shop in town is **Aqua Sports Center** at El Cid Hotel, Tel. 33333, ext. 1341. Open daily from 9:00 A.M. to 5:00 P.M., they offer one- and two-tank trips to Venados and Pajaros islands. Tanks filled.

SHORE FISHING

Despite thousands of miles of shoreline that surround Mexico, Mexicans as a whole are not sports fishermen. For the most part, they either make a living from fishing or hardly ever go fishing, even when they live right next to the most prolific fishing grounds. If you are an avid fisherman, you will find yourself pleasantly surrounded in Mazatlán by miles of shoreline with no competitors whatsoever. There are as many fish out there as you can catch. The trick as usual is what bait, lures, techniques, etc., to use in a given spot. Frankly, I am a jack-of-all-trades-and-master-of-none when it comes to fishing. I do as most fishermen do. I try a number of lures and baits and when I get good results I act like a real pro and give knowledgeable advice. So here goes: Before coming down to Mexico, go to a reputable, large fishing shop and simply tell them, "I am going to Mazatlán, what are the best lures I can use there for shore fishing?" The "fish worms" behind the display cases usually know more about fishing in Mexico than casual visitors do. Not only do they get feedback from returning customers, but they always have new or redesigned lures that are sure to give results. Just in case you talk to a clerk not familiar with the fishing, here are a few do's and don'ts. Do not bring down salmon eggs, tied flies, or anything to do with trout or salmon fishing. Do bring Kast, Masters, or Hopkins lures (2–3 oz.), particularly those with tied feathers to simulate tail movement. Look for good casting spots along the rocky shoreline edging the southern end of the Malecón (Paseo Clausen and Olas Altas) and at Punta Camaron and Punta Sabalo.

SNORKELING

Most of the shoreline along Mazatlán is sandy beach, unsuitable for good snorkeling. Some of the rocky areas such as Puntas Camaron and Sabalo offer good snorkeling, but only in very calm seas. The only good and protected snorkeling area in Mazatlán is the leeward side of Isla Venados. Take the amphibian of your choice, the ocean express (the one with the most frequent departures) from the Las Flores Hotel, or "El Tiburon," from the El Cid Hotel. Once on the island, you have two areas to choose from for your snorkeling. The first is north of the beach. This area north of tiny Los Venados Beach is a rocky shoreline made up of mostly rough, sharp rocks. Snorkel in this area only when the visibility is good enough so you can see the rocks in order to stay clear of them. At first the depth is only about 4 feet and increases gradually as you swim toward the open sea. The second area is south of the beach. The rocky shoreline here is made up of smooth, round rocks, which are a blessing on snorkelers' knees and legs. This area is the recommended choice for inexperienced snorkelers because it is very protected from currents and waves. The depth of this area increases gradually as you move away from the rocks. You can snorkel for about 300 yards south of the end of Isla Venados, and then continue on snorkeling along the adjoining Isla Chivos. The two islands are separated by a tiny water channel only about 10 feet wide. (See also "Beach Hikes" section.)

WATER SKIING

For water skiing arrangements ask your hotel's travel agency, or call **Aqua Sports**, Tel. 33333, ext. 1341, for information.

WINDSURFING

Aqua Sports, next to the El Cid Hotel, offers the best selection of standard and high-fly boards. Rentals are approximately $6 an hour, which includes the cost of your transportation to Venados Island for your windsurfing pleasure.

TOURS

When you are sunburned or simply burned out from the beach scene, consider the soothing effects of sightseeing through mysterious mining towns in the legendary nearby Sierra Madre. Or a visit to the historical beach town of San Blas with a boat tour to La Tovara Springs. Mazatlán offers a great variety of land tours conducted by English-speaking guides in buses equipped with air conditioning and restrooms. With all land tours you will be picked up at your hotel half an hour before the tour's scheduled departure. A couple of short sea tours are also available. Reserve at the travel agency in your hotel.

City and Shopping Tour You are taken to a number of the city's main sights such as the Malecón, the old part of town, the cathedral, the market, etc., and to several craft shops. Departures are daily at 10:00 A.M. and 3:00 P.M.; tour lasts about 3 hours and costs approximately $5 per person.

Mountain Tour In this interesting all-day tour you are taken to a couple of small mountain towns nestled among the Sierra Madre, and visit Concordia and Copala, a small mining town founded in 1571. The tour price includes lunch at Copala. Departures are daily at 10:00 A.M.; tour lasts about 6 hours, and costs approximately $13 per person.

Rosario Tour This tour includes a visit to Villa Union and the hot springs town of Agua Caliente. The highlight of the tour is the old mining town of Rosaro. Departs Tuesdays at 9:00 A.M. The duration of the trip is 5 hours and it costs approximately $13 per person including lunch.

San Blas Jungle Tour In terms of time and miles traveled (about 300 round trip), this is the longest tour but the most interesting one you can take from Mazatlán. For first-time visitors to Mexico it is a good way to see the varied and beautiful Mexican countryside. At San Blas, your destination, you will be taken on a boat tour to La Tovara Springs, where you will have time for a refreshing swim and lunch (included in the cost). Departures are Wednesdays and Saturdays. The trip lasts about 12 hours and costs approximately $20 per person.

Bay Cruise This tour offers a fish-eye view of Mazatlán. You have a choice between the *Fiesta Mazatlán* and the *Bahía* tour boats to cruise around the city's harbor and along the city's shorefront to view the lighthouse, the sea lion rocks, and the Three Islands. Departures are daily at 10:00 A.M. (*Bahía*) and 11:00 A.M. (*Fiesta Mazatlán*) from the port. The trip lasts about 3 hours and costs approximately $4 per person. Children ages 5 to 14 are charged half fare.

Deer Island Tour An ideal sea tour for even the most confirmed landlubber. Your transportation for the short, smooth 10-minute ride to the island is an amphibious U.S. army surplus vehicle called the *Ocean Express*. Board it right on the beach in front of Las Flores Hotel (Zona Dorada). It goes back and forth every half-hour or so. Make sure you catch the last departure from the island.

A TO Z

AIRLINES
Aeromexico *Ave. Del Mar 117.* Tel. 17804.
Mexicana *Paseo Claussen 101-B.* Tel. 27722.
Western *Ave. Camaron Sabalo at Hotel El Cid.* Tel. 32709.

AIRPORT
The Mazatlán airport is located 23 km (14 miles) south of Mazatlán on the main highway. It has several car rental offices (Avis, Budget, Hertz, and National), baggage lockers, two restaurant-bars, a duty-free shop, and a couple of small souvenir shops. Surprisingly there is no money exchange or bank here.

Transportation from the airport into town is provided by yellow-and-white cars and VW buses. Fares vary depending on your destination in town.

AQUARIUM

Acuario Mazatlán, *Ave. de Los Deportes 111,* consists of two sections, one with about thirty tanks of small tropical fish and a smaller section exhibiting shells, coral, and marine artifacts. Open daily 10:00 A.M. to 6:00 P.M.

BANKS

Like any large city, Mazatlán has no shortage of banks. Although banks are open from 9:00 A.M. to 1:00 P.M., most change money only until around noon or earlier. There are several banks on the corner of Ave. Camaron Sabalo and Calle R.T. Loaiza at Zona Dorada.

There are a number of money exchange booths around town, but they usually offer lower rates than the banks.

BASEBALL

Mazatlán has a first-class baseball stadium and its own home team, Los Venados (The Deer), belonging to Mexico's Pacific Baseball League. The season runs from the beginning of October to the end of December.

BOAT RAMP

Club Nautico Mazatlán has a boat ramp that can be used by nonmembers for a fee. Club Nautico is located by the sports fishing fleet.

BULLFIGHTS

Mazatlán is real bullfight country and the locals are passionate aficionados of the sport. Bullfight season goes from mid-December to April. There are two bullfight rings in Mazatlán and fights are held every Sunday alternating between one and the other. Ask your hotel desk or travel agency for booking information.

BUS TERMINAL

The **Central de Autobuses** is on *Boulevard de Las Americas and Calle Tamazula.* In the first-class section you will find a post and telegraph office, money exchange, and baggage lockers. There is a nice clean buffet-style restaurant between the first- and second-class sections. In front of the bus station there are three inexpensive hotels.

There are many departures from here to Guadalajara and Mexico City as well as to Durango, Chihuahua, and Zacatecas.

CAR RENTAL

Avis *Ave. Camaron Sabalo in the Zona Dorada.* Tel. 36200.
Budget *Ave. Camaron Sabalo 402.* Tel. 32000.
Hertz *Hotel de Cima, Ave. Del Mar 1111.* Tel. 36060.
National *Ave. Camaron Sabalo in the Zona Dorada.* Tel. 36000.

CONSULATES

Canadian Consulate *Calle Albatros 705.* Tel. 37320.
United States Consulate *Calle Circunvalacíon 6 Poniente.* Tel. 12685 or 16988.

DRY CLEANER

Glemnsa *Ave. Camaron Sabalo 160.* In Mexico you know you are in a big city when you can find a dry cleaner, and Mazatlán has one.

FERRIES

Ferries go from Mazatlán to La Paz daily at 4:00 P.M. Ticket sales start at 9:00 A.M. but to secure a place, it's best to get in line by 7:00 A.M. Strictly one ticket only for each person in line. (This means that a family of five must all line up.) Fares are a bargain, for passengers as well as for vehicles.

GOLF

El Cid Hotel, *Ave. Camaron Sabalo,* has a golf course. For information and reservations phone the hotel at 33333.

Club Campestre has a 9-hole course and is located on the highway to the airport. For information, Tel. 25702.

HORSEBACK RIDING

Horses can be hired at the end of *Calle Gaviotas* (which is the continuation of Calle R.T. Loaiza) *in the Zona Dorada.* Hours are 9:00 A.M. to 3:00 P.M.

JOGGING

The Malecón's seaside sidewalk is a continuous concrete track that stretches for about 4 miles from the Zona Dorada south to

Olas Altas. As the sun sinks into the ocean, dozens upon dozens of joggers of all ages merge into this busy runway. Join them. The ocean breeze will cool you off and blow away the car fumes from the busy Malecón's traffic.

LAUNDROMATS

Las Palmas *Centro Comercial, Ave. Camaron Sabalo 333.* One-day service. Hours 8:00 A.M. to 8:00 P.M. Drop off your clothes in the morning, pick them up in the evening. Closed Sundays.

Lavandería Sabalo, *Ave. Camaron Sabalo 160.* Drop off your clothes in the morning, pick them up in the evening.

LONG DISTANCE

Most hotels provide long-distance service. If yours does not, ask the desk for the nearest long-distance office (*caseta de larga distancia*).

MARKET

The market looks more like a train station than a market. The building, which dates from around the turn of the century, occupies a whole block on *Ave. Serdan and Calle Melchor Ocampo*. It is interesting to see, but for shopping convenience, **Supermarket Ley** has ample parking and is closer to the hotel zones, and offers a larger variety of products.

MEDICAL SERVICES

Dr. Miguel R. Guzman *Calle Guillermo Nelson 1808.* Hours: 10:00 A.M. to 2:00 P.M. and 5:00 to 8:00 P.M. Tel. 12587; Home Tel. 15117.

Should you need one, the United States Consulate has a list of specialists.

POST OFFICE

The main post office (*correos*) is located downtown at the *Plaza Principal at the corner of Calles Benito Juarez and Angel Flores*. There is also a post office at the central bus station. The post office is open through lunch hour.

SUPERMARKETS

There are numerous small supermarkets throughout the city, particularly along the Malecón. The largest one is **Supermarket Ley**, located on *Boulevard de Las Americas and Calle Rio Piaxtla*.

TENNIS
Many of the larger hotels have their own courts and usually only guests are allowed to play on them. The following hotels rent courts to nonguests.

Las Gaviotas Racquet Club *Calles Ibis and Río Bravo at Las Gaviotas.* Five Lay-Kold courts. Tel. 35939.

Tequila Charlie's *R. T. Loaiza.* Two Lay-Kold courts. Tel. 32031.

TELEGRAPH OFFICE
The main Oficina de Telegrafos is located downtown at the *Plaza Principal* right next to the post office. It is open through lunch. A smaller telegraph office is at the central bus station.

TRAINS
Trains are the cheapest, although the slowest, means of land transportation in Mexico. There are two daily departures, at 11:30 A.M. and 11:00 P.M., from Mazatlán to Nogales, Sonora, at the United States border. Trains leave Mazatlán for Guadalajara at 8:30 A.M. and 5:00 P.M.

TRAVEL AGENCY
Most of the major hotels have travel agencies.

Wagon-Lits Mexicana *Angel Flores 806 Poneniente.* Provides full travel service. Tel. 16294.

TRAVELER'S CHECK REFUND OFFICES
American Express is located upstairs at *Ave. Camaron Sabalo 310* and **Wagon-Lits Mexicana** (for Thomas Cook traveler's checks) is on *Calle Angel Flores at the Plaza Principal.*

WATER SLIDE
Fun for kids as well as for adults is **Tobogan Acuatico** at *Ave. Camaron Sabalo across from the El Cid Hotel.* Open daily 10:00 A.M. to 8:00 P.M.

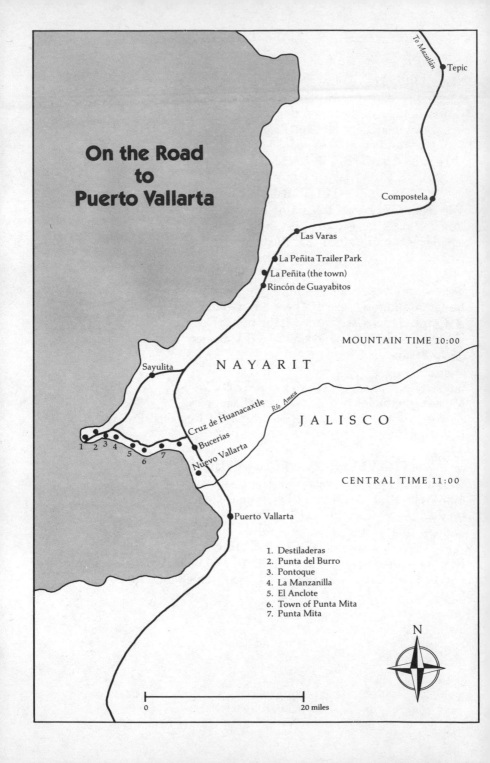

On the Road
to
Puerto Vallarta

To Mazatlán

Tepic

Compostela

Las Varas

La Peñita Trailer Park

La Peñita (the town)

Rincón de Guayabitos

MOUNTAIN TIME 10:00

Sayulita

N A Y A R I T

Cruz de Huanacaxtle

Río Ameca

J A L I S C O

Bucerias

1 2 3 4 5 6 7

Nuevo Vallarta

CENTRAL TIME 11:00

Puerto Vallarta

1. Destiladeras
2. Punta del Burro
3. Pontoque
4. La Manzanilla
5. El Anclote
6. Town of Punta Mita
7. Punta Mita

N

0   20 miles

ON THE ROAD TO PUERTO VALLARTA

Mexico's Highway 15 starts at the border city of Nogales, Sonora, and passes through Mazatlán on its way to Tepic and Guadalajara. It is one of the most heavily traveled highways in Mexico and you should exercise the utmost caution while driving on it. As you drive toward Tepic (180 miles south), the first 125 miles are, for the most part, over flat terrain and low, rolling hills. There are plenty of long, straight stretches, but just the same, don't step on it. Potholes, pedestrians, and cattle grazing on the edges of the road are common. For the remaining 50 miles between Río Santiago and right up to the outskirts of Tepic, the highway twists and climbs through a steep mountain range. The grade slows trucks and trailers to a crawling speed of 10 miles an hour. Behind them follow endless caravans of cars whose drivers behave as if they were driving an ambulance to the site of an accident. Blind curves follow one another and the traffic coming from the opposite direction is as heavy as that in your lane. The best thing to do is to be patient, play your favorite tape, and go with the flow of traffic.

The junction to San Blas is 33 km (20 miles) from Tepic and is well marked. Several Pemex gas stations can be found between Mazatlán and Tepic.

As soon as you reach the outskirts of Tepic, your heavy-traffic headache will be over. For one thing, there is a bypass that avoids the traffic of Tepic, capital of the state of Nayarit. Better yet, the traffic from here to Puerto Vallarta is reduced to about a quarter of what it was on the previous stretch of the highway.

Highway 200 starts at Tepic, goes through Puerto Vallarta and along the Pacific coast, ending at the Guatemalan border. From Tepic the road works its way down the Sierra Madre, and 81 miles later reaches the coast at La Peñita-Rincón de Guayabitos. This is the northernmost of the beaches grouped in the chapter "On the Road to Puerto Vallarta."

From Guayabitos, the highway curves through low mountain ranges alternating with flat straight stretches. Along the highway are huge tobacco plantations interspersed with large, open-sided barns where rows and rows of tobacco leaves are hung to dry. South of Guayabitos, the highway runs fairly close to the sea but seldom within sight of it. From Guayabitos to Puerto Vallarta, there is only one gas station, in Guayabitos, until you reach Puerto Vallarta.

Kilometer markers begin at the city of Tepic. The distances given under each locality indicate the kilometer marker number and the number of kilometers from Puerto Vallarta.

SAN BLAS

San Blas was founded in the year 1530 by the Spanish conquistador Nuño Beltran de Guzman. For the next two centuries San Blas was nothing but a settlement visited by Spanish ships. It wasn't until the last half of the eighteenth century that the town started to develop, when it became the departure port for ships to Baja and Alta California and Sonora. In March 1768, Fra Junípero de Serra departed from San Blas to establish the first missions in Alta California. Toward the end of the eighteenth century, a number of expeditions departed from San Blas to explore the Pacific coast as far north as Alaska. At this time the once forgotten settlement of San Blas reached a population of around 20,000 inhabitants and was one of the most important ports of the Pacific coast of what was then New Spain.

San Blas became an important center of trade and commerce for ships transporting goods along the Pacific coast and was the first port of call and commerce for ships making the long journey from the Philippines. But the glory days of San Blas were soon to be over. After the War of Independence from Spain in 1810, the town's commerce and population dwindled to nothing. At present the town's main sources of income are its small shrimp and fishing fleets and tourism.

As a tourist destination, San Blas does not compare to the

larger, more popular spots such as Puerto Vallarta and Mazatlán. But San Blas has a number of tourist attractions that no other town or resort can match—it simply has the best surfing, bird watching, and beachcombing on the west coast of Mexico. Its beaches are as beautiful as any in the larger tourist towns mentioned in this guide. The boat tour to La Tovara Springs is unique. And best of all, San Blas is remote, laid back, easygoing, and cheap.

GETTING THERE

Bus There are about half a dozen direct daily buses from Tepic to San Blas. From Guadalajara there are two direct daily buses. To reach San Blas from Puerto Vallarta, change buses at Tepic. Coming from Mazatlán, you can either take a bus to Tepic and then transfer to one for San Blas, or get off at the San Blas junction and wait for the San Blas bus to come by. The problem with this is that you may have a 2- or 3-hour wait and then the bus may be full. Keep in mind that the last direct bus to San Blas goes by the junction before 5:00 P.M.

Car A large Pemex station marks the junction for San Blas, 35 km (22 miles) north of Tepic. From there it's another 35 km to San Blas over a very winding, narrow, paved road with no shoulders. Keep your speed around 40 mph, as cattle graze on the vegetation growing on the edges of the pavement. There is a Pemex station at the arch marking the entrance to town.

Airplane Puerto Vallarta is the closest and most convenient international airport to San Blas. The VW airport vans that service Puerto Vallarta can take you to San Blas. For the best price, negotiate with a couple of different drivers.

WHERE TO STAY

San Blas has no more than a dozen hotels, all of which are in the cheap and budget ranges. The hotels in the budget range far surpass in quality and service those in the cheap range. All of the town's hotels are within six blocks of the Plaza Principal.

CHEAP

Hotel El Bucanero *Calle Juarez.* The cheapest of the cheap and also one of the ugliest in the country. Even worse, there is a loud disco right next door. Try it as a last resort. Fans; no hot water.

Hotel Los Flamingos *Calle Juarez.* In the glory days of San Blas, this used to be the German consulate. Now it's an old and decaying building, but as a hotel it's pleasant, clean, and friendly. Miraculously it has fewer mosquitoes than the more expensive hotels in town. Fans; no hot water.

Hotel Posada del Rey *Calle Campeche.* A small, family-run hotel with about 10 new rooms. Fans; pool.

Posada Casa Morales *Calle Cuauhtemoc.* Also a small family-run hotel, with about 15 cabanalike rooms. It's the only hotel in town located on the waterfront. Pool; fans; hot water.

BUDGET

Motel Las Brisas *Calle Cuauhtemoc.* Las Brisas is just a short breeze from the waterfront and offers ample green areas, swimming pool, and air conditioning.

Marino Inn Motel *Calle H. Batallon.* Large and brand new, the Marino Inn provides the most conveniences. Lots of greenery, a swimming pool, air-conditioned rooms, and restaurant-bar. Write for reservations. Four blocks from El Borrego, the town's beach.

Hotel Suites San Blas *Calle Aticama.* With 43 rooms, this is the town's biggest hotel. Rooms are air-conditioned and have a kitchenettelike area without cooking utensils. Green areas and a swimming pool, but no restaurant-bar. Write for reservations. Four blocks from El Borrego.

Trailer Park Los Locos *Calle H. Batallon.* The only trailer park in San Blas and an attractive and shady one at that. It has 100 full hook-up spaces, showers, and a nice little bar. Located one block from El Borrego beach.

RESTAURANTS

The selection of restaurants in San Blas is limited. Not only will you find little choice of restaurants, but quite often a number of dishes on the menu will not be available. As a rule, the larger the menu, the more dishes that will be unavailable. When the waiter hands you the menu, ask him: *"¿Que platillos no hay?"* (What plates don't you have?) Besides the restaurants listed, in high season a couple of other restaurants open their doors to the public.

Taqueria El Faro *Corner of Calles Canalizo and Mercado. Taqueria* is the word for an eatery specializing in tacos. Order by the piece and the service is superfast. Also serves quesadillas and *tortas* (the Mexican version of a sandwich). Serves beer. Open only in the evenings.

Restaurant Amparo *West side of Plaza Principal.* A small family-run restaurant where grandma does the cooking. The menu is limited; includes one fish, one chicken, and one beef dish among others. Open all day.

Restaurant MacDonald's *Calle Juarez.* MacDonald is the family name of the owners of this restaurant and they make a hamburger that would put their famous competitor to shame. They have an ample menu of seafood, meat, and chicken plates. Open all day. Serves beer.

Restaurant La Isla *Corner of Calles Mercado y Paredes.* Specializing in seafoods, this is the best restaurant in town and the only one with atmosphere and decent décor. Prices here are not much higher than in the other restaurants in town and the air conditioning alone is worth the difference. Serves beer and wine. Open 2:00 P.M. to 9:00 P.M., or so. Closed Sundays. Formerly called Chef Tony's.

BEACHES AND ACTIVITIES

For a small town, San Blas certainly has its share of nice, fine-sand beaches, all within easy reach of town. There is a bus service from the Plaza Principal in San Blas to the village of Matanchen and Los Locos. The bus leaves from the corner outside the bus station but the "schedule" is too vague to give actual departure times here. You would do well to inquire about departures well ahead of time. And make sure you pack mosquito repellent if you plan to stay on the beach around, and particularly after, sunset.

Playa El Borrego El Borrego (the lamb) is located on the southern edge of town and can be easily reached by a 10-minute walk down Calle H. Batallon (starting at the Plaza Principal). El Borrego is about a mile long and it is a wide stretch of fine grayish sand. The water is shallow for a ways and fairly calm, due to a series of rock wavebreakers jutting out to sea. During the rainy season, the ocean water is very brackish, but once the dry season sets in, the water's clarity can be upgraded to mildly brackish. There are a number of *palapa* restaurants on the north end of the beach. Besides food and drink, they provide the only shade found on the beach.

Playa Isla del Rey Isla del Rey is just a stone's throw from San Blas's waterfront across the Del Rey estuary. To get there, take the *panga* that leaves from the customs house (*aduana*) at the west end of Calle Juárez. The *panga* goes back and forth daily as passengers arrive, between 6:30 A.M. and 5:30 P.M. The fare is about 25¢. There is no food, water, or shade on the island.

When you land on the island, follow the dirt road, bear right at the fork, and in 5 short minutes you will be on the long and desolate Playa del Rey. The beach is a wide expanse of fine sand. As with the other beaches in the area, the water is brackish and shallow for a ways, with 1- to 2-foot waves.

Few tourists visit Isla del Rey despite its proximity to San Blas. Its more numerous visitors are the Huichol Indians of certain mountain regions of the state of Nayarit. In their religion, which has taken in many elements of Catholicism, the island is considered a sacred ceremonial ground. Here they perform marriages, baptisms, and other ceremonies and make offerings to Aramara, their sea goddess. The town's people have seen on occasion a large group of Huicholes going to the island with a cow they brought along with them to be slaughtered and served at the feast following an important wedding. The Huicholes visit the island in small groups throughout the year, but in Semana Santa (Easter Week) they pour onto the island in large numbers.

Playa Las Islitas To get to Las Islitas from the Plaza Principal, take the road to the main highway for 3.5 km (2 miles) to the junction marked Matanchen, Los Cocos. Two km down is the village of Matanchen. There the road splits: to the left a paved road goes to Playas Matanchen and Los Cocos; the dirt road straight ahead goes to Las Islitas. Total distance to Las Islitas is 7 km (4 miles).

Las Islitas takes its name from the small rock promontories located along the beach. At high tide, during certain times of the year, water surrounds these promontories, turning them into little islands (*islitas*). This is the surfers' hangout as the mile-long wave that draws them to San Blas goes past Las Islitas. The water is generally very calm and clearer than in any of the beaches in the area. There are several *palapa* restaurants along the beach and some even offer shade for your car.

Playa Matanchen To get to Playa Matanchen, follow the instructions for Playa Las Islitas. Playa Matanchen is the name given to the long, curving stretch of beach along the northern half of the Bay of Matanchen. The road runs parallel and right next to the beach. There are a number of spots along the road to park your car to walk on this lonely beach or swim in its lazy waves. There is no food, drink, or shade on this beach.

Playa Los Cocos Despite its abundant, towering coconut trees, Playa Los Cocos is the least attractive of the area's beaches. From a distance it looks attractive and shady, but once you get there you find out that the ocean is gnawing on the land and there is practically no beach left. If you wish to see it for yourself, see instructions for Playa Las Islitas.

BEACHCOMBING AND HIKING

You don't have to be a beachcomber to be a beach hiker, but you have to be a beach hiker to be a beachcomber in San Blas, where the same beaches that are good for hiking are also excellent for beachcombing. Playa del Rey and Playa Matanchenh are wide, sandy beaches ideal for both activities.

Playa del Rey, the longest beach in the San Blas area, stretches north for about 10 miles and can be hiked in its entirety. It's a desolate beach where on occasion a lone local can be seen clamming. Remember, there is no shade or water on this beach. Matanchen can be hiked starting at Playa Las Islitas, south for about 5 miles to a point halfway down the Matanchen bay.

As for beachcombing, both beaches are littered with driftwood in sizes ranging from twigs to whole tree trunks. Many tropical trees grow with fascinating twists, knots, and in a variety of shapes not found in North American trees. A given branch of tropical driftwood can, for example, be alternately round and flat, then make a loop and twist around itself. With a little luck and a good eye, you can find a piece of wood that is a natural sculpture and small enough to take home with you. The rainy season is the best time of the year for beachcombing on these beaches. During this period (June through October) rivers empty their waters and flotsam into the ocean. The mouth of Río Santiago, one of the largest rivers on the west coast of Mexico, is located only a few miles north of San Blas's Playa del Rey.

Likewise, the rainy season is the best time of the year to beachcomb for shells. The high waves caused by the season's tropical storms sweep into the beach thousands of shells from the shallow ocean floor. Matanchen Bay is a large shallow bay with a sandy bottom. It is a good breeding ground for bivalve shells, clams, cockles, scallops, and the best find in the area, the comb Venus (not to be confused with the Venus comb). The best part of the bay to beachcomb is the middle, where the waves are the highest during a storm. The best part of this wide beach to comb immediately after a storm is the high water mark. With time, the shells brought out to the beach by high waves will be buried by windblown sand. If you are a persistent beachcomber, look for prize shells well beyond the high-water mark in calm-water seasons. Your efforts may be well rewarded.

Playa del Rey has far fewer shells than Playa Matanchen. However, since it is a land point, it receives the impact of sea currents, winds, and swells throughout the seasons and is therefore a good year-round spot for shell finds.

BIRD WATCHING

With its variety of bird habitats, beaches, mangrove swamps, estuaries, forests, mountains, plantations, and grasslands, the area of San Blas provides a home to dozens of land and water bird species. Birds are everywhere, and you don't even have to make special bird-watching trips to spot them. As you lie on the beach you'll see magnificent frigate birds hovering overhead. As you sit in the patio of your hotel you'll notice a swallow (or is it a swift?) landing in its nest on the ceiling beams, and as you travel around the countryside in San Blas you will see entire flocks of egrets.

If you are a dedicated bird watcher and you wish to spot rarer species, you will find very professional help here. Señor Manuel Lomeli has been conducting bird-watching tours of the area for many years. He can take you to places where you can spot the San Blas jay, mangrove cuckoo, anhinga, and in the evening the ferruginous pygmy owl. His tours, according to your request, may involve car and boat transportation. Although they are reasonably priced, they are nevertheless an expense which many featherweight bird watchers would prefer to fly by. The best thing to do is to take Señor Lomeli's standard bird-watching tour, just to see if, according to your needs, he pecks as hard as he crows. Inquire for Señor Lomeli at La Tovara Springs. Boarding points: El Conchal or Matanchen.

The best time of the year for bird watching in the San Blas area is from December to March, when the local as well as the foreign species partake of the water, air, and land regardless of race, screech, or color.

FISHING

Due to the area's shallow sandy bottom and brackish waters, the most likely catch with bait would be a blowfish. They are as exciting to catch as a dead twig. About the only place worth fishing from the shore is the man-made rock edges of the Del Rey estuary by the *aduana*. Cast with light, silvery spoons for small jacks, or whatever else may come along when the tide rushes in and out of the estuary.

For a day of real fishing, try hiring one of about three *pangas* that are moored by the *aduana*. Their owners are experienced fishermen who make a part-time living taking out amateur fishermen. They will always come back with a good catch, except in very adverse fishing conditions. As long as you hire them to go out to fish what they know is most available at the time, you, too, are likely to come back with a good catch.

Try to make arrangements for your fishing trip a day or more before you plan to go out. A 4- to 6-hour fishing trip should cost $50 with about four riders allowed on the boat.

SURFING

My knowledge of surfing is very limited. In fact, a few years back, before I knew anything about surfing, I was amazed to see young North American travelers lugging around their own ironing boards. I thought to myself, "Why don't they just buy wash-and-wear clothes?"

What little I know about surfing at present is still insufficient to be of any use to surfers, who for the most part have a pretty good idea of the best times of the year to visit and the type of waves and surfing spots that are found in San Blas. Visitors to San Blas wishing to try their luck at surfing may find the following information of some use.

For years San Blas has been a mecca for devoted North American surfers. Its proximity to the United States West Coast, inexpensive accommodations, laid-back atmosphere, and warm waters are a powerful magnet to most surfers. Add to that the longest wave on the west coast of Mexico and no surfer could resist the temptation of visiting San Blas at least once during his life. This wave starts at the northern point of the bay of Matanchen around the area of Playa Las Islitas and can be ridden for about a mile before it breaks.

In a way, surfing is something like fishing: you get the best equipment possible, but the big wave, like the big fish, might just never materialize. Unlike fishing, good weather does not lend itself to good surfing. In San Blas, as well as on the whole west coast of Mexico, the best surfing months are during hurricane season from June through October. Don't panic; hurricane season is just a name for weather conditions that can potentially produce a hurricane. A normal hurricane season produces a couple of dozen tropical storms, the precursor of a hurricane.

Tropical storms kick up high winds, which in turn cause high waves in areas covering thousands of square miles high at sea. Fortunately the great majority of tropical storms die at sea four days or so after they are born. But fortunately, too, for surfers, the big waves they make travel hundreds of miles until they reach the little town of San Blas, where, ironically, the last mile in the life of a former tropical storm wave may be a hurricane of an experience for a surfer.

Surfers may rent boards from Juan Banana at the **Team Banana Surf Shop** at Playa Las Islitas. Juan Banana's name comes from the fabulous banana bread he and his American wife make and bake right at Playa Las Islitas. You can buy it by the loaf or by the slice. Anyway, Juan Banana, little known as Juan Francisco Garcia Rodriguez, is the foremost surfing expert in San Blas. He knows the waves and tides as well as anyone in town and is also an excellent source of information on any subject of interest to visitors.

TOURS

La Tovara Springs boat tour One of the greatest attractions in San Blas is the natural springs of La Tovara. Even better, in my opinion, is the boat ride through the mangrove swamps to get to the springs. For years the local boatmen have cut a path through the mangrove vegetation to allow passage for their boats. The result is a maze of tunnels about 5 feet high by about 10 feet wide. The vegetation mirrors itself in the still swamp water and as your boat moves along you get the impression that you are sliding down a cylinder painted in silver and green. About halfway to La Tovara, the boat comes out of the tunnel and the rest of the way your boat glides through a wider, open-air waterway. Keep your eyes open for birds and, on the edges of the mangrove tunnel, for turtles. Your boat stays at La Tovara Springs for about an hour to give you time for a swim. There is a little restaurant there serving fish and shrimp dishes, soft drinks, and beer.

There are two points for boarding the boats: the closest from town is at El Conchal, next to the bridge at San Cristobal estuary, or at the village of Matanchen. The price is the same at both, but from El Conchal it takes an hour longer for the round trip than it does from Matanchen. The boats that take you on the tour are outboard *pangas* with a capacity for about ten people. The tour price is approximately $17 for five passengers. No reservations are necessary. Boats leave from 8:00 A.M. to 2:00 P.M. Two bits of advice. Some of the boatmen think they are driving an ambulance to the scene of an airplane crash. Before you even board the boat, tell them to go slow (*"Por favor, vaya despacio."*) so you can appreciate the scenery and wildlife. And second, when riding through the mangrove tunnels, watch your head. Don't make sudden movements that will upset the balance of the boat and don't stick your arms out when you are too close to the vegetation.

See "Bird Watching" section for other tours.

A TO Z

BANKS

Banamex *Calle Juárez, a few steps from the Plaza Principal*, is the only bank in San Blas, and gives the best exchange rates in town. Exchange hours are only 8:30 to 10:00 A.M.

BUS STATION

San Blas's *terminal de autobuses* is located on a corner of the Plaza Principal next to the church. There are several direct buses to

Tepic and two to Guadalajara. All buses serving San Blas are second class and usually fairly crowded. Buy your ticket ahead of time.

ICE

Bags of ice cubes made from purified water can be bought at the La Brisas and Marino hotels. Ice blocks are not made with purified water.

LAUNDRY

Lavomatic *H. Battalon, three blocks from the main plaza.* Overnight service.

LONG DISTANCE

The *larga distancia* office is located on *Juarez at the Plaza Principal.* Open 9:00 A.M. to 2:00 P.M. and 5:00 P.M. to 9:00 P.M.

MARKET

The town's only market is located on a corner of the Plaza Principal next to the church. Inside, as well as on the side street facing the church, you will find grocery stores, a bakery, vegetable and fruit stands, butchers, fish stands, and a couple of live chicken stands where the chickens are sold to you live, slaughtered and defeathered right before your eyes. The market closes around 2:00 P.M.

MEDICAL SERVICES

Dr. Jorge Ascensio Medina *Calle Sinaloa 16.* Dr. Ascencio receives patients at this address, which is home and office, from 1:00 P.M. on. Before 1:00 P.M. he may be seen at the Navy Hospital or reached at Tel. 50180.

POST OFFICE

The tiny local *oficina de correos* is located on the *corner of Calle Michoacan and H. Batallon.* Open 9:00 A.M. to 1:00 P.M. and 3:00 to 6:00 P.M., except Saturday when it's open till noon.

TAXIS

Taxis can be hired at the Plaza Principal, across from the church, for local service or special trips to Tepic, etc. They have no meters, so negotiate with the drivers.

TELEGRAPH OFFICE

The *oficina de telegraphos* is located on *Calle Canalizo, three blocks south of the Plaza Principal.* Open 8:00 A.M. to noon and 2:00 to 5:30 P.M. On Saturdays it closes at 11:00 A.M.

RINCÓN DE GUAYABITOS—LA PEÑITA

KM 95 Tepic Highway (74 km north of Puerto Vallarta)

Rincón de Guayabitos and La Peñita are 1 mile from each other but for all practical purposes they are like one town, with Guayabitos being the residential area and La Peñita the commercial one. Guayabitos is a land development that was started about 10 years ago and is now dotted with private homes, hotels, and trailer parks. In time, Guayabitos may well become an important tourist center but for now it's content to simply offer rest and relaxation.

GETTING THERE

Bus The bus station is located at La Peñita. The only bus line that makes scheduled stops here is Autobuses Pacífico. Buses stop about every hour on their way south to Puerto Vallarta and north to Compostela, Tepic, and Guadalajara.

Car Guayabitos is an hour north of Puerto Vallarta.

GETTING AROUND

Guayabitos and La Peñita are approximately 2 kilometers from each other, with the main highway as the only road connecting the two towns. La Peñita's streets are laid on a north-to-south grid. Emiliano Zapata is the main street and begins at the highway. Guayabitos's main street is Ave. Sol Nuevo and runs parallel to the sea. The streets branching out from Ave. Sol Nuevo on the sea side are *retornos* (dead end) streets. Although there are no local buses for transportation, there is a taxi stand in La Peñita across from the Pacifico bus station.

WHERE TO STAY

The main point to emphasize regarding Guayabitos's accommodations, whether they be hotels, bungalows, or trailer parks, is the high standard of cleanliness and the rates offered by most hotels and bungalows. Not only are the rates considerably lower than comparable accommodations in Puerto Vallarta, but also they are often negotiable, depending on your length of stay and how full they are. The emptier they are, the better your power of negotiation will be. All accommodations at Guayabitos are within a small area two blocks from the beach.

Establishments such as Suites-Bungalows Diana offer discounts ranging from 30 percent for a week to 50 percent for up to 5 weeks, based on a double occupancy rate of around $15 per day.

Besides those listed here, there are plenty of other hotel and bungalow accommodations available at Guayabitos, with a few in the budget and moderate ranges.

The Hotel Rosita and Motel Russell are in La Peñita; the others are in Guayabitos.

CHEAP

Hotel Rosita *On the highway, south of Pacifico bus depot.* Very clean and centrally located, with several rooms facing side streets and convenient, motel-like parking. Caution: The bathroom light switches are too close to the sink faucets and when wet could be an electrifying experience.

Motel Russel *Calle Ruben Jaramillo.* Right on the beach and only a couple of blocks from downtown La Peñita. It's quiet, nice, clean, and friendly. The best deal for the money.

BUDGET

Hotel Peña Mar *Ave. Sol Nuevo and Jacarandas.* The largest of Guayabitos's hotels with 100 clean, air-conditioned rooms, two swimming pools, restaurant-bar, and tennis court (no charge for guests). All rooms are equal in quality including the more expensive ones with a sea view. For reservations write to: Hotel Peña Mar, P.O. Box 369, Tepic, Nayarit.

Suites and Bungalows Diana *Ave. Sol Nuevo and Huanacaxtle.* Pool, squash court, barbecue grills. Offers the best off-season rates of any hotel-bungalow accommodations in Guayabitos. Excluding the months of April, July, August, and December, discounts range from 30 to 50 percent on stays of one to five weeks.

Bungalows El Delfin *Retorno Ceibas.* New, very quiet, nice pool. Just a jump from the beach and Villanueva's restaurant.

MODERATE

Hotel Fiesta Mar *Ave. Sol Nuevo and Ceiba.* Among the top ranking of Guayabitos's superclean hotels, offering a pool, restaurant-bar, squash court, and a disco on Friday and Saturday nights. All rooms are air-conditioned.

Costa Del Sol Hotel and Bungalows *Retorno Tabachines.* A spotless, efficiently run hotel-bungalow accommodation right on the beach, complete with air conditioning, restaurant-bar, and a large pool. All rooms have an ocean view. The bungalows are fully equipped and have parking spaces. Bungalow rates depend on number of occupants, length of stay, and season. For reservations, write: Costa Del Sol, Hidalgo #3 Nte., Compostela, Nayarit.

TRAILER PARKS

Guayabitos has more trailer parks than any town in this region. The ones mentioned here are very clean, efficient operations with full services. All are right on the beach and can handle even the largest of trailers. Reservations are not accepted; it's first come, first served. Given the large number of trailer parks here, if first-rate parks are full, you can always get a space in one of the other ones. The better parks charge approximately $6 a day for trailer space and two occupants.

La Peñita Trailer Park and Campground *77 km north of Puerto Vallarta, Km marker 92.* Without a doubt, this is the best in the region with a swimming pool, clubhouse, store, money exchange, tennis courts, etc. The park's 140 spaces are situated on a terraced hillside overlooking the ocean and receive its ocean breezes. All spaces are level, have full hook-ups, and are shaded by the abundant jungle greenery. Just a few steps down the hill, a beachful of sun awaits you. Tent spaces are available with showers, restrooms, and barbecue grills. Reservations not accepted. Rates vary with length of stay.

El Dorado Trailer Park *Retorno Tabachines.* The cleanest, most attractive of Guayabitos's trailer parks. Twenty-four full hook-up spaces with lots of tall trees for shade and a boat ramp.

Paraiso Del Pescador Trailer Park *Retorno Ceibas.* Thirty shaded spaces, slightly cramped. Boat ramp available.

Villanueva Trailer Park *Retorno Ceibas.* Twenty-eight spaces, some shaded. There's a good restaurant.

Tropico Cabaña Trailer Park *Retorno Palmas.* Thirty spaces, no shade.

RESTAURANTS

The restaurants listed here are a sampling of the choices available at Guayabitos and La Peñita. Most of the hotels and bungalows at Guayabitos have their own restaurant. Some are open for one or two meals a day, others for all meals. La Peñita's main street, Ave. Emiliano Zapata, houses about half a dozen restaurants serving inexpensive Mexican food. At night, numerous eateries and taco stands open up along Zapata and cross streets. Don't hesitate to ask other Americans to recommend other places to eat. Many of them (particularly in the middle-aged group) spend several months a year here and know the area well. The first two are in La Peñita; the others in Guayabitos.

Restaurant Jayme Wong's *Ave. Zapata and Bahía de Manzanillo.* Despite its name, Wong's does not serve Chinese food. The menu has about a dozen items, including shrimp cooked in various styles and sirloin steak. Open for breakfast, lunch, and dinner. Beer only.

Restaurant-Bar La Plazita *Ave. E. Zapata and Salina Cruz.* The dimly lit atmosphere, good food, and service make this one of the classiest little restaurants in the region. The menu consists of about 20 entrées priced under $5 each, as well as nightly specials.

Restaurant-Bar Diana *Retorno Ceibas.* This restaurant is so spotless and attractive that you'll feel like going in even if you're not hungry. The house specialty is pizza and a small one will feed two. Also on the menu are brochettes and shrimp dishes and hamburgers. Hours: 1:30 to 10:00 P.M. Closed Thursdays.

Restaurant-Bar Villanueva *Retorno Ceibas at Trailer Park Villanueva.* Right on the beach with a great sea view plus good food and service. Prices are reasonable. Shrimp dishes, fish fillets, and breaded oysters, an unusual dish to find in the region, are the specialties. For a splurge, try the lobster. Hours: 9:00 A.M. to 8:00 P.M.

THE BEACH

The beach is a 2-mile stretch of fine golden sand that spans from Guayabitos on the southern end of the Bay of Jaltemba to La Peñita on the northern end. The water is shallow for about 20 feet and free of tricky tides or currents. The calmest part of the beach is the southern end, where it's safe for children to play in the shallow waters with gentle 1-foot waves. Along the beach are several restaurants offering fresh seafood at reasonable prices.

A TO Z

La Peñita's main street, Emiliano Zapata, is a total of five short blocks. It contains two banks, several drugstores, restaurants, six grocery stores and supermarkets. The long-distance phones, post and telegraph offices are located at the west end of Zapata. The bus station is located on the corner of E. Zapata and the main highway. Across the highway, on Calle Colon, is the laundromat. Mechanic (*taller mecanico*) and tire repair shops (*llantera*) are located on the highway, a short way from E. Zapata. In Guayabitos there is a long-distance phone office at Retorno Ceibas. A couple of mini-supermarkets can be found at Sol Nuevo and Calle Cedro. Most businesses close from 2:00 to approximately 5:00 P.M.

SAYULITA

Km 123 Tepic Highway (44 km north of Puerto Vallarta)

Sayulita is a seaside village of about a thousand inhabitants. Its sources of income include small-scale fishing, cattle ranching, and, to a limited degree, tourism. Although it is connected by highway and has electricity, water, and sewage systems, Sayulita resembles the much less urbanized village of Yelapa in the southern half of the Bay of Banderas.

Like Yelapa, Sayulita is set in the midst of dense jungle with hillside houses overlooking the sea. Here, too, North American visitors who come for the winter are looking for sun, sea, sand, and low-cost living that go with the simplicity of the Mexican village life-style.

There are two well-stocked grocery stores, a drugstore, and a liquor store. Fresh fish can be bought daily on the beach as fishing boats return throughout the afternoon.

GETTING THERE

Autobuses Pacifico leave hourly from the Puerto Vallarta bus terminal on Calle Insurgentes (south end of town).

WHERE TO STAY

Houses are available for seasonal or year-round rental at various prices. The best time to rent a house for the high season is before December.

Overnight visitors should try the **Bungalows Las Gaviotas,** one block from the beach. Units for up to four persons rent for $12.

By the time this guide is published, Sayulita's first hotel may be finished. The local gringos have dubbed it cell block H because of its tiny, dimly lit rooms.

RESTAURANTS

There are three *palapa* restaurants on the beach that serve fish and shrimp dishes for very reasonable prices. **Cuca's Restaurant**, for example, serves a delicious, filling helping of fresh shrimp ranchero for only $3. These restaurants close around 6:00 P.M. Then a couple of spots open in the vicinity of the main square (two blocks from the beach). They serve tacos, tostadas, *pozole*, and other typical Mexican specialties. A generous portion of *carne asada* costs less than $1.

BEACHES AND ACTIVITIES

Sayulita's beach is over a mile long and can be divided into two areas: the calm one and the rough one. The calm area is at the left end of the beach as you face the sea, and is bordered on the right by a shallow rock area. It is free of currents and undertow and has 2- to 3-foot waves, good for a short surfboard ride if you happen to have one.

The rough section starts to the right of the shallow rock area and stretches north for most of the length of the beach. The waves here crest, roll, and crash, and can twirl and strip you with the greatest of ease. Avoid this area on rough days.

ALONG THE PUNTA MITA HIGHWAY

Junction at Km 136 Tepic Highway (30 km north of Puerto Vallarta)

The Punta Mita highway is a narrow two-way asphalt strip with no shoulders. During the rainy season, the vegetation along the sides of the highway grows unchecked and takes an extra foot off the width of the highway. Add to this sharp curves and hidden cattle foraging in the vegetation, and you have a scenic highway made for slow, leisurely driving. But don't despair, the highway is only 22 km (13.5 miles) long from where it begins at the main highway to its end at Punta Mita. The beaches along the Punta Mita highway are among the most beautiful in the Bay of Banderas.

There is a new bus service to Punta Mita. For details, see "A to Z," Puerto Vallarta, but the best way to reach these beaches is by car.

Cruz de Huanacaxtle Km. 2. Cruz de Huanacaxtle is a tiny, pleasant town of approximately 2,000 inhabitants. *Huanacaxtle* is the name of an indigenous tree with long, thick horizontal branches that provide large amounts of shade (there are a couple of them in

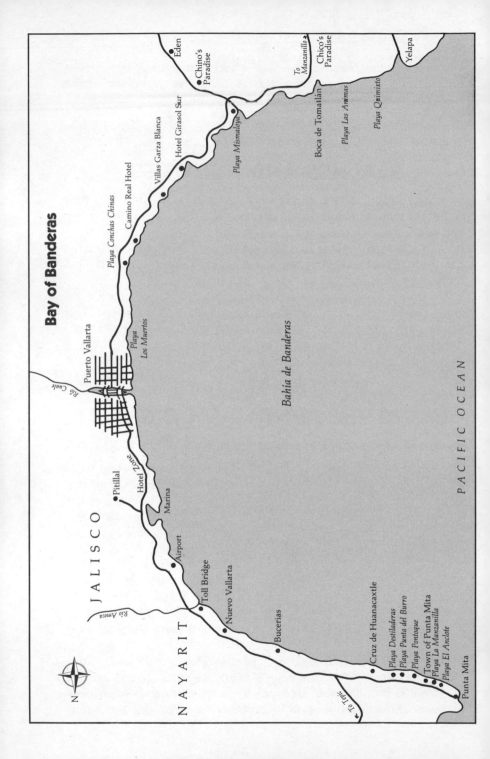

Bay of Banderas

JALISCO

NAYARIT

Río Ameca

Río Cuale

Puerto Vallarta

Pitillal

Hotel Zone

Marina

Airport

Toll Bridge

Nuevo Vallarta

Bucerias

To Tepic

Cruz de Huanacaxtle

Playa Destiladeras

Playa Punta del Burro

Playa Pontoque

Town of Punta Mita

Playa La Manzanilla

Playa El Anclote

Punta Mita

Playa Los Muertos

Playa Conchas Chinas

Camino Real Hotel

Villas Garza Blanca

Hotel Girasol Sur

Eden

Chino's Paradise

To Manzanillo

Chico's Paradise

Yelapa

Playa Mismaloya

Boca de Tomatlán

Playa Las Ánimas

Playa Quimixto

Bahía de Banderas

PACIFIC OCEAN

N

the town's main square) and *cruz* is the Spanish word for cross. Along the town's main two-way cobblestone street you'll find the Hotel Miramar and its seafood restaurant and bar, a well-stocked grocery store, and the main square. The main street leads to the town's protected harbor where the beach is ideal for nonswimmers, children, and anyone with a deep dislike for waves.

Playa Destiladeras *Km. 8.* The soft, whitish sand, the long, rolling waves, the shallow blue water and, best of all, the tranquility, make Destiladeras one of the nicest beaches in the Bahía de Banderas. The beach is about a mile long with no trees for shade.

The sea is very safe on calm days; you can walk into it for 20 yards and the water will still only be at chest level. Beyond this point the waves crest and break and are about 3 feet high. On rough days, they reach 5 feet or more and at the breaking point are unsafe. It's like being inside a blender, which can be fun but can also hurt you badly. If you're caught by surprise at the foot of a large breaking wave, dive under it and paddle fast to come out behind it. Destiladeras is a great beach for boogie board riding and body surfing but only fair for short surfboard rides. Inexperienced riders should avoid riding on the crest of high waves, as they can flip you when they break.

A *palapa* restaurant by the parking area serves the usual fare of seafood specialties.

Playa Punta Del Burro *Km. 10.5.* The dirt road to this beach is easily recognizable, as it's topped with broken pieces of white coral. It's only a third of a mile from the highway to the beach.

Punta del Burro is a private land development that will include a beach club with a swimming pool, restaurant-bar, and tennis courts. The project, however, may be grounded for a number of years due to the lack of fresh water.

Punta del Burro is one of the most private, unspoiled beaches in the whole Bay of Banderas. The main beach is a 400-yard stretch of soft sand. As you walk in the water the grade is gentle; the waves break at about 4 feet. Watch out for rocky areas on the bottom, particularly on days when the water is not clear. North of the main beach there are a series of coves where the bottom is covered with more and sharper rocks. There are no restaurants; bring your own food and drinks.

Fonda Las Amapas *Km. 13.5. Fonda* is another Spanish word for restaurant. Las Amapa's menu is without a doubt the most unusual in the region, featuring the day's catch—that is, the jungle day's catch. You will find iguana a la Veracruzana, fried rattle-snake, boar in green sauce, and baked possum. Less exotic dishes such as rabbit (*conejo*) and duck (*pato*) are also available.

Playa Pontoque *Km. 13.5.* This beach is 600 steps from the highway on a path through the jungle. Park your vehicle at Fonda Las Amapas; the path is across the highway and to the right. The walk from the highway to the beach is a great deterrent to picnickers carrying beach paraphernalia, which is why Pontoque is often deserted. The beach is sandy, but in the water it is rocky in areas. The waves break about 5 feet from the water's edge and are the tricky, rolling type described under Playa Destiladeras. If the waves are 5 feet or higher it's best to stay out. Both ends of this tiny beach are rocky, but the fascinating black rocks along the northern shoreline make for good exploring.

Town of Punta Mita *Km 19.* The tiny town of Punta Mita consists of a group of uniform white brick houses with red tile roofs. The main entrance to the town is a two-way cobblestone street on the sea side of the highway. A tiny store sells refreshments and a few staples, but not much else.

Playa La Manzanilla *Access Km 19.* Take the cobblestone street at the entrance to the town of Punta Mita. Turn left at the bust of Zapata and follow the road to the beach. It's 700 yards from the highway to the beach, which is an extension of El Anclote Beach a half-mile to the north. La Manzanilla, however, is more private. Here, a woolly carpet of soft, warm, white sand blends in with the ocean's fresh, curly blue waves. Plenty of shade is provided by the beach's namesake, manzanilla trees. Bring your own food and beverages or walk north to El Coral Restaurant.

Playa El Anclote *Km 19.5.* Half a kilometer past the entrance to the town of Punta Mita, a sign on the left side of the road reads "Restaurant El Coral—Sandy Beach." El Anclote Beach is a short 300 yards from this sign. "Sandy Beach" is an understatement for the baby-skin softness of the sand. Unlike the ground-up rock sand of other beaches in the Bay of Banderas, the sand here is coral and shells ground to a fine powder. The water is safe and shallow, with 2-foot waves that are ideal for surf and boogie boards and general fun and frolic. To the right of the restaurant the shoreline is rocky and risky.

El Coral Restaurant, with its fine and reasonably priced seafood dishes, is a good complement to this beautiful beach.

Punta Mita *Km 22.1.* Punta Mita is the arid, northern point of

Bahía de Banderas (quite a contrast to its lush, green southern end called Cabo Corrientes), and is also the name of the tiny fishing village found there. This is a postcard image of a small Mexican fishing town: a row of *palapa*-roofed huts built at the water's edge with fishermen mending their nets and cleaning their fish while sea gulls flutter overhead hoping for a share of the catch.

The beach at Punta Mita is beautiful but not perfect. Due to the coral reefs off the point, there are sharp, broken pieces of coral in the sand and water. Wear sandals when strolling or beachcombing. There are a couple of restaurants offering the day's catch.

A word of caution about Sayulita Road at Km 18.5: The road from Punta Mita to Sayulita is paved only in parts, interrupted abruptly and without warning by streams and gullies. Until it is totally paved, it's advisable to avoid this road entirely as there have been robberies reported on it. If you want to go to Sayulita, travel on the main highway.

HERMIT CRABS

When exploring the Punta Mita area, you might see what looks like bicycle-tire tracks in the sand. These are made by hermit crabs who live in empty shells washed ashore by the waves. As a hermit crab grows, it simply moves into a larger shell.

BUCERIAS

Km 142 Tepic Highway (25 km north of Puerto Vallarta)

Bucerias is a long, narrow town inhabited by a few thousand people and sandwiched between a nice stretch of beach on the Bay of Banderas to the west and the Tepic Highway on the east. It's a quiet, mostly residential town with little to offer party-going tourists.

Bucerias can be divided into three sections: southern, central, and northern. The southern part consists mainly of expensive residences, many of which can be rented through Puerto Vallarta's real-estate agencies. Access to this area is best over the southern-most set of *topes* (traffic bumps) on the highway.

In the central section you'll find the grocery, produce, fish, and meat stores, telegraph, post, and telephone offices along or near the highway. There is no gas station; gasoline is sold by the 5-liter container at the *farmacía* and they pour it into your tank. Restaurants on the beach offer the usual fare of fried fish, shrimp, and other seafood at prices comparable to those in Puerto Vallarta.

The northern section is made up mostly of Fraccionamiento Cruz de Huanacaxtle (a land development not to be confused with the town of Cruz de Huanacaxtle a couple of miles to the north). This area consists of residential homes, bungalow complexes, and, in the near future, time-share condos and other resort developments. The only access is through the Fraccionamiento Cruz de Huanacaxtle entrance over the northernmost traffic bumps.

Despite its proximity to Puerto Vallarta and the beauty of its beaches, Bucerias has been slow to catch on to its potential as a tourist town. But this is good news for those looking for quiet, economical accommodations.

GETTING THERE

Bus Pacifico buses leave hourly from the Puerto Vallarta bus terminal on Calle Insurgentes.

Car Bucerias is only a few miles away from Puerto Vallarta.

WHERE TO STAY

At present, tourist accommodations in Bucerias are limited to one trailer park in the south section and three bungalow hotels in the northern section. Except for peak vacation periods, it's easy to get a room in Bucerias.

CHEAP

Bucerias Trailer Park, formerly Elizabeth Taylor's beach property, is the only one on the beach in the Puerto Vallarta area. It has 46 full hook-ups, purified water, restroom-shower facilities, and a restaurant specializing in charcoal-broiled meats. Rates: $8 a day for a trailer with two occupants; $7 a day for vehicle and tent with two people.

BUDGET

Bungalows Los Picos *Retorno Playa Pontoque.* Twenty-seven large bungalows, half of them brand new.

Bungalows La Martoca *North end of Fraccionamiento.* Up to 40 percent discount in low season. Cozy and private. Ten bungalows. Reservations required for high season: P.O. Box 556, Puerto Vallarta.

MODERATE

Bungalows Princess *Retorno Destiladeras.* Forty dollars plus tax for up to four people. Each bungalow is a two-level new house with living/dining/kitchenette on the lower level and two bedrooms and a bathroom upstairs.

THE BEACH

The Bucerias beach, of fine, white sand, is ideal for hiking. You could probably walk about 4 miles to the south without seeing another soul. A few shells and small pieces of driftwood can be found here and there. The waves are small and the bluish water is safe for swimming.

NUEVO VALLARTA

Km 151 Tepic Highway (16 km north of Puerto Vallarta)

Nuevo Vallarta is a land development ambitiously started about 4 years ago that includes a marina and a network of canals that in theory should be lined with fancy residences. Today, Nuevo Vallarta remains a ghost town of wide, clean, tree-lined avenues. Ironically, they are well marked with large street signs so that you can easily find your way to the nonexistent houses.

But recently, Nuevo Vallarta has started to come alive and two new hotels are planned for the future. Considering its vast beautiful beach, potential to grow, and its proximity to the slowly but surely rapidly expanding Vallarta, Nuevo Vallarta may, as the name implies, become the New Vallarta.

GETTING THERE

Car The main access is Nuevo Vallarta's second entrance as you drive from Puerto Vallarta. The sign reads: "Nuevo Vallarta, Main Street." It's 4 km (2.5 miles) from the highway to the beach.

Bus Autobuses Pacifico leave about every hour from Vallarta and stop at the entrance to Nuevo Vallarta. From there, it's a 2.5-mile walk to the beach.

WHERE TO STAY

At present there is one brand-new hotel right on the beach and several more are under construction.

Condotel Marival Double rooms cost $50. Rooms with or without kitchenettes available. Air conditioning, sea view, restaurant-bar, pool, tennis courts. For reservations write: 4085 Boul. St. Elzear East, Duvernay, Laval, Quebec, Canada H7E 4P2, or call Tel. (514) 323-3366 in Montreal.

THE BEACH

Nuevo Vallarta has an expanse of desolate beach of fine, white sand stretching for miles north and south. For about the first 30 feet, the water is knee deep and gradually gets deeper. The waves are about a foot and a half high.

PUERTO VALLARTA

The first written records of Puerto Vallarta date from the sixteenth century when Spanish ships carrying supplies and people from Manzanillo and Barra de Navidad en route to Alta, California (now the state of California), and Baja California to form settlements stopped in Puerto Vallarta to replenish their water reserves. But it wasn't until 1851 that Guadalupe Sanchez formed the first settlement in the bay and named it Las Peñas. Over the years the settlement grew, and in 1918 Las Peñas was declared a municipality and rebaptized as Puerto Vallarta in honor of former Jalisco governor Ignacio L. Vallarta.

Isolated and ignored, Puerto Vallarta went on with its business of agriculture, which by then was practiced on a large scale in the Valle de Banderas that spans to the north of Puerto Vallarta. Corn, beans, and tobacco were shipped to other parts of Mexico and bananas to the United States.

Communications were slow to arrive in Puerto Vallarta, a little town so sleepy that it was hard to wake it up. Regular air flights to and from Puerto Vallarta did not begin until 1954 and the highway to Compostela and Tepic wasn't paved until 1970. What really brought Puerto Vallarta out of its slumber was the filming in 1963 of the movie *Night of the Iguana* with Richard Burton and Ava Gardner, directed by John Huston. The film put Puerto Vallarta in the limelight and overnight a new star beach resort was born.

At present, Puerto Vallarta has a population of 150,000 and is growing. Despite its growth, Puerto Vallarta retains the charm of its cobblestone streets, red-tiled roofs, palm trees, and brightly colored flowers plus the congeniality and flavor of a small town.

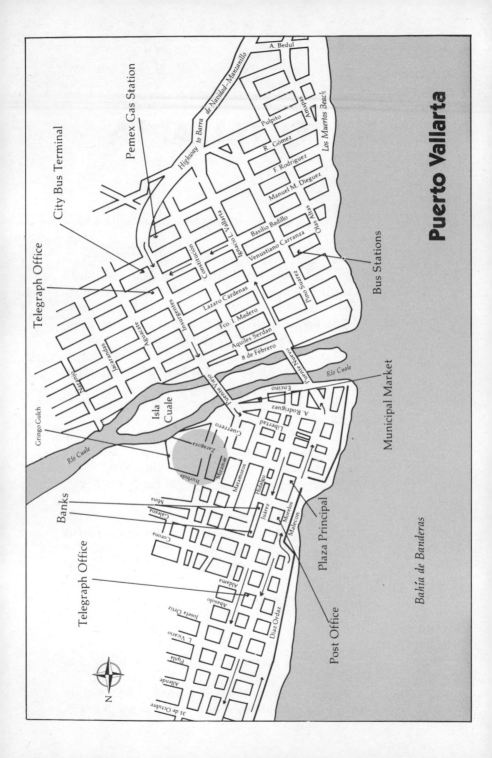

Puerto Vallarta

It's common to see the locals going about their business with burros carrying their wares, women doing laundry in the river, and to hear church bells chiming and roosters crowing.

During the Christmas season, festivities abound in the town square and throughout the city. On December 12, the Day of the Virgin of Guadalupe, people dressed in costumes and carrying torches form processions that lead to the church of Guadalupe to give thanks. In the streets, commencing on December 18, children and their families gather to sing and dance and to try to smash the *piñatas* that they've hung from trees outside their homes. Blindfolded, they swing wildly with sticks in the hope that they'll connect with the *piñata* and out will fall the candy and fruit that's inside.

There is no end to the festive mood of Puerto Vallarta. When it's not the locals celebrating one of their holidays, it's the North Americans celebrating the most revered of all holidays—a well-earned vacation.

GETTING THERE

Airplane Puerto Vallarta can be reached by direct flights from several major cities in the United States and Canada. Aeromexico and Mexicana Airlines offer the greatest number of flights from Seattle, San Francisco, Los Angeles, Denver, Chicago, Dallas, and San Antonio. Other airlines with direct flights to Puerto Vallarta are American, Continental, Frontier, Republic, and Western. Flights from Canada usually include one or more stopovers in American and Mexican cities.

Bus Tres Estrellas bus line has a direct daily run from Tijuana (a few miles south of San Diego, California) to Puerto Vallarta. Travel time is about 32 hours. Buses also go to Puerto Vallarta from Tijuana via Cabo San Lucas and continue by ferry from there. From Guadalajara to P.V. it is a 4- to 5-hour bus ride via Tres Estrellas, Estrella Blanca, Norte de Sonora, or Transportes del Pacifico bus lines. They depart from the first- and second-class sections of the Central de Autobuses, downtown Guadalajara.

Car Highway 15 starts at the Mexican border city of Nogales, Sonora (below Nogales, Arizona), and stretches south 1,500 km

(930 miles) to Tepic, in the state of Nayarit. From Tepic it's 170 km (109 miles) to Puerto Vallarta on Highway 200.

An alternate route is Highway 1 from Tijuana along the 1,690 km (1,050 mile) length of Baja California to Cabo San Lucas. From there, a ferry leaves for Puerto Vallarta on Sundays and Wednesdays. Buy tickets a day ahead of time for the 20-hour cruise.

Despite long ticket lines, conflicting and confusing information, and other bureaucratic hassles (the ferries are government owned and operated), the ride from Cabo to P.V. can be fun and interesting.

GETTING AROUND

The main part of the city of Puerto Vallarta is shaped much like a banana, longer than wide, and contoured by the Bay of Banderas.

Puerto Vallarta has only two main streets (both one way) traveling the length of the city and connecting with the highway to Manzanillo on the south and the highway to Tepic on the north. They change names every few blocks and twist around a bit but don't let that confuse you; just follow their general direction.

Downtown, the city is divided into north and south by Río Cuale (Cuale River). Two bridges cross the river: Puente Viejo (Old Bridge), the one farthest from the sea, with traffic going south to north; and Puente Nuevo (New Bridge) one block from the sea, with traffic traveling north to south.

The tiny Isla Cuale is located under the bridges and houses a number of souvenir shops, restaurants, and a small regional museum. The market and the greatest concentration of businesses, banks, offices, etc., are located on the north side of the river.

CITY TRANSPORTATION

To get around inexpensively, although not in the height of comfort, take the city's public transportation buses and VW vans. They stop at corners every two blocks and their destinations and route numbers are chalked on the windshield. To inquire if the bus is going your way, ask the driver, "*¿Pasa por* _____ ?"

Ruta 11 buses (also marked Pitillal) and VW vans marked Ruta 1B and Ruta 03 go by the large hotels and to the nearby marina north of town. Ruta 03 VW vans go as far as the airport. To ensure a seat, the best spot to catch VW vans and buses to Mismaloya is at their departure point at Plaza Lázaro Cárdenas (at the corner of Calle Lázaro Cárdenas and Olas Altas) as here they fill to capacity. Fares are inexpensive.

TAXIS

Vallarta's taxis, all painted yellow and white, are easily found throughout town, outside the big hotels, or cruising the streets. Since they have no meters, the rates are set by zones and increase about once a year. It's best to inquire before boarding the taxi "¿Cuanto cuesta a _____?"

WHERE TO STAY

Puerto Vallarta may be a small city but the choice of accommodations is plentiful and choosing one can be confusing, particularly to first-time visitors.

Rather than attempt to describe all the various accommodations, I offer a selection of the best values in categories to suit every budget. The list does not include hotels that are overrated or have deficient security or poor service.

CHEAP

Hotel Azteca *Madero 473.* Ceiling fans, hot water, nice and clean.

Hotel Villa Del Mar *Madero 440.* Ceiling fans, hot water, clean.

Hotel Chula Vista *Juárez 263.* Ceiling fans, hot water, clean.

Hotel Marlyn *Ave. Mexico 1121.* Ceiling fans, hot water, very clean, some rooms with sea view. The superstar of P.V.'s one-star hotels. Tel. 20965.

Hotel Belmar *Insurgentes 161.* Clean, airy rooms, ceiling fans, balcony. Rooftop garden. Tel. 20572.

Hotel Yazmin *Basilio Badillo 168.* Courtyard, ceiling fans, half a block from Los Muertos Beach. Very popular with budget travelers. Tel. 20087.

Hotel Posada Don Miguel *Insurgentes 322.* Ceiling fans, air conditioning at a slightly higher price. Small pool. Tel. 20668.

Hotel Plaza *Malecón and Calle Allende.* Eight clean, ample rooms, air conditioning.

Hotel Posada de Roger *Basilio Badillo 237.* Pool, restaurant-bar, garden/courtyard, ceiling fans. Two blocks from Los Muertos Beach. In its historical 15 years of existence, Roger's has grown from a 10-room guest house to its present capacity of 50 rooms and is one of the nicest, cleanest, and most sociable hotels in town. From the end of Easter Week to the end of October, rates drop to about half. A money order with one day's deposit is required. Tel. 20836.

BUDGET

Hotel Rio *Morelos 170.* Ceiling fans, pool, restaurant-bar. An older hotel but nice and offers good service. Located on one of the main streets, so it can be noisy. If available, ask for a room in the back. Tel. 20366.

Hotel Rosita *Diaz Ordaz 901.* Pool, restaurant-bar, patios, ceiling fans, or air conditioning. The Rosita, together with the Oceano, is one of the oldest, most respected hotels in town. It's on the northern end of the Malecón. Tel. 21033.

Hotel Fontana del Mar *M. Diguez (just off Olas Altas).* Rooftop pool, air conditioning, telephones. One block from Los Muertos Beach. Guests of the Fontana may use the facilities of Hotel Playa Los Arcos, including beach chairs and towels, as they are under the same ownership. Tel. 21712.

Hotel Oceano *Galeana 103.* Air conditioning, balconies, restaurant, bar, view, small rooftop pool. Founded in 1955 (originally named Posada Gutierrez), Hotel Oceano was the pioneer hotel in Puerto Vallarta. The Oceano has been host to such famous personalities as John Huston, Richard Burton, and Elizabeth Taylor. Tel. 21322.

Hotel Torre de Oro *Calle Pulpito 138.* One block from Los Muertos Beach, with spacious rooms originally built as suites, many with an ocean view. Tel. 24488.

Hotel Eloisa *Lázaro Cárdenas 179.* Pool, restaurant-bar, clean, view, ceiling fans, air conditioning, large but quiet. On Los Muertos Beach. Tel. 20286.

Hotel Encino *Juárez 122.* Restaurant-bar, rooftop pool, air conditioning, telephones in rooms, many rooms with view. Tel. 20051.

Hotel Tropicana *Amapas 214.* Pool, restaurant-bar, quiet, clean, friendly. Right on Los Muertos Beach, most rooms have an ocean view. Reservations are a must as the Tropicana receives large groups of Canadian tourists. Tel. 20912.

MODERATE

Hotel Club Tenis Vallarta *Km 3 Tepic Highway, P.O. Box 598.* Eleven new suites, kitchenettes, pool, restaurant-bar, six tennis courts. Small, very friendly, secluded. Guests are allowed 1 free hour of tennis a day. Tel. 22767.

Los Arcos Hotel *Olas Altas 380.* Pool, two restaurants, bar, rooftop tennis. Los Arcos is one of the best medium-priced hotels in Puerto Vallarta. It's right on Los Muertos Beach, has an abundance of shady coconut trees, and is within easy walking distance of downtown. Los Arcos is very protective of its female guests and will not permit them to bring men to their rooms after 11:00 P.M. Tel. 21583.

Condominiums Girasol Sur *Km 8 Manzanillo Highway, P.O. Box 124.* Pool, restaurant-bar, mini-grocery store, balconies, kitchenettes, air conditioning, telephones in rooms. On a beautiful stretch of beach, Girasol is one of the most attractive condo-hotels in Puerto Vallarta and, for the facilities it offers, a real bargain. Tel. 22350.

Hotel Las Palmas. *Km 2.5 Tepic Highway, P.O. Box 55.* Pool, restaurant, bar. The minute you arrive at Las Palmas's large Polynesian-style *palapa* lobby, you will feel the coziness and friendliness of the hotel. All rooms face one of the nicest palm-lined beaches in Puerto Vallarta. Tel. 20650.

Hotel Oro Verde *Corner of Calles Amapas and R. Gomez.* Pool, two restaurant-bars. Previously a two-star hotel, the Oro Verde changed owners, who remodeled to make it a pleasant four-star hotel. Located on a crowded stretch of Los Muertos Beach. Tel. 21555.

Hotel Playa Conchas Chinas *Km 2.5 Manzanillo Highway, P.O. Box 346.* On the beach, 40 rooms, mini-kitchenettes, sea view restaurant, bar, plenty of greenery on the grounds. Tel. 20156.

Hotel Buenaventura *Ave. Mexico 1301.* Two restaurants, bar, pool. On the beach, ten blocks from the Malecón. The Buenaventura is a fairly new addition to the moderately priced hotels in Puerto Vallarta. It's attractive and cozy, which is more than I can say for a couple of the more expensive, big-name hotels at the north end of town. Depending on the season, its beach changes from sandy to rocky. Tel. 23727.

DELUXE

The following hotels have five-star and grand tourism ratings and are the cream of the crop. They are full-service hotels with several restaurants, bars, shops, car rental, travel agency, a nightclub, and a variety of other facilities.

In addition to the basic double rate, other accommodations are available, such as master and junior suites and penthouses.

Hotel Buganvilias Sheraton *P.O. Box 333.* Tel. 23000. Telex 065544.

Hotel Camino Real Tel. 20002. Telex 065503.

Hotel Fiesta Americana *P.O. Box 270.* Tel. 22010. Telex 65538.

Hotel Playa de Oro Tel. 20348. Telex 065513.

Hotel Plaza Las Glorias Tel. 22224.

Hotel Plaza Vallarta *P.O. Box 36/B.* Tel. 24360. Telex 65559.

Hotel Posada Vallarta Tel. 21459. Telex 065504.

Villas Garza Blanca *Km 7.5 on the Manzanillo Highway. P.O. Box 58.* Garza Blanca's deluxe accommodations include chalet suites with private pools for about $200 per day and luxury villas, each one unique in taste and elegance, with private pool, Jacuzzi, breathtaking view, room service, etc., for approximately $400 per day for up to six persons. Tennis court, restaurant, bar, and private beach. Write for additional information. Tel. 21023. Telex 65515.

RESTAURANTS

Leave your diet at home with the celery sticks and the Jane Fonda exercise tape, because in Puerto Vallarta temptation is the order of the day. Who could resist a meal starting with tortilla soup, followed by a steaming plate of red snapper Veracruz, washed down with creamy piña coladas, topped off with rum-soaked chocolate cake, and, to ease the guilt, a diet cola.

In the area between the Malecón and Olas Altas Street alone there are over fifty tourist-oriented restaurants. Many are popular because of their location and advertising, but the quality of food and service can be inconsistent. You sometimes get the impression their main concern is to feed you, clean the table, and seat the next tourist in line. The following restaurants generally offer good service and good food.

DOWNTOWN
El Jardin Restaurant-Bar *Malecón and Calle 31 de Octubre.* As its Spanish name implies, this is a garden where dinner is served in

an informal but elegant candlelit atmosphere. The menu is fairly small, divided between American steak cuts and seafood dishes. Backgammon room. Open 6:00 P.M. to 1:00 A.M. Tel. 20342.

Moby Dick Restaurant-Bar *31 de Octubre, just off the Malecón.* A large seafood restaurant with an ample menu. The combination seafood plate for two consists of lobster, shrimp, fish fillet, and frog legs. Open 1:00 to 11:00 P.M. Tel. 20655.

Restaurant-Bar Las Palomas *Malecón and Aldama.* Set in a true Mexican décor, Las Palomas is one of the nicest and most popular spots downtown. Ample menu includes such unusual dishes as lobster tacos, sweet and sour roast pork loin, and avocado soup. Standard fare includes crepes, steak, and lobster, and assorted seafood platters. Open 8:00 A.M. to midnight.

Restaurant-Bar Hotel Oceano *Malecón and Galeana.* Located on the second floor overlooking the bay. A very popular place for breakfast for the locals and Vallarta's regular visitors. Breakfast is reasonably priced. Also open for lunch and dinner. Bar is located on the main floor and offers live music every night from 7:00 to 11:30 P.M. Tel. 21322.

Brazz Restaurant-Bar *Morelos and Galeana.* A spacious room with a tall, tile-topped roof where you sit in comfortable *equipales,* typical Guadalajara leather chairs, and listen to live mariachi music. In contrast, the dining area is an incongruous, air-conditioned glass enclosure. Specializes in American steak cuts and offers a salad bar. Mariachis every night. Lunch menu includes sandwiches and hamburgers. Tel. 20324.

Restaurant-Bar Casa Del Almendro *Galeana 180.* One of Vallarta's newest restaurants, where the emphasis is on fine food served in the quiet, romantic, candlelit atmosphere of a Mexican patio setting. House specialties include almond lobster, veal saltimbocca, and chicken cardinal. For a special treat, order the Chateaubriand Bouquetière for two, which is prepared at your table. Open 5:00 to 11:00 P.M. Closed Sundays. Tel. 24670.

Pietro's Fonda Italiana *Zaragoza 245.* Offers a menu of about fifteen entrées including delicious pastas and the best wood-oven pizzas in Mexico. The four-season pizza with mushrooms, ham, bell peppers, and salami is delicious and enough for two. Beer and wine only. Great service. Open noon to 11:30 P.M. Tel. 23233.

ISLA CUALE

Franzi's Café Restaurant-Bar *Isla Cuale, new bridge.* A pleasant, open-air restaurant serving good food at reasonable prices in a relaxed garden atmosphere. The dinner menu is ample and includes several original house specialties. The breakfast menu has about twenty different choices and you can have your omelet made to order from twelve ingredients. For dessert, Franzi's offers pies, cakes, ice cream, and about ten different coffee- with-liqueur drinks, not counting real espresso and capuccino. Open for breakfast, lunch, and dinner. Closed Mondays.

Le Bistro Jazz Café Restaurant-Bar *Puente Viejo, Isla Cuale.* Few restaurant-bars in town offer the unique combination of good cuisine, tasteful décor, good (taped) music, and excellent service found in the affordable elegance of the jazzy and classy Le Bistro. House specialties include steak Isabel, shrimp gabardina, and chicken au champagne. Try the Pomeroys, Bellinis, and other exotic drinks. Indulge in the crepes with fudge sauce for dessert. Open for breakfast, lunch, and dinner. Tel. 20283. Closed Sunday.

SOUTH OF TOWN

Restaurant-Bar El Torito *I. Vallarta 290.* Features nightly movies on its gigantic TV screen and live broadcasts of baseball, basketball, and football. Choose from a charcoal-broiled T-bone, New York, or sirloin steak, or Mexican combination plates. And to toast your favorite team, try one of Torito's gigantic margaritas. Open for dinner only. Tel. 23784.

Restaurant La Cabaña de Pancho Villa *Ignacio Vallarta.* Villa's has more branches than any restaurant in town, but they are dead tree branches nailed to every available inch of wall and ceiling space. Frankly, the décor is so ugly that it's quaint. Steaks, beef fillet, barbecued chicken, pork chops, and skewered beef are offered. Watch for the very spicy veggies and chips with sauce served before dinner. Beer and wine only. Pancho Villa's is one of Puerto Vallarta's few late-night dinner spots. Open 9:00 P.M. to 4:00 A.M.

The Toucan *Ignacio Vallarta 332.* The Toucan is my modest contribution to good, unpretentious food in a fun, hospitable atmosphere. The menu consists of a little something of everything (beef, poultry and seafood) and I change the menu frequently. Breakfast, lunch and dinner are served. Drop by during happy hour from 5:30 to 6:30 P.M. For reservations and nightly specials, ask for Memo when you call. Tel. 20836.

Restaurant-Bar Felipe's *Located on the hillside at the beginning of the Manzanillo Highway.* With a great view of the city and the bay, and fair to good food to go with it, Felipe's is a pleasant spot for wining and dining. Open for dinner only. Tel. 24599.

Restaurant-Bar El Set *Km 2.4 Manzanillo Highway.* El Set overlooks the ocean and is one of Puerto Vallarta's traditional spots to sip a piña colada and watch, as they say, "another lousy sunset in Paradise." The menu is small but adequate—soups, salads, and entrées such as conchas chinas seafood plate, barbecued spareribs, and pork loin. Open 2:00 to 11:00 P.M. Tel. 20302.

CALLE OLAS ALTAS

Restaurant Los Pingüinos *Olas Altas 391.* Offers fast, efficient service and good Mexican food. The owner is your host, waiter, and troubador and will delight you with the songs he sings along with the radio. Open 8:00 A.M. to 1:00 P.M. and 3:00 to 9:00 P.M. Tel. 20505.

Restaurant-Bar Andale *Olas Altas 425.* One of the newest restaurants-bars on Olas Altas and popular from the day it opened. The bar, with a lively atmosphere and full-volume videos, is conveniently separated from the quieter and more ventilated dining area on the second floor. The menu consists of pasta, seafood, and meat dishes. Open 5:00 P.M. to 1:00 A.M.

Restaurant Las Tres Huastecas *Olas Altas 444.* A simple restaurant catering mostly to locals, with seafood and Mexican dishes. Open for breakfast, lunch, and dinner.

Restaurant Luigi's *Olas Altas 508.* A branch of Pietro's Restaurant downtown, but fancier and pricier. Offers a more varied menu than does its counterpart.

Restaurant Acapulco *Olas Altas and R. Gomez.* Despite its plain looks and tacky décor of velvet paintings, this is one of Vallarta's best little restaurants, with a good selection of seafood dishes plus a couple of dozen meat and Mexican specialties. Open for breakfast, lunch, and dinner. Tel. 21279.

NIGHTLIFE

Most of you northern birds will not know how much of a night owl you are until you migrate south to the enticing nights of the tropics. Some early birds start their nightlife by bar hopping from one happy hour to a happier one.

Less thirsty ones go to their hotel, take a shower, have a siesta, and then head for one of the town's many restaurants. If you are definitely in the party mood, then head for the Malecón. There, lined up one after another, are **El Jardin, Ciao,** the **Red Onion, Il Mangiare, Mogambo,** and **Las Palomas,** restaurant-bars with a pleasant atmosphere where you can people watch, socialize, and talk under bearable levels of background music.

If, on the other hand, you want a ringside seat at the action, go straight to **Carlos O'Brien's** or **Casablanca** (also on the Malecón). These are the places you go to see and be seen, and you shout your order to the waiter.

If you are south of the river and wish to avoid the commotion and crowds downtown, try **Andale's Restaurant-Bar** on Calle Olas Altas. It has a publike atmosphere not found in any other bar in P.V., nonstop music videos, and fast, friendly service. A few blocks toward the new bridge is the restaurant-bar **El Torito,** another of Vallarta's loud and lively bars, where the entertainment is spurred on by both the waiters and the customers. The house specialty is the deadly giant margarita; one or two is all you'll need.

Now that you have revved your engines, you are on the right side of town for the discos. Next to Torito's is **The City Dump,** the oldest disco in town. Two blocks down on Lázaro Cárdenas #329 is the **Sundance,** and not far up the hill, but a bit tricky to get to, is **Capriccio's.**

The discos start to simmer at about 11:00 P.M. and reach the boiling point around 1:00 A.M. If you want to get there before everyone evaporates into the night, make sure you arrive before 4:00 A.M.

HAPPY HOUR DIRECTORY

The restaurant-bars that have happy hours usually serve two drinks for the price of one or at reduced prices. Beer and imported liquors are not included in happy hour prices. This list does not include the major hotels. Check happy hour times, which are subject to change.

Try the following bars at Los Muertos Beach.

Barba Roja all day, all week.

Bar El Pirata 4:00 to 5:00 P.M.

Bar La Palapa 8:30 to 9:30 A.M., 2:00 to 3:00 P.M., and 6:00 to 7:00 P.M.
Bar El Marinero *Hotel Oro Verde* 5:00 to 7:00 P.M.
Bar Andale *Calle Olas Altas* 4:00 to 7:00 P.M.

From Ignacio Vallarta St. to New Bridge there are several bars with happy hours.
The Toucan 5:30 to 6:30 P.M.
El Torito 6:30 to 7:30 P.M.
Franzi's 5:00 to 7:00 P.M.
Vista Cuale *Encino Hotel* 5:00 to 6:00 P.M.
Oceano Bar 2:00 to 3:00 P.M. and 6:00 to 7:00 P.M.
Zapata 6:00 to 7:00 P.M.
Carlos O'Brien's 5:30 to 6:30 P.M.
El Jardin 6:00 to 7:00 P.M.

MEXICAN FIESTAS

Mexican fiestas or Mexican nights are a combination of buffet dinners, Mexican folklore dances, songs, and customs. They are offered at five locations on various days of the week. The cost includes the buffet, open bar, and show. Reservations are required. Since they are all different, no one can be said to be better than the other.

Posada Vallarta's Fiesta Mexicana begins with Mexican carnival games where the fiesta-goers take part in prize-winning games such as throw the hoop around the tequila bottle and sink two balls into the milk jug. This is all done in good spirit aided by a tequila-testing and -toasting open bar.

The buffet dinner—a table laden with salads, Mexican specialties, barbecued ribs, pork roast, plus French pastries and fresh fruits for dessert—before the show is more than worth the price of admission.

The show includes colorful dances depicting various regions of Mexico, rope tricks by a professional *charro* (Mexican cowboy) and, the grand finale, a celestial display of fireworks that paint the night with an array of colors. Mexican fiesta locations are:

Camino Real Hotel Fridays, 7:00 P.M. Tel. 20002.

La Iguana Restaurant Thursdays and Sundays, 7:00 P.M. Tickets available at travel agencies.

Las Palmas Hotel Wednesdays, 7:30 P.M. Tel. 20442.

Posada Vallarta Saturdays, 7:00 P.M. Tel. 21459.

Sheraton Hotel Thursdays, 7:00 P.M. Tel. 23000.

OTHER ENTERTAINMENT

Brazz Restaurant-Bar *Malecón and Calle Galeana.* A mariachi group plays nightly in the bar. For performance times, call Tel. 20324. No cover.

Zapata Restaurant-Bar *Malecón 522, upstairs.* One of the few places in town that features a Latin American folklore music group. The performers are good, with a large repertoire; however, the volume is kept so high to attract the passers-by below that it's difficult to chat with your companion. No cover.

The following bars in the major hotels usually feature a tropical combo, guitarist, or singers. Call for information regarding current entertainment.

Bar El Marinero *Hotel Oro Verde* Tel. 20387.

El Embarcadero Night Club *Sheraton Hotel* Tel. 23000.

Bar Kon-Tiki *Hotel Playa de Oro* Tel. 20348.

Lobby Bar *Hotel Plaza Vallarta* Tel. 24360.

Lobby Bar *Hotel Posada Vallarta* Tel. 21459.

DANCING

Capriccio's Disco *Pulpito 170.* Capriccio's is Vallarta's "in" disco for the beautiful people, no matter what they look like. It's busy every night but to ensure they're never "out" of it, Capriccio's also features a dance contest on Mondays, beach party (bikinis and suntans are highly recommended) on Tuesdays, and a beauty contest on Wednesdays. Tel. 21593.

City Dump Disco *I. Vallarta 278.* The oldest disco in town and one of the most popular, with a dance floor the size of a boxing ring but without the ropes to bounce off.

The Lion's Den *Km 1 on the Tepic Highway, next to the Sheraton Hotel.* Aptly named because it is a regular zoo. The largest disco in town offers plenty of room to roam, making it easy to avoid rubbing elbows with people you don't want to meet. Tel. 24601.

Sundance Disco *Lázaro Cárdenas 329.* This is the high temple of sun worshipers in Puerto Vallarta, where night after night natives and palefaces meet to do the Sundance. And it never fails, for give or take a few clouds, the sun always rises in P.V. Sundance is one of the largest and most popular discos in town and has a comfortable seating area that surrounds an ample dance floor. There is also a separate backgammon room with well-lit tables. Tel. 22296.

All discos have a cover charge.

DANCE THE NIGHT AWAY

A little common sense and the following advice will spare you a lot of heartache when you are out for a night on the town.

1. Don't wear expensive jewelry.
2. Don't carry your passport, tourist card, traveler's checks, large amounts of cash, or more than one credit card.
3. Don't leave your purse unattended. A small shoulder bag that can be worn while dancing is a wiser choice.
4. In discos, shorts are acceptable wear for women, but men wearing shorts may be turned away at the door.
5. Have a good time but, as in your own country, do not tolerate behavior that is offensive.
6. Check your bill for accuracy.
7. Taxis are cheap in P.V. and as in any city it is advisable to take one late at night.

SHOPPING

Anyone who goes to Puerto Vallarta with the false impression that all he or she is going to find is *sarapes*, sombreros, and sandals is in for a pleasant surprise. The city is a mecca of fine shopping, whether you're looking for ethnic art, clothing, or jewelry or designer-label fashions, jewelry by internationally known craftsmen, or art by up-and-coming artists. In fact, of the resorts included in this guide, Puerto Vallarta offers the best shopping.

It seems that all roads lead to the main market (*mercado municipal* at the Río Cuale) just across Puente Viejo (Old Bridge) with its festive atmosphere and wide array of ethnic goods. On a smaller scale is the Tropical Mall beneath the Puente Viejo. Throughout town are many shops that have similar merchandise at varying prices.

Although some merchants in tourist towns tend to have a take-it-or-leave-it attitude, bartering is still common. But keep in mind that bartering is not an argument and should not be conducted with disgruntled groans and rolling of the eyes. It is a polite discussion of the price.

The shops included in this section are a guide to exclusive and specialty shops. In all establishments, there is at least one person on the premises who speaks English.

CLOTHING AND SHOES

La Zanahoria *Corner of Ignacio L. Vallarta and Lázaro Cárdenas.* T-shirts, dresses, pants, shirts, all with the Zanahoria label.

Viva *Corner of F. Madero and Ignacio L. Vallarta.* Great shop for browsing or shopping. The many unique items include pottery, antique belts, brightly colored tin soldiers, and butterflies and purses made of brass, silver, and copper. Most of the clothes are made in the store and range from cotton dresses with crocheted insets and collars to flamboyant dresses of gauze material with detailed sequined flounces in a multitude of colors. A section in the back has ethnic clothes from all parts of Mexico. Hours: 10:00 A.M. to 2:00 P.M. and 4:00 to 8:00 P.M.

Vallarta 13 *Corner of Basilio Badillo and Ignacio L. Vallarta.* High-fashion clothing designed and made by the owner. Good selection of bead and brass jewelry and leather belts with large brass buckles. They also carry ethnic clothes from Oaxaca. There's also a hair salon in the back.

Marta's Boutique *Calle Olas Altas.* Hand-picked selection of elegant and casual women's clothing at very reasonable prices.

Casa "Aoam" Modas *Francisco I. Madero 365.* Look for a small passageway, and down there you'll find a small shop with men's and women's clothes, shoes, and accessories. It's crowded, so dig deep. The best designs are for men.

La Zapatilla de Cristal *Francisco I.Madero 364.* A small selection of shoes but it appears they've been chosen carefully, as they're all beautifully designed and in great colors.

De Rizo's *Corner of Aquiles Serdan and Insurgentes.* Men's and women's sporty active-wear—jackets, T-shirts, shorts, etc. Most clothes carry the store's label.

Designer Bazaar Two locations, *Calles Juárez 350* and *Morelos 500.* One label, Vercellino Design, has both stores all sewn up, so to speak. They claim their clothes have "rhythm, art, and new expressions in how to think and be." Judge for yourself.

Deorela Boutique *Calle Juárez 178.* Fashion and accessories from head to toe—sunglasses, hair clips, lingerie, bathing suits, clothes, and shoes.

D'Karlo *Calle Juárez 188.* Shoes and boots made from elephant, iguana, buffalo, and snake skins, and the more mundane leather pants, vests, and skirts. To accessorize, there's silver and turquoise jewelry, and if you have any money left, they also have onyx ashtrays, ornaments, etc.

Filios Boutique *Calle Juárez 428.* Designer clothes by Oscar de la Renta for men and women. Some shoes for men. Hours: 9:00 A.M. to 10:00 P.M.

Max Three locations—*Calle Juárez 487; corner of Calles Juárez and Galeana; and Calle Morelos 582.* You won't go unnoticed with clothes from Max's. All clothes are made exclusively for their stores and lean toward chic women's designs. A large selection of silkscreened dresses, tops, and pants, plus matching shoes and coordinated belts. Coats are hand-woven 100 percent wool and wool-and-rayon blends and have sweaters to match.

D'Leo *Calle Aldama 112.* Stores in Acapulco, Mazatlán, Cancun, Manzanillo, and now Puerto Vallarta, with formal, casual and sports wear for men and women. A variety of designer labels such as Givenchy, Yves Saint Laurent, Gloria Vanderbilt, Christian Dior, Bill Blass, as well as Hang Ten and Crayons. Friendly and helpful staff.

Mykonos *Calle Mina 178.* Comfortable classy clothes in beautiful fabrics for women by Paris designer Joss Iff. Hours: 9:00 A.M. to 2:00 P.M. and 5:00 to 9:00 P.M.

The Rolling Stone *Calle Morelos 525.* Beautiful exotic skin goods for men and women—shoes, boots, purses, wallets, briefcases, watchbands, and, to take it all home, carry-all bags.

Aries *Calle Morelos 201.* This boutique is a joy to shop at. Not only are the clothes, accessories, and leather goods of good design and quality, but the staff is very nice. Hours: 10:00 A.M. to 2:00 P.M. and 5:00 to 8:00 P.M.

Polo *Calle Aldama 109.* Everything you could ever want with the Ralph Lauren label is there, including fragrances and clothes for the whole family. Hours: 10:00 A.M. to 2:00 P.M. and 5:00 to 9:00 P.M.

Genesis Boutique *Calle Juárez 783.* A little off the beaten downtown track but worth the stroll. It is small and has a limited stock of shoes and clothes for men and women plus accessories, but every single item is high fashion. Hours: 10:00 A.M. to 2:00 P.M. and 4:00 to 8:00 P.M.

Ocean Pacific *Corner of Calles Abasolo and Morelos.* Everyone will know where you bought your clothes, as everything has "Ocean

Pacific" or "OP" incorporated into the design, but at least it's done with style and in some cases a lot of flash. One of the more interesting shops. T-shirts, jackets, dresses, plus children's clothes.

Cocaine *Plaza Malecón.* T-shirts, jackets, dresses, tote bags, etc., right down to the tiniest bikini, have either the label sewn on or the word emblazoned across the front. As befits the name, prices are not cheap. Hours: 10:00 A.M. to 2:00 P.M. and 5:00 to 10:00 P.M.

ACA Joe *On the Malecón.* Fashionable, trendy, and popular. Shelves and shelves of T-shirts, pants, and jackets with the ACA Joe label. Be prepared to serve yourself as the staff is nonchalant, to say the least.

Rags Boutique *Lázaro Cárdenas 245.* Many of the clothes are made and designed on the premises, so alterations are readily available. Good selection of casual skirts, pants, shorts, etc., interspersed with dressy attire. Hours: 10:00 A.M. to 2:00 P.M. and 4:30 to 8:00 P.M.

Bambino *Plaza Malecón.* Children's clothing. You'll find the ideal gift here for your favorite toddler back home.

JEWELRY

Ric *Calle Juárez 207.* Teamwork makes this business successful with internationally known designer Erika Hult de Corral designing and her husband acting as manager and administrator. Many unique and beautifully crafted pieces in silver and gold. Some unset stones for sale. Take your time here, there's a lot to see.

Arodi Six locations—*Calle Juárez 252* and *Hotels Fiesta Americana, Camino Real, Sheraton, Plaza Vallarta,* and *Plaza Las Glorias.* Original and classy pieces. Eighty percent of their gold and precious-gems jewelry is designed and made at their downtown store. Silver also available. Major credit cards accepted.

ART

When perusing the art shops and galleries, you might keep in mind original art is duty-free. If you're wondering how you'd get that giant brass elephant head you've fallen in love with home, no problem, all art establishments are experienced in shipping and take the utmost care to ensure that your purchase arrives intact. They also will inform you of the paperwork that's required and the easiest way to expedite the exporting process.

Studio Zoo *Corner of Francisco I. Madero and Ignacio L. Vallarta.* It's a brass, papier-mâché, and ceramic jungle in here with designs by Guadalajara's Carlos del Conde. There are brass monkeys climbing trees, unicorns, parrots on perches, and small animals climbing on and out of fruit. Also a small collection of brass by Mexico City's Enrique Zavala.

Galeria de Laura Two locations—*Lázaro Cárdenas 237* and *Insurgentes 272*. A broad selection of ceramics and pottery including pre-Columbian reproductions, hand-painted stoneware by Ken Edwards, and black clay sculptures—mothers cradling babies, hunters with bows arched—from Oaxaca. A wide range of blown glass is available at the Lázaro Cárdenas location.

La Coleccion *Calle Morelos 529*. As you enter this gallery your eyes will travel immediately to the Pegasus under the waterfall. This is the world of Sergio Bustamante, including his early works of papier-mâché ostriches, zebras, etc., and more recent works of ceramic animals escaping from seashells, frogs cracking through eggshells, and surrealistic men of the sea and sky. There's even a huge monkey who bears a striking resemblance to George Burns, complete with cigar. Take your time or you'll miss a lot. Hours: 10 A.M. to 2 P.M. and 4:30 to 9:30 P.M.

Galeria Uno Two locations—*Calle Morelos 561* and *Plaza Malecón*. Mini-museums that carry the works of Mexico's best contemporary artists. Among them, Tamayo, Maximino Javier, Manuel Felguerez, Colunga, Toled, and Ramiz Barquet. The Plaza Malecón location has small framed works perfect for collecting or gifts. Winter hours: 10 A.M. to 2 P.M. and 4 to 10 P.M. Summer hours: 10 A.M. to 1 P.M. and 5 to 8 P.M.

El Dorado *Calle Morelos 631*. The new kid in town. Not only will you be visually enthralled by the sculptured world of fantasy in ceramics, brass, and copper signed by Mario Gonzalez, but the staff is ready and willing to describe the origin, history, and medium of the pieces. Some speak for themselves and others inspire the imagination. Hours: 10 A.M. to 2 P.M. and 5 to 9 P.M.

ICE CREAM

Bings *Calle Juárez 280*. A shopping strip is not complete without a stop at Bings. You can browse over their list of twenty ice cream flavors, various sherbets, and house specialties. A few steps away is the main square where you can enjoy your ice cream and rest after shopping.

BEACHES AND ACTIVITIES

The beaches on the Bay of Banderas offer plenty of amenities and opportunities for getting a good tan and having a good time.

From Los Muertos Beach, in the heart of P.V., to the Playa de Oro Hotel, 5 miles south, the beaches are a hothouse of activity where you can windsurf, water ski, ride horseback, mingle, socialize, or simply people watch.

Beach talk is simple and just about any line could be the beginning of a torrid affair, a lasting friendship, a business contact or, possibly, a boring conversation. But you can always excuse yourself, take your beach chair for a walk, and start all over.

If on the other hand, you prefer vast stretches of empty beaches, the northern half of the bay offers a wide choice. From Nuevo Vallarta to Punta Mita, you will find miles and miles of beautiful, sandy beaches. It's here that you get the most for your tan dollar as the beaches are always sunnier. In the rainy season, you can actually watch P.V. get drenched by a downpour while you are singing in the sun.

Whatever beach you choose, have a good tan.

BEACHES IN TOWN

Playa de Los Muertos, parallel to Calle Olas Altas on the south end of town, means Beach of the Dead and got its name from the casualties left on the beach after a pirate attack. Other reasons for its name could well be the numerous inert bodies that lie on the sand recharging their solar batteries, or the hangover victims sprawled on beach chairs, or the masses of deathly pale gringos that descend upon this terrestrial paradise every day.

But in spite of these signs, Los Muertos is definitely alive and well. Los Muertos is a music fair where strolling musicians— mariachis, quartets, trios, duets, and solos—will play the music your ears desire except for tunes requiring a piano, trombone, or lyre. With its continuous caravan of beach vendors, it is also a market on feet. If you hate shopping, and prefer that it come to you, just choose your beach chair, order your piña colada, and wait. In a few minutes, one of the Seri Indian wood sculpture salesmen will appear with pelicans, roadrunners, sailfish, and sea lions all carved from a beautiful dark wood called *palo fierro*.

Then comes the acrylic sweater man or the blanket lady, uncomfortably wrapped in layers of her multicolored cotton blankets, followed by various silver-jewelry vendors (the ones with the black attaché cases). Señor Canasta (Mr. Basket) arrives with woven reed baskets of every size and color and a magic act of small baskets appearing from larger ones, followed by Mr. Mat Reed, as he calls his reed mats.

In between souvenir vendors you may be approached by kids with fishcicles (fish on a stick) or fruit cocktails, and in the busier spots (Hotel Los Arcos, restaurant-bars La Palapa, El Dorado, and La Carreta) by the beer, piña colada, Coca-Cola, coco loco kids who work independently and normally give you faster and better service than some of the waiters working there. But don't pay them in advance; some of them may be pirates among pirates.

Finally, when the strolling musicians and beach vendors seem to have disappeared, you welcome the chance for a siesta. As you form a dream of blue skies and fleecy clouds, you're startled by a parachute that seems to have zeroed in for a landing on your belly button. Then you hear a prolonged whistle and shouts of "Pool eet! Pool eet!" It's another gringo parasailing and the commands come from the on-land navigator instructing the parasailer to pull the strap to tilt the parachute toward the beach for a perfect landing. But the airborne person is either too nervous, distracted, dumbfounded, or all of the above to pull the correct strap and lands, not very graciously, in the water. Immediately the parachute helpers scramble to the water to save the parachute, naturally, and to scorn the flunky.

Meanwhile, the whole beach is on its feet clapping, shouting, laughing, and making toasts, and once again Playa de Los Muertos shows, with a splash, that it's truly alive and well.

The sandy beach is about a mile long and the depth at the water's edge varies from stretch to stretch. At the north and south ends the grade is steep and after a few steps into the water, you can't reach the bottom. Here, on rough days, the waves are about 6 feet high and you can get hurt if caught where they crest and break. The safer, shallower part of the beach is between the Tropicana and Oro Verde hotels.

There are about a dozen restaurants on the beach. Most serve a variety of seafood, meat, and Mexican dishes. The larger, more popular ones are La Palapa, El Dorado (P.V.'s most popular beach hangout), and La Carreta. They all have good lunch menus, but El Dorado has even better breakfasts. Smaller but with great service and good food are Tito's (blue chairs) and Barba Roja (yellow chairs) on the southern end of the beach. For dessert, wait for Catalina, the pie lady, to come by with her delicious pies and muffins.

Sheraton Hotel to Playa de Oro The 2-mile stretch of beach between these hotels is a beautiful blanket of soft sand. It is the best-kept beach area in P.V. as most of the big hotels are located there and take responsibility for the upkeep. In some cases, they are so conscientious that they go to the extent of sifting the sand. In the rainy season the water can be murky and uninviting. Despite the fact that this beach stretch houses several large hotels, it still remains relatively uncrowded.

BEACHES SOUTH OF TOWN

Between P.V. and Mismaloya (12 km south) there are several small beaches that are among the prettiest in the bay. Some of these are hotel beaches, but not exclusively so, as the law establishes that the first 60 feet of land closest to the water is open to the public. Keep in mind, however, that while hotel facilities (beach chairs, showers, etc.) are for the exclusive use of guests, their bars and restaurants serve the general public.

These beaches are nestled between the rocky shoreline that is prevalent in the southern half of the bay. They are: **Playa Conchas Chinas** (2.5 km south of P.V.), **Playa Hotel Camino Real** (3 km south of P.V.), and **Playas Gemelas**, the site of Condominiums Girasol (8 km south of P.V.).

Playa Mismaloya *12 km south of P.V. on the Manzanillo Highway.* This beach can be reached by car or bus. The route numbers change, so ask the driver if he goes to Mismaloya. Once a public beach much like Los Muertos, but with its own personality, Mismaloya is now being built into a large beach-hotel development. The movie *Night of the Iguana* was filmed here. The movie set still stands at the southern end of the tiny Mismaloya Bay.

Boca de Tomatlán *16 km south of P.V. on the Manzanillo Highway.* Boca de Tomatlán is the tiny village located at the mouth of Los Horcones River. In the dry season, when the river's flow is greatly reduced, a small but pleasant beach forms. The water is fairly shallow for a short distance and then dips steeply. Except for the weekends, this beach is usually empty. The two restaurants serve a few seafood dishes. Boca de Tomatlán is also a departure point for chartered outboard motorboats (*pangas*) for special trips to Las Animas, Quimixto, and Yelapa.

At Playa Boca de Tomatlán, the Manzanillo Highway leaves the coast and goes up into the mountains. The following beaches south of Boca can be reached only by boat. (See "Boat Tours.")

Playa Las Animas Las Animas is the first beach south of Boca de Tomatlán, a 10-minute boat ride from Boca and a 40-minute ride from P.V. It's a sandy beach about a quarter of a mile long with clear water and calm waves. Las Animas is the destination of the *Bora-Bora* tour boat and a stopping point for the *Buenaventura*. Two restaurants on the beach serve the usual seafood fare.

Playa Quimixto Quimixto is only about a mile north of Las Animas and 50 minutes from P.V. The *Buenaventura* day-tour boat comes here, as do Chico's and Silent World's day-long diving and snorkeling trips. The sandy beach is about half a mile long and it is not unusual to see the village pigs burying themselves in the sand or simply taking a stroll. Stay out of the water; the bottom is quite rocky and the waves can throw you off balance and scrape you badly. A little restaurant on the south end of the beach serves fish and more fish.

Playa Yelapa The beach at Yelapa has a sharp drop-off three or so steps into the water. On the side of the Lagunita Hotel, the sand is coarse and quite abrasive on tender feet, while on the town side the sand is finer. The beach is a sand bar behind which is a small lagoon where egrets and sea gulls hover. In the rainy season, the lagoon swells and cuts its way through the sand bar. To reach the path to town, it is necessary to wade through the upper part of the lagoon.

BEACH HIKES

Playa Los Muertos to Playa Conchas Chinas A short, scenic 1-mile hike through rocky terrain alternating with sandy beach stretches. You'll definitely need footwear, and you might also consider packing a towel, suntan lotion, etc., as there are some very inviting sunbathing spots along the way.

The path to Conchas Chinas starts at the south end of Playa Los Muertos at the foot of the steep rocky hillside. It quickly disappears and from there you'll be walking along the shoreline. In the rocky areas, look for tide pools where you can find sea chitons, crabs, fish, and other small forms of sea life. At the end of your hike you'll reach the Hotel Conchas Chinas. Its restaurant, El Set Playa, is open from 7:00 A.M. to 11:00 P.M.

Playa Punta del Burro Km 10.5 Punta Mita Highway. Tennis

shoes or good sandals are recommended for this 1-mile hike although about a third of the way can be done in bare feet. Bring your own food and drinks.

The first leg of the hike is over a fine, white-sand beach. Look for hermit crabs that live in empty shells of various sizes, some as small as a pea, others as large as a fist. Hermit crabs do not live long outside of their natural environment. Watch them, have races with them, but leave them where you found them.

After the sandy beach you will come to a couple of small coves with a mixture of stones, solid rock, and sand where many varieties of shells can be found, including cockles and arks.

Nuevo Vallarta 16.5 km from P.V. on the Tepic Highway. From the Marival Condotel at Nuevo Vallarta, you can hike either south for approximately 1½ miles to the rock jetty or 5½ miles north to the town of Bucerias. In both directions, parts of the beach become a steep slope that runs to the water's edge. Along the surf line there is a strip of beach where the sand has been packed by the waves. Walking here instead of on the soft sand will be easier on your ankles.

Sheraton Hotel to Playa de Oro Hotel This short 2-mile hike can make for a pleasant excursion as there are many water holes along the way. The terrain is flat and the sand is soft; the only obstacle is during the rainy season when the Pitillal River (located between the Holiday Inn and Posada Vallarta) forges its way through the beach, making it necessary to wade across. To reach this area from downtown, take the buses or VW vans marked "Pitillal." They can be boarded at various points along Calle Juárez. Of course, taxis are another option.

CAMPING

The best spot in the area for camping and recreational vehicles is **Tacho's Trailer Park**, located across from the ferry terminal, 5 km north of downtown P.V. on the Tepic Highway. Tel. 20979.

Tacho's has 155 spaces with full hook-ups, restroom and shower facilities, swimming pool, barbecue grills, and lawn games. Rates: R.V.s with two occupants, about $7 per day; a car and two people, about $6 per day.

Besides Tacho's, the only other trailer park/campground is the **Bucerias Trailer Park** in Bucerias.

DEEP-SEA FISHING

A day before Puerto Vallarta's 1984 International Sailfish Tournament started, a tourist out fishing in the bay caught a giant 1,100-pound sailfish. One can only imagine the groans that accompanied the account of that situation when he told his fishing buddies back home, "I almost won first prize at P.V.'s Sailfish Tournament but I got a bit overanxious and caught a record-breaking fish a day early."

Puerto Vallarta has one of the largest sport-fishing fleets in Mexico, ranging from 15-foot outboard motor boats (*pangas*) renting for approximately $100 a day to 42-foot twin-engine cruisers going for about $300 a day plus 15 percent tax.

Before you embark on your fishing trip, check around with several fishing boat operations to compare prices and services. Also, ask questions such as: Does the crew speak English? How many people can fish? How many can go for the ride? Is there a bathroom on board? Does the price include food or drinks? How much of the catch can you keep? Does the cost include the 15 percent tax? Do they carry life preservers and how many?

For inexpensive fishing trips for not more than six people (only two can fish at one time), try the outboard *pangas* for hire at Los Muertos Beach and at Progreso Turístico Fishing Co-op on the Malecón. They rent for around $60 a day and the equipment is geared mainly for smaller species (albacore, yellow fin, dorado, etc.).

Lone fishermen can join the fishing party boats run by Big Al Tours and Miller Travel Agency. Both cost $50 plus tax and include bait and tackle, box lunches, and soft drinks. Daily departures; reserve the day before.

Big Al Tours *Hotel Posada Vallarta*, Tel. 22818, and *Hotel Playa de Oro*, Tel. 21251. Seven cabin cruisers available from 32 to 42 feet and renting from $180 to $300 plus 15 percent tax.

Miller Travel Service Main office, *Paseo Las Garzas 100*. Tel. 21397. Branches at Hotel Las Palmas, Tel. 20585, and Hotel Plaza Las Glorias, Tel. 20586. They offer a fleet of six 34- to 40-foot cruisers ranging from $180 to $200 plus 15 percent tax.

Progreso Turístico Fishing Co-op *On the Malecón across from Hotel Rosita*. Tel. 21202. Ten owner-operated boats from 30 to 40 feet renting for $110 to $180. They claim the cost includes the 15 percent tax.

SHORE FISHING

Every year during the month of June (the start of the rainy season), the Bay of Banderas teems with jacks, bonitos, and other small tunas. At times, the schools of feeding fish are so large that their prey, sardines, have no escape route other than to swim to the shore. With their prey cornered in water a foot or less deep, the hunters begin a feeding frenzy, thrashing about and lunching on helpless sardines. Then the hunters become the hunted when lurking fishermen, curious bystanders, and anyone with a dormant hunting instinct runs to the water employing beach towels, picnic baskets, and even their bare hands to catch a fish.

The big fish withdraw, their numbers somewhat depleted, not to mention the poor sardines who've been attacked not only by schools of fish but also by flocks of pelicans from the air. Meanwhile, on the beach, fish are counted and fish stories recounted.

Now, this may sound like a tall tale, but notice I didn't say *I* caught any of those fish with my bare hands. When I witnessed this episode I was on the beach, busy holding hands with a statuesque, beautiful, blond mermaid and couldn't have cared less.

Beaches such as Playas Los Muertos and Mismaloya with a fast drop-off are good for casting with lures of various weights.

Shallow, sandy beaches where the surf breaks about 10 to 30 feet in knee-high water are best for bait fishing. Nuevo Vallarta, Playas Destiladeras, Punta Del Burro, and La Manzanita at the north end of the Bay of Banderas are of this type.

For best results when fishing with lures use shiny, silver lures or a combination of silver and red or other colors as long as silver is included. White feather jigs with red eyes work well. Red lures can be very effective for catching needlefish, which are great leaping fighters. For best casting, use lures that weigh 2 to 3 ounces. Common catches when casting with lures are jacks and sierras.

For bait casting use shrimp, conch, or cut fish. Shrimp, complete with shell, always gives good results and can be bought at the market in Vallarta. The cheapest shrimp is *camaron coctelero* (cocktail shrimp). A quarter kilo (about half a pound) is enough for a good day's fishing. Because it is tough, conch is a good bait as it stays on the hook. Cut fish works well if the flesh is fresh and firm.

To cast your baited hook, add a couple of ounces of sinkers and make sure it goes out 15 feet or more from the breaking waves. The catch with bait can vary from surf perch to cabrillas and groupers when closer to rocks. Blowfish are unavoidable at some beaches.

There is always an unexpected catch. On my last visit to Tenacatita, I had a 15-minute fight with a big one that kept taking yards and yards of line every time I got it close to shore. When I finally landed it and was able to get a close look, I discovered I'd caught a 30-pound sting ray.

SCUBA DIVING

There are probably as many species of fish in the waters of the Bay of Banderas as there are bird species above. The only problem in viewing the fish and other forms of sea life is visibility. Due to silt, brought down by rivers, the bay's visibility in the best of conditions is around 30 feet in the dry season. In the rainy season (June through October), it's about 20 feet or less, depending on how heavily it rains.

Often, the best sights of your dive aren't under the water but rather on the water's surface en route to your dive. The Bay of Banderas is a natural habitat for gigantic manta rays with wing-spans up to 12 feet. This harmless plankton-eating creature may occasionally be seen leaping out of the water, some say for the pure joy of jumping, others say to shake parasites from its skin.

If you see one or several fins sticking out of the water, don't gulp and cry "shark!" Grab your camera and say "cheese," as the bay is full of smiling dolphins and a dolphin a day keeps the sharks away.

Buzos de Vallarta and Silent World Diving are P.V.'s major diving operations. They both have short trips (3 hours) and day trips (8 hours). Short trips are conducted on the same days and go to the same spot, the huge Los Arcos rock formations south of town. Day trips are also conducted on the same days by both shops, but with different itineraries. At the end of the dives both stop at Playa Quimixto for lunch. Optional for Silent World divers, at no extra charge, is a hike to a beautiful waterfall about 20 minutes up into the jungle.

Divers are advised to bring their own masks and wetsuits for the months of December through March, as the water can get very nippy.

Buzos de Vallarta *Malecón 772.* Tel. 21895. One-hour beginners diving instruction is offered at the Fiesta Americana Hotel. Departures are from the shop on Malecón downtown. Short trips leave Monday, Tuesday, Thursday, and Friday at 10:30 A.M. and are back by 2:00 P.M. Day trips go Wednesday and Saturday at 9:00 A.M. and return around 5:00 P.M.

Silent World Diving *Travel Agency, Holiday Inn.* Tel. 21700. One-hour beginners diving instruction is offered at Las Palmas Hotel. Departures are from Holiday Inn beach, or make arrangements to be picked up at your hotel's beach. Short trips leave at 10:00 A.M. and 3:30 P.M., Monday, Tuesday, Thursday, and Friday and last 2½ hours. Day trips leave Wednesday and Saturday at 8:00 A.M. and are back by 4:00 P.M.

Prices at both operations include the following: Short trips— equipment, a one-tank dive, and soft drinks. Full day trips— equipment, a two-tank dive, lunch, and a couple of beers after diving.

A word of caution to novice divers. The 1-hour diving course taught by Buzos and Silent World gives you sufficient information for your escorted one-tank dive. If you have any doubts, ask your instructor to clear them up for you. If you feel insecure or afraid, don't go diving. It would be ideal to pair up with a certified diver, particularly when the guide has several beginners to oversee.

SNORKELING

Snorkeling in the Bay of Banderas is best in the dry season (November through May), in the rocky shoreline areas south of Playa Los Muertos as far as Cabo Corrientes (the southern point of the bay) and at Punta Mita (the northern point).

In the best of conditions, visibility is around 20 to 30 feet throughout the bay, and mostly before noon. The types of sea life that inhabit the rocky shoreline here are the same as those found along most of the Pacific coast. Up to a depth of 20 feet, snorkelers may spot various species of sturgeon, butterfly, angel, damsel, trigger, and trunk fishes. Very common throughout the area are long, skinny cornet fish, mullet, yellow goatfish, sea cucumbers, and queen parrotfish.

There are a couple of boat snorkeling tours to Los Arcos and points along the shore in the vicinity of Quimixto. The combination of snorkeling and the scenic boat ride along the coast are worth the price of the tour. These tours are combined with scuba-diving trips. (See "Scuba Diving" section.)

There are, however, several other prime snorkeling spots along the road between P.V. and Boca de Tomatlán. Depending on their proximity to Puerto Vallarta, these spots can be reached by hiking, automobile, or the Mismaloya mini-buses.

Playa Los Muertos to Conchas Chinas is a mile-long stretch of beach providing ample underwater vistas. You can hike here from Playa Los Muertos. (See "Beach Hikes.")

Villas Garza Blanca, *6.5 km south of P.V.,* has a snorkeling area that stretches about a quarter of a mile across from the steep cobblestone road to the villas. You should be able to judge the visibility conditions from the rocks before getting in. The calmer the sea, the better the visibility. Do not risk entering from the rocky shoreline if the waves are over 3 feet high.

Girasol Sur Condotel, *8 km south of P.V.,* has good snorkeling spots along the rocks that flank its beautiful beach. As you have to go right through the hotel's lobby to get to the beach, just pretend you are one of the local fish and swim right past the security guys.

Mismaloya Beach, *12 km south of P.V.,* offers good snorkeling on both sides of the rocky Mismaloya Bay. The southern side is more interesting, as you can hike at the foot of the hill where the buildings from the set of the movie *Night of the Iguana* still stand.

WINDSURFING

Windsurfing has become a popular water sport along the beaches of Puerto Vallarta. With good, constant breezes and gentle waves, the bay is ideal for this sport.

Aqua Sport Windsurfing has shops at the Fiesta Americana, Holiday Inn, Las Glorias, and Las Palmas hotels. Lessons are approximately $30 per person and include 1 hour of on-shore instruction plus 4 hours of water instruction. Board rentals are $8 an hour. Open 10:00 A.M. to 5:00 P.M. Aqua Sport shops also make reservations for deep-sea fishing, scuba diving, and snorkeling.

WATER SKIING

Water skiing arrangements can be made either through the big hotels' travel agencies or on the beach with the speed boat operators. Although the boats operate until around 3:00 P.M. the best skiing hours are before noon when the water is calm.

TOURS

Vallarta's travel agencies offer guided land tours combining sight-seeing through the city and visits to Mismaloya Beach and Boca de Tomatlán on the south end of the bay. Additionally, there are ten boat tours to various beaches in the Bay of Banderas. (See "Boat Tours.")

Guided land tours are conducted in English in either air-conditioned motor coaches or VW vans. You'll be picked up and returned to your hotel. These tours are the easiest way for sight-seeing the city and beaches south and north of P.V. If, however, you choose the freedom and mobility of a rented vehicle or the economy of public transportation, refer to the "Sightseeing on Your Own" sections.

GUIDED LAND TOURS

City tour and Mismaloya Beach This 3-hour tour costs around $5 per person and leaves daily at 10:00 A.M. and 3:00 P.M. from major hotels. You'll visit the downtown area and drive by the major hotels and the marina south of town, then turn around and head south, stopping at Mismaloya Beach before returning to town.

Tropical tour Departs daily from major hotels at 10:00 A.M. for a 5-hour tour at a cost of about $7 per person. It's a variation of the previous tour with a swim stop at Mismaloya, continuing on to Boca de Tomatlán and concluding at Chino's Paradise. There you can have lunch (not included) and take a dip in the river pools.

SIGHTSEEING ON YOUR OWN WITH PUBLIC TRANSPORTATION

City sights Puerto Vallarta's downtown area is small enough that you'll automatically see the sights (the cathedral, the Malecón, the Cuale Island) as you go about town. If you wish to check out Gringo Gulch, a neighborhood inhabited mostly by Americans where Elizabeth Taylor and Richard Burton once lived, walk up the hill on Calle Miramar next to Banco Internacional at the Puente Viejo (Old Bridge). Three blocks up, turn right at Calle Iturbide and then right again at Calle E. Carranza. At the end of this block there is a spectacular view of the southern end of the city. Continue down the street to Calle Zaragoza and turn left. The bridge that spans across the street connects the houses that

were once occupied by Burton and Taylor. Continue on down
Zaragoza which connects with Calle Guerrero. Here, turn right to
return to Calle Miramar where you began.

Mismaloya Beach *12 km south of town.* A mini-bus departs
every 15 minutes from the square of Lázaro Carreras and Olas
Altas streets (by Los Muertos Beach).

Boca de Tomatlán and Chico's Paradise To reach these points
south of Mismaloya, take the Cihuatlán buses, which leave for
Manzanillo about every hour from the station at the corner of
Constitución and Madero streets. The fare is less than 50¢. For
the return trip, stand by the roadside and lift your hand to flag
down the bus. (For individual descriptions of Boca de Tomatlán
and Chico's Paradise, see "Beaches" and "Sightseeing On Your
Own in a Car" sections.)

**Bucerias, Cruz de Huanacaxtle, Playa Destiladeras, and Punta
Mita** Bucerias can be reached from Puerto Vallarta on Transportes
del Pacifico. They leave from Calle Insurgentes 282 about every
half-hour and the fare is about 50¢.

Points from Cruz de Huanacaxtle to Punta Mita can be reached
on bus service provided by Transportes Medina. Departures are
from Calle Brasil 1269 almost at the corner of Calle Honduras (a
few blocks behind the Buenaventura Hotel) at 8:00 A.M., 12 noon,
and 5:00 P.M.

SIGHTSEEING ON YOUR OWN IN A CAR

There are plenty of beaches and sights to visit by vehicle north
and south of P.V. along the bay. On the first day, the full gas
tank and 200 free kilometers that are included in the rental will
allow you to visit, for example, points north as far as Punta Mita
and back to Vallarta, a total of 100 km. The next day you could go
south to Chico's Paradise and back, using up around 50 km and
still have 50 km to spare.

Chino's Paradise and El Eden at Mismaloya Beach *12 km from
P.V. on the Manzanillo Highway.* Access is at the cobblestone road
parallel to the river on the left side of the bridge.

Chino's Paradise is 2 km in from the highway. Open noon to
6:00 P.M. Built on and around huge boulders on the banks of the
Mismaloya River. Swim in natural river pools and lunch on the
combination seafood plate for two that includes half a lobster,
shrimp, octopus, fish fillet, etc., for $20 or scallops for $7.

El Eden Restaurant *4 km from the highway.* Hours: 11:30 A.M. to

6:00 P.M. A brand-new restaurant under a huge *palapa*. El Eden's best attraction is getting there through the jungle. It, too, offers natural river pools. The menu includes a seafood combination plate for $12, barbecued chicken for $5, and other standard menu items.

Le Kliff *15 km from P.V. on the Manzanillo Highway.* Le Kliff offers an impressive ocean view from the multilayered levels of its no less impressive, huge *palapa*. It was originally designed to be a take-off of Acapulco's high divers' La Quebrada. The 110-foot dive, however, was obviously too risky and only an occasional kamikaze pelican has been known to dive from it.

Chee Chee's Beach Club *15 km from P.V. on the Manzanillo Highway.* Hours: 10:00 A.M. to 7:00 P.M. Chee Chee's is a multistage beach club project that includes restaurants, bars,and sea-water swimming pools.

Chico's Paradise *22 km from P.V. on the Manzanillo Highway.* Hours: 11:00 A.M. to 11:00 P.M. Like other river restaurants, Chico's also offers freshwater pools and giant boulders where you can sit and enjoy the jungle scenery. Chico's menu is quite original, with such delicious dishes as rabbit in adobo sauce, cornish hen in pipian sauce, stuffed crab, and oyster paradise. A live marimba group plays from 2:00 to 4:30 P.M.

El Tuito *40 km from P.V. on the Manzanillo Highway.* The highway past Chico's continues to climb through dense, tropical vegetation and gradually changes to a mixture of semitropical and pine forests. As you are watching this transformation you will arrive at the town of El Tuito. To most tourists this town is no more than a wide spot on the road to turn around and head back toward P.V. But to connoisseurs of *raicilla*, this is the spot to buy a few liters of this unusual moonshine. If you're interested in the stuff, ask around on the main street.

DAY TRIP TO GUADALAJARA

Occasionally during the winter months, cloudy, rainy days will interrupt your tanning weather, offering a good opportunity to take a trip to Guadalajara.

Guadalajara is the second-largest city in Mexico and has many shopping and sightseeing possibilities. The obvious spot for one-stop shopping is the huge Mercado Libertad, easy to find as you only need to mention the name to a taxi driver and he will deliver you to the entrance. Here, you will find sections with everything from leather goods, pottery, birds, medicinal herbs from every part of Mexico, jewelry, and traditional clothing, to the necessities of life—food and drink. Bargaining is customary and part of the fun, but be sure to first shop and compare.

To combine shopping and sightseeing ask a taxi driver to take you to Tlaquepaque, a neighborhood that was once a separate town but is now part of cosmopolitan Guadalajara. The shops on Calle Independencia are transformed private homes that now house antiques, glass and pottery vases and figurines, and original works of art—paintings, carvings, and sculptures. The clothing boutiques have designer fashions and accessories for the most discriminating shopper.

At Independencia 237 is the Regional Ceramic Museum (open from 10:00 A.M. to 4:00 P.M., closed Sundays); very interesting and no entrance fee. Across the street is a glass factory where not only can you purchase the wares but watch them being created.

The main square at Tlaquepaque has a conglomeration of restaurants serving traditional dishes such as *birria* (goat meat cooked in a red chile sauce), *carnitas* (pork meat deep-fried in lard), enchiladas, tostadas, etc. While you eat, strolling mariachis will offer to play; don't miss the chance to hear "Guadalajara" or "Cielito Lindo," especially played for you by these traditional musicians.

To fly to Guadalajara, Mexicana Airlines leaves Puerto Vallarta at 8:35 A.M. and returns from Guadalajara at 8:20 P.M. The cost round trip is $40.

BOAT TOURS

From Puerto Vallarta several boat tours will take you to various beaches within the large Bay of Banderas. Tour boats range in size from a 50-passenger catamaran to a 550-passenger ship. All depart from the marina at Km 5 on the Tepic Highway and are full day trips, with the exception of the sunset cruises, which are 3 hours.

Upon reaching your destination, you will be transported from the boat to the beach in either small dugout canoes or outboard motorboats, which may be difficult for physically handicapped persons. If you are prone to seasickness, Dramamine tablets can be bought at local pharmacies.

Boat tour tickets can be purchased in advance at travel agencies around town and at the major hotels, or at the last minute at the marina. Children's fares are as follows: up to 8 years of age, free; 9 to 11, half price; 12 and up, full fare.

Sarape. Capacity: 550 passengers. Leaves for Yelapa at 9:00 A.M., returns to P.V. at 4:00 P.M. Drinks, sandwiches, live music, dancing on board. Three hours at the beach with horseback riding, hiking, parasailing available. Price: $5, includes two beers or soft drinks.

Princess Yelapa. Capacity: 300 passengers. Leaves for Yelapa at 9:00 A.M., returns to P.V. at 4:00 P.M. Bar, sandwiches, live music on board. Three hours at the beach. Horseback riding, hiking, parasailing available. Price: $4.

Vagabundo. Capacity: 90 passengers. Leaves for Yelapa at 8:45 A.M., returns to P.V. at 4:00 P.M. Bar on board. Horseback riding, hiking, parasailing available during 2 hours at the beach. Price: $11, includes buffet lunch.

Bora-Bora trimaran. Capacity: 90 passengers. Leaves for Las Animas at 8:45 A.M., returns to P.V. at 4:00 P.M. Bar on board. Two hours beach time. Price: $13, includes buffet lunch.

Shamballa trimaran. Capacity: 30 passengers. Leaves for Quimixto at 8:45 A.M., returns to P.V. at 4:00 P.M. Bar on board. Three and a half hours at the beach. Hike to nearby waterfalls. Price: $8, includes beach lunch.

Buenaventura. Capacity: 45 passengers. Leaves for Quimixto and Las Animas at 8:45 A.M., returns to P.V. at 5:00 P.M. Bar on board. Two hours at each beach. Hike to nearby waterfalls. Price: $12, includes beach lunch.

Cielito Lindo trimaran. Capacity: 30 passengers. Leaves for Piedra Blanca at 8:45 A.M., returns to P.V. at 4:00 P.M. Three hours beach time. Price: $11, includes beach lunch.

Simpatica catamaran. Capacity: 60 passengers. Departs for Chee Chee's at Boca de Tomatlán at 9:30 A.M., arrives in P.V. at 3:30 P.M. Bar and snacks on board. Three hours at the beach, where snorkeling is available. Twenty-five percent discount on food and beverages at Chee Chee's. Price: $7.50.

Sombrero sunset cruise. Three-hour tour of the bay departs at 5:00 P.M. Price: $9, includes buffet dinner.

Simpatica sunset cruise. Departs at 4:45 P.M., returns at 7:30 P.M. Bar and snacks available on board. Price: $8.

A TO Z

AIRLINES

Aeromexico *Calle Juárez 255*. Tel. 20031. *Airport*: Tel. 21055.
American Airlines *Airport*: Tel. 23707.
Continental Airlines *Airport*: Tel. 23096.
Frontier Airlines *Airport*: Tel. 23166.
Mexicana Airlines *Calle Juárez*. Tel. 21878. *Airport*: Tel. 20138.
Republic Airlines *Calles Morelos and Agustin Rodriguez*. Tel. 21422.
Western Airlines *Airport*: Tel. 23919.

AIRPORT

Puerto Vallarta International Airport is located 8.5 km north of the Plaza Principal on the Tepic Highway. Transportation into town is provided by VW vans carrying about six passengers each. The fare per person, including a reasonable amount of luggage, depends on the destination point. To find out how much it costs to your destination, ask the driver *"¿Cuanto cuesta a _____?"* Transportation is also provided to points surrounding the P.V. area, such as Nuevo Vallarta, Bucerias, and outside of it to points about 3 hours away, such as San Blas to the north and Hotel Plaza Careyes to the south. Try to negotiate the best rate possible in these cases. Taxi fares from town into the airport also depend on distance to be covered.

The airport has several souvenir shops, restaurant, bar, duty-free shop (inside the boarding area), seven car-rental agencies, and a money exchange booth which sells and buys pesos at less than the official rate.

Remember to save about $10 to pay the international departure tax, which is not included in the price of your ticket. This fee is collected at the security checkpoint.

BANKS

Most of the banks in P.V. are downtown, within two blocks of the Plaza Principal. One block north on Calle Juárez are Comermex, Serfin, Refaccionario, and Bancomer. All banks are open from 9:00 A.M. to 1:30 P.M. Monday through Friday.

Exchange booths are located throughout the city and offer a few cents less per dollar than the banks. Likewise, money may be exchanged at hotels at lower rates than banks offer. Most hotels, restaurants, and shops will accept American currency.

BULLFIGHTS
Bullfight season runs from the beginning of December to about the middle of March. Bullfights are held every Wednesday at 5:00 P.M. at La Paloma Bullfight Ring (in front of the marina) and last approximately 2 hours.

Usually two bullfighters are featured and each one fights two bulls (one at a time, in case you were wondering). The bulls are killed at the end of each fight, so be prepared.

The price of admission depends on where you sit. The higher you sit the cheaper the seats. If you notice a lack of Mexicans in the crowd, don't be too surprised. This part of Mexico is more into soccer, baseball, and discos. Tickets can be purchased in advance at travel agencies.

BUS TERMINALS
Puerto Vallarta doesn't have a central bus station for out-of-town buses. The individual terminals for each bus line are located along a three-block stretch of the Calle Insurgentes south of the old bridge.

Departures to Guadalajara and Mexico City leave about every hour up until 1:00 A.M. on one of the bus lines. Tres Estrellas, first-class bus line, has two daily departures to Mazatlán and points north as far as Tijuana. The most comfortable buses to Manzanillo are Tres Estrellas (one daily departure) and Norte de Sonora (two daily departures). Auto-Transportes Cihuatlán, a second-class bus line, has departures to Barra de Navidad and Manzanillo every hour. These buses also stop at Mismaloya Beach, Boca de Tomatlán Beach, and Chico's Paradise. Transportes del Pacifico, second-class buses, leave about every half-hour for Tepic and Guadalajara and stop to drop off and pick up passengers at the following points north of P.V.: Nuevo Vallarta junction, the town of Bucerias, the junctions of Cruz de Huanacaxtle, Sayulita and San Francisco, and the town of Rincón de Guayabitos.

Autotransportes Cihuatlán *Corner of Calles Madero and Constitución.*

Autobuses Estrella Blanca *Calle Insurgentes 180.* Tel. 20613.

Transportes Norte de Sonora *Corner of Calles Insurgentes and Madero.* Tel. 21650.

Transportes del Pacifico *Calle Insurgentes 282.* Tel. 21015.

Autotransportes Tres Estrellas de Oro *Calle Insurgentes 216.* Tel. 21019.

Transportation Medina *Calle Brasil 1269, corner of Calle Hondu-*

ras. Service to reach points from Cruz de Huanacaxtle to Punta Mita. Departures are 8:00 A.M., 12 noon, and 5:00 P.M.

CAR RENTALS

The following companies have rental offices in Puerto Vallarta:
Avis Tel. 21412 (no jeeps).
Budget Tel. 22680.
Hertz Tel. 20056.
Odin Tel. 20887.
Quick Tel. 23505.
Travis Tel. 22217.
AHMSA (no phone) office at the airport offers one-way rentals to Manzanillo.

CONSULATES

There are no consulates in Puerto Vallarta. The closest American consulate is in Guadalajara, and the closest Canadian consulate is in Mexico City. Mrs. Jenny McGill is the acting United States consular representative. Her office is located above Banco Internacional, next to the old bridge. Tel. 20069. Office hours are 9:00 A.M. to 1:00 P.M., weekdays only.

Mr. North Johnson is the volunteer Canadian representative approved by the Canadian embassy in Mexico City. Tel. 20969. Office hours: 9:00 A.M. to 1:00 P.M. and 4:00 to 7:00 P.M., Monday through Friday.

Mrs. McGill and Mr. Johnson are extremely busy and will be glad to help you with valid tourist problems. Please do not call them for trivial information; they are not tourist bureaus.

FERRY TERMINAL

The ferry terminal is at the marina located 5 km north of downtown P.V. (Tel. 20476). Ferries depart from Puerto Vallarta to Cabo San Lucas (Baja California) on Tuesdays and Saturdays at 4:00 P.M. Purchase tickets on the day before departure. Ferries return from Cabo San Lucas on Sundays and Wednesdays and arrive in P.V. around noon the following day.

GOLF

The 18-hole course at **Los Flamingos Club de Golf** was designed by Percy Clifford and is located 25 km north of Puerto Vallarta. The greens fee is $15. Free transportation is provided to and from the club. Departures are every hour (8:20, 9:20, 10:20 A.M., etc.) from the main gate at Unided Deportiva (across and to the right of the Sheraton Hotel). For reservations and additional information, contact your hotel's travel agency or call Tel. 22703 and 20959.

HORSEBACK RIDING

There are several spots to rent horses along the beach in front of the big hotels north of town and at Plaza Lázaro Cárdenas, by Los Muertos Beach.

IMMIGRATION OFFICE

Oficina de Poblacion *Morelos 600.*

JOGGING

Puerto Vallarta's cobblestone streets can be unsafe for joggers with weak ankles, so do as the locals do and run along the Manzanillo Highway (facing the traffic), on the beach, or for those who are in top condition, up and down the steps at the far end of Los Muertos Beach.

LAUNDRIES

There is no self-service laundromat in P.V., but you can leave your clothes in the morning and pick them up in the afternoon.

Lavandería Ada *Morelos 860.*

Lavandería Roger *Olas Altas 385.* Open 8:00 A.M. to 7:00 P.M. Closed Sundays.

LONG DISTANCE

Long-distance calls can be made at most hotels, except for those in the budget category, and at the following *larga distancia* stations:

Hotel Posada de Roger *Basilio Badillo 237.* Hours: 8:00 A.M. to 10:00 P.M. English-speaking clerk.

Telefonia Avanzada *Juárez 124.* Hours: Monday to Friday, 9:00 A.M. to 2:00 P.M. and 4:00 to 7:00 P.M. Saturday, 9:00 A.M. to 2:00 P.M.

MARKET

The **Mercado Municipal** is located at the north end of the Puente Viejo downtown in a two-story building topped with a red-tile roof. A small section (downstairs in the west end) is filled with seafood and meat shops and one grocery store. Two large produce stores are located just outside the market. A large area of the upstairs section is made up of food stands (see "Restaurants" section). The rest of the market (actually over half its total space) is a conglomeration of souvenir, craft, and trinket shops with the best one-stop shopping you'll find in town. Hours: 9:00 A.M. to 8:00 P.M. daily. Closes around 2:00 P.M. on Sundays.

MEAT SHOPS

The best meat shops in town are **Carniceria Chico's,** *Madero at Insurgentes,* Tel. 21115 (English spoken), and **Carniceria Wakakari,** *Ave. Mexico 49.* Both have American beef cuts, pork, and chicken. To buy meat after 3:00 P.M. and on Sundays, see "Supermarkets."

MEDICAL SERVICES

Dr. John Mabrey *Edificio Malecón 11-T-8, corner of Libertad and Morelos.* Tel. 22969. Office hours: 9:00 A.M. to 1:00 P.M. Monday through Saturday. Dr. Mabrey, American born, is a family practitioner who specializes in tropical medicine and infectious diseases. He is a graduate of the Universidad Autonoma de Guadalajara with a degree in tropical medicine obtained in San Ramon, Costa Rica. Currently he is a resident physician in P.V. who also volunteers his services to the local Red Cross and an isolated rural clinic north of the city. Call for appointments or home/hotel visits.

Centro Medico Quirurgico *Basilio Badillo 365.* Tel. 23572 or 24395. Hours: 9:00 A.M. to 2:00 P.M. and 4:00 to 8:00 P.M. Call 24 hours a day for emergencies. The clinic has specialists in pediatrics, traumatology, orthopedics, and gynecology, plus general practitioners.

MUSEUM

Museo del Cuale is located on the west end of the Cuale Island downtown. It's a small, one-room exhibit made up mostly of weapons (axes, bows and arrows, obsidian knives, etc.) from various Mexican Indian groups. Admission is free. Open daily: 10:00 A.M. to 3:00 P.M.

PHOTO DEVELOPING

60 minutes *Calles Aldama and Juárez.* Hours: Monday to Saturday 9:00 A.M. to 9:00 P.M. Drop off your film, do your errands, and pick it up an hour later.

POST OFFICE
Oficina de Correos *Morelos 444, downtown.* Hours: 9:00 A.M. to
6:00 P M

PRODUCE STORES
La Quemada and **Legumbres y Frutas** Located across from each
other at Calles A. Rodriguez and Matamoros adjacent to the main
market downtown, these stores have the best selection of fresh
fruits and vegetables. La Quemada closes at 6:00 P.M. while
Legumbres closes around 3:00 P.M. On Sunday both close around
2:00 P.M.

SUPERMARKETS
There are several small supermarkets around town but the largest
and best stocked is **Gutierrez Rizo** at *Constitucion 136.* Hours: 6:30
A.M. to 10:00 P.M. daily.

TELEGRAPH OFFICES
Downtown office *Calle Corona (just off Calle Juárez).* Hours: Mon-
day to Friday 9:00 A.M. to 7:30 P.M., Saturdays 9:00 A.M. to 4:00
P.M., Sundays and holidays 9:00 A.M. until noon.
   Emiliano Zapata office *Basilio Badillo 377.* Hours: Monday to
Friday 9:00 A.M. to 1:00 P.M. and 3:00 to 6:30 P.M.; Saturday,
Sunday, and holidays, 7:00 A.M. to noon.

TENNIS
Tennis buffs may play at the following clubs:
   Hotel Club Tennis Vallarta *1 km east from Km 3 on the Tepic
Highway.* Tel. 22767. Six Lay-Kold courts, two lit. Restaurant, bar,
and swimming pool available to players.
   John Newcombe Tennis Club *Plaza Vallarta Hotel.* Tel. 24360,
ext. 500. The most popular in P.V. tennis circles. Tournaments
periodically organized. Four covered Lay-Kold courts and four
open-air clay courts. Reserve the day before, and arrive a half-
hour before playing time.
   Los Flamingos Golf Club *Tepic Highway, 22 km north of P.V.*
Two clay courts. For transportation information, see "Golf."
   Vallarta Racquet Club *On the beach between the Sheraton and the
Plaza Vallarta hotels.* Tel. 22526. Five clay and three Lay-Kold
courts. Hours: 7:00 A.M. to 7:00 P.M. Small restaurant-bar.

TIME-SHARE CONDOMINIUMS
Almost as obnoxious as the beach vendors who wake you from your nap trying to sell you a siesta hammock are the people trying to sell you vacation time while you're on vacation. If you look affluent, married and/or gringo, you'll be approached by half a dozen condo time-share sellers as you stroll around town. Check the facts before you invest. Write to: The Federal Trade Commission's Consumer Protection Bureau, Pennsylvania Ave. N.W., Washington, D.C. 20580, and request their brochure "Ten Time-Share Tips."

TRAVELER'S CHECKS
The following are the only companies in P.V. who will replace lost or stolen traveler's checks:

American Express: *Servicios Turisticos Miller, Paseo de Las Garzas (Posada Vallarta Hotel).* Tel. 21197.

Thomas Cook: Wagons-Lits Viajes *(Camino Real Hotel lobby).* Tel. 20002.

For lost or stolen Bank of America traveler's checks, call collect 56-67811 in Mexico City.

TRAVEL AGENCIES
Travel agencies are found in all the major hotels and in town. The following are located in town.

Promociones Viajes Y Recorridos *Peru 1306.* Tel. 24512.

Viajes Tortuga *F. Rodriguez 280.* Tel. 22992.

Asesores de Viajes Internacionales *Hidalgo 119-203.* Tel. 21991 and 23883.

Viajes Mismaloya *Serdan 493.* Tel. 21896.

WARNING
For safety's sake, avoid the city's beaches at night. It's not against the law but it should be against your better judgment, as Ali Baba and his forty thieves have claimed these areas as their stomping grounds.

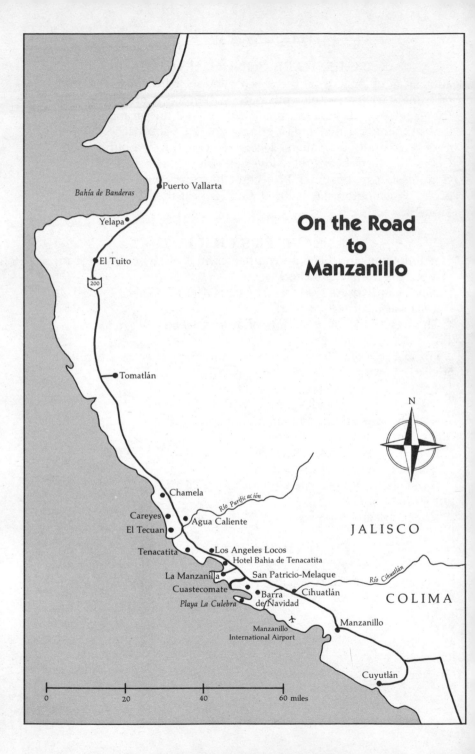

On the Road
to
Manzanillo

Bahía de Banderas

Puerto Vallarta

Yelapa

El Tuito

200

Tomatlán

Chamela

Río Purificación

Careyes

Agua Caliente

El Tecuan

Tenacatita

Los Angeles Locos

Hotel Bahia de Tenacatita

JALISCO

La Manzanilla

San Patricio-Melaque

Río Cihuatlán

Cuastecomate

Cihuatlán

COLIMA

Playa La Culebra

Barra
de Navidad

Manzanillo
International Airport

Manzanillo

Cuyutlán

N

| 0 | 20 | 40 | 60 miles |

ON THE ROAD TO MANZANILLO

South of Puerto Vallarta the highway (Route 200) follows the coast for 16 km (10 miles) as far as Boca de Tomatlán. There it makes a sharp turn to the left and begins to climb up the mountains to Manzanillo. For the next 127 km (79 miles) the highway climbs away from the ocean to altitudes of up to 3,000 feet.

At Chamela, 144 km (89 miles) from P.V., the highway descends again to ocean level and runs fairly parallel to the coast. The beaches, beach hotels, and beach towns found between Chamela and Manzanillo are located at the end of roads branching off the main highway.

The distances given under the heading for each locality indicate: 1. Kilometers from P.V. (set/check your km counter at the Pemex gas station right at the beginning of the Manzanillo Highway). 2. Kilometer marker (when available). One set of kilometer markers starts at Barra de Navidad at Km 0 and ends in Puerto Vallarta at Km 216. Between Barra and Manzanillo, kilometer markers are almost nonexistent. Larger localities, i.e., Hotel Plaza Careyes and Barra de Navidad, are usually indicated by signs, but smaller places such as Tenacatita Beach are totally unmarked, thus the importance of setting/checking the km counter of your car. 3. Kilometers from Manzanillo airport.

The highway is in excellent condition between P.V. and Barra de Navidad, a total of 216 km (132 miles), and is a pleasant drive, as it's lightly traveled. The scenery is magnificent with plenty of long, straight stretches, but remember to keep your speed under 80 kph (50 mph) as there are plenty of cattle grazing along the edges. When you see turkey vultures on the highway, slow down to a minimum speed as they are very sluggish in taking flight.

The highway between Barra and Manzanillo is very heavily traveled as it's the main artery connecting Guadalajara (the country's second-largest city) with Mexico's largest port on the Pacific coast, Manzanillo. This highway stretch is only 64 km (40 miles) long.

GETTING THERE

Airplane The Manzanillo International Airport, 40 km (25 miles) north of the city, is the closest arrival point for the beaches between Manzanillo and Chamela. The connecting land transportation to your beach destination is by communal VW vans. The rates per person depend on the destination and the number of passengers (normally up to five) sharing the total cost of the ride. In some cases, land transportation is included in the price of your excursion fare, for which you should have a voucher. Other excursion deals include a set rate regardless of destination or number of riders. Get the facts from your travel agent.

Bus Buses run about every hour between Puerto Vallarta and Manzanillo and vice versa. Cihuatlán buses, which have the most runs between these cities, stop in most towns and connecting junctions along the main highway. From the junction to a beach or beach hotel, you would have to hitch a ride or catch a passing taxi. Distances from the junction to the beach or hotel are given at the beginning of each locality.

Car A private vehicle is the best way to reach the many hidden beaches found south of Puerto Vallarta. Pemex gas stations are located on an average of about every 50 km. *Llanteras* (tire repair) and *talleras mecanicos* (mechanic shops) are found in even the smallest villages along the highway.

GETTING AROUND

Without a vehicle, transportation between the beaches south of Puerto Vallarta is via taxis or public transportation. Taxis can be found in the towns of Chamela, Agua Caliente, and Barra de Navidad and at Hotels Plaza Careyes and Fiesta Americana at Los

Angeles Locos de Tenacatita. There is also a car rental at Plaza Careyes. Buses run along the highway between Manzanillo and Puerto Vallarta about every hour and can be flagged down. These means of transport will enable you to get from one location to another to take advantage of different amenities offered by the various hotels.

YELAPA

Yelapa, about 25 miles down the coast south of Puerto Vallarta, can be reached only by boat. It's a town of about six hundred inhabitants, often outnumbered by the crowds of tourists that arrive daily on the tour boats. The town's houses, built on the steep sides of the jungle-covered mountains surrounding the tiny Bay of Yelapa, are made of stones, bricks (handmade from cement and sand carried by horseback from the beach), and topped with *palapa* roofs.

Yelapa has no vehicles, not even a motorcycle, and, of course, no roads. The town's communication network consists of a maze of paths on which tourists can easily get lost, particularly at night since there is no electricity. There are no telephones, no telegraph office, and no plans to change.

In town, there is a liquor store and two restaurants, The Yacht Club and El Tule are open at night and are the gringo social centers during the high season. There are several restaurants on the beach but they're open only during the day.

A 3-hour visit to Yelapa is enough time to walk around town and hike up to the waterfall (or water trickle in the dry season), which can also be reached by horseback.

If you want to work on your tan, have lunch at one of the many beach restaurants. Domingo's offers delicious langostinos for $6 and other dishes for under $4.

On your way to the falls you'll pass Javier's wood-carving shop. From the outside it looks like just another carpenter's shop, with wood shavings piled up under a *palapa* roof. Once inside, however, you'll fall captive to the sweet-scented *tampinziran* rosewood that Javier so masterfully shapes into wine goblets, salad bowls, and vases.

GETTING THERE

See "Boat Tours" for scheduled daily trips. Outboard motor-boats may also be chartered at Boca de Tomatlán, 16 km from P.V. on the Manzanillo Highway. Prices negotiable.

If you think Yelapa is a nice place to visit but you wouldn't want to live there, make sure you're back on the beach before 3:00 P.M. to get in line for the boat you came on.

WHERE TO STAY

If you wish to escape traffic jams, television, and telephones, consider renting a *palapa* in Yelapa. **Nuevo Lagunita Hotel** (Yelapa's one and only), right on the beach, has about 20 clean, *palapa*-roofed rooms that rent for around $20 for a double. The hotel has a restaurant serving all meals, a full bar and its own electricity generator which is shut off about 11:00 P.M.

In town, there are a variety of houses for rent that range from one-room "Yelapa rustic" (cement floor, bathroom, and some furnishings) for around $200 a month to "gringo rustic" (gringo-owned and furnished backyard annexes with bedroom, living room, kitchen-dining area, and bathroom) for up to $600 a month. Ask the locals on the beach for *"casas para rentar."* In the high season your chances of renting a "gringo rustic" are fairly slim, as they are often rented for months at a time. It's generally easier to find an available "Yelapa rustic." You can rent one for a couple of days and look for a better one in the meantime. Another source of rental information are the local gringos. They're the ones who stay bolted to the beach chairs at Domingo's Restaurant while everyone else is running to the boat lines.

WHAT TO BRING

Once you have a place to stay in Yelapa, your list of necessary supplies could include anything from pots and pans to water purification tablets. There are a few general stores that stock a little bit of everything. A quick overnight shopping trip to P.V.

may be required. Musts on your list should include a flashlight and mosquito repellent (particularly in the rainy season).

Depending on your interests, you may wish to bring snorkeling gear, fishing equipment (mostly for casting), binoculars, and *A Field Guide to Mexican Birds* by Peterson and Chalif.

CHAMELA BAY

143 km from P.V. (Km marker 72)
102 km north of the Manzanillo Airport

This is the first beach area to be reached after a 2-hour drive from Puerto Vallarta. Here, the village of Chamela consists of a few houses along the sides of the highway. The village "center" is the bus stop located between Kms 71 and 72 of the highway. At the bus stop there is a restaurant, supermarket, and a bank (Banamex). Next to the bank is a dirt road that leads to the beach, 1.5 km (approximately 1 mile) down.

Chamela is the place for people looking for a beautiful, quiet beach with inexpensive accommodations. Bring enough reading material, fishing gear, and whatever else you need to entertain yourself.

WHERE TO STAY

Motel-Trailer Park Chamela *Km 72, right on the highway.* Double, $10. Fans, pool, tennis court. Trailer spaces have full hook-ups and cost $1 per person.

Villa Polinesia Camping Club *1½ km from Banamex.* Villa Polinesia is a brand-new campground and trailer park located right on the beach. The camping section is huge and has shaded picnic areas with barbecue grills and dishwashing facilities. The showers and restrooms are located in two spectacular *palapas* that also serve as the Villa's social centers. For people without tents, the Villa offers solid masonry cabañitas of the same shape and size as a tent for two.

The Villa has 16 shaded trailer spaces with full hook-ups. Rates are $2 per person for trailer occupants and tent campers. Cabañitas rates not available.

Bungalows Mayar *1½ km from Banamex*. These bungalows are the best beach accommodations in Chamela. They are clean and economical with fans, kitchenettes, shaded grassy areas, and there's also a pool. Rates are $25 for two to four occupants.

Hotel Suites Chamela *½ kilometer north of Bungalows Mayar*. An unfinished, run-down hotel that normally would not be included in this guide, but it is right on the beach and Chamela's accommodations are scarce. The "suites" have tiny kitchenettes (ask for cooking utensils at the desk) and ceiling fans. Pool. Rates: $25 two to four people; $50 up to eight people. Includes tax.

BEACHES AND ACTIVITIES

Chamela Playa *1½ km from Banamex*. The Bay of Chamela has two main beaches but the southernmost beach is private and inaccessible; the northernmost beach is Chamela proper. It's about 5 miles long and 50 yards wide with hard-packed sand at low tide ideal for bike riding (if you happen to have one in your luggage) and jogging. From the high-tide point to the vegetation line, the beach is a steep sand dune of soft gold dust. The water is blue and clear and the waves are only about a foot high. No food is available on the beach. Buy beverages at the giant *palapas* at Villa Polinesia.

Playas La Fortuna and *La Pérula* *Km marker 76, 139 km from P.V.* These beaches, actually the northern end of Chamela Beach, 2 km from the highway, are good for people bringing their own boats as they can drive right up to the water's edge on the hard-packed sand. There are a few *palapa* restaurants serving fish, rice, and beans.

BEACH HIKE

After noon, the blue waters of the Pacific retreat from the beach and uncover a wide avenue that leads to a pleasurable, lonely beach hike. In the areas where the sand is wettest, the ground is almost as hard as concrete. The soles of your feet may get sore if you are not used to walking barefoot. Higher up, toward the drier sand, there is a softer area where your feet will sink in about a quarter inch, making walking more comfortable.

The easiest spot to begin this hike is from Villa Polinesia, located at about the middle of the beach. From there, it's 2 miles either to the northern or southern end of the beach.

SHORE FISHING

See "Puerto Vallarta" as the fishing conditions and catch are similar. See "Hotel Plaza Careyes" for other activities, deep-sea fishing, sailing, scuba diving, and snorkeling.

A TO Z

BANK

The Banamex branch is open Monday through Friday from 9:00 A.M. to 1:30 P.M. Sometimes they won't cash Canadian currency when the current exchange quotations haven't arrived from the head office.

BUS STOP

Most buses traveling to Manzanillo and Puerto Vallarta stop at Chamela. Boarding one is a different story as they may be full, particularly on Saturdays and Sundays.

OUCH AND ITCH

Every human being is a blood bank and every square inch of exposed skin is a teller's window from which mosquitoes can draw funds to their hearts' content. The beach areas south of Puerto Vallarta, from Chamela to Manzanillo, are dotted with numerous lagoons that are ideal breeding grounds for mosquitoes and gnats.

Save your blood for the Red Cross and take the following precautions:

1. Don't be a sucker by thinking that mosquitoes won't get you. Wear long pants, sleeves, socks, and a scarf around your neck after sunset, particularly near swampy areas.
2. Use a good mosquito repellent.
3. When camping, stay as close as possible to the beach. Generally, the breeze will keep mosquitoes safely away.

GAS STATION

The Pemex gas station is 400 yards south of the Chamela bus stop. It's open from 7:00 A.M. to 9:00 P.M. with regular gas and diesel only.

LONG DISTANCE

The long-distance phone booth operates at the back of the restaurant next to Banamex. Hours: 8:00 A.M. to 2:00 P.M. and 4:00 to 8:00 P.M.

RESTAURANT

There is a large, clean restaurant at the bus stop with a menu that offers a little bit of everything at reasonable prices. There is no food at Chamela Beach.

SUPERMARKET

This supermarket is surprisingly large and well stocked for such a tiny village. They sell ice in blocks about the size of a portable typewriter, but it is not made with purified water. The attendant at the meat section will weigh your fruits and vegetables.

TENNIS

There is a tennis court at the Motel Chamela on the highway.

HOTEL PLAZA CAREYES

162 km from P.V. (Km marker 53)
85 km north of the Manzanillo Airport
1.5 km from the highway over a cobblestone road

Plaza Careyes is a jewel of a hotel set in the emerald greenery of the Careyes Coast. Tucked in a tiny tranquil bay of aquamarine water, Plaza Careyes is an oasis of peace and quiet. It has a total of 90 units, rooms, suites, and apartments, and considering the deluxe facilities and the beauty of its natural surroundings, the rates are surprisingly reasonable. A double room is $50. (Similar accommodations in P.V. can be almost twice as expensive.)

Besides horse rentals, pool, tennis courts, mini golf course, a car rental and a 4,000-foot airplane landing strip, Plaza Careyes has the most complete array of water-sport facilities (scuba diving, deep-sea fishing, windsurfing, and sailing) between P.V. and Manzanillo.

BEACHES AND ACTIVITIES

The hotel's beach area consists of two small cribs of golden soft sand. The larger of the two is about 200 yards long and is shaded by tall, swaying coconut trees. The water is among the bluest and clearest of the beaches covered in this book. The waves are about as large as those your toes make when you're testing the temperature of the water. But this tiny beach doesn't end here; it's the gateway to many other beautiful beaches hidden in coves and bays of this fascinating and exotic coast.

Calypso Nautic Club is the hotel's water-sports shop owned and operated by French-born Bertrand Pequignot, a certified PADI/ dive master. He personally checks his top-of-the-line equipment and schedules and conducts scuba-diving and deep-sea outings. You could not find better and more professional services in this region. He has two 25-foot, 75 hp outboard motor *pangas* with a capacity for 10 passengers.

DEEP-SEA FISHING

A full day (6 hours) trip with four fishermen rotating action is approximately $140. A 4-hour trip for two fishermen is $70. Rates include all equipment and bait but no food or drinks.

SCUBA DIVING

The waters of Costa Careyes are very clear with the average visibility at 40 feet and quite often up to 60 feet. Since it rains very little in this area you can count on good diving even in the rainy season. The extensive rocky shoreline with its many coves and calm waters make for the best scuba-diving conditions in this region.

One-tank dives are $30, two-tank $40. Prices include equipment but no food or drink. If you want to discover the pleasure of scuba diving, you are in good hands with Bertrand, who gives a 1½-hour course at the hotel's swimming pool for $20.

BEACH PICNIC

The beach picnic is a combination of fishing and scuba diving or snorkeling. As you boat to Paraiso Beach, the site of your picnic, you'll troll for fish that later will be cooked over a coal fire. Along the way, the boat will stop for your choice of a one-tank dive or snorkeling. The picnic for divers is $40 or $30 for snorkelers. Included in the price is equipment, lunch, beer or soft drinks. Departure time is 10:30 A.M., returning by 4:00 P.M.

SNORKELING

A short walk from your room to Careyes beautiful little beach and you are in for hours of pleasurable, easy snorkeling. On both ends of the beach are shallow, rocky areas that are home to hundreds of fish species. Visibility right off the beach is approximately 30 feet and better as you round the point at the beach's southern end. Once you have explored the underwater life of these calm waters, you may want to join the snorkeling on the picnic tours organized by Club Nautico Calypso. The snorkeling tour is $15 per person and includes equipment (see "Beach Picnic"). Quality snorkeling equipment is for rent at Calypso for $5 a day.

SAILING

A 16-foot Hobiecat can be rented for $15 an hour. Two windsurfers are also for rent at $10 an hour. Individual instruction is $20.

See "Rancho El Tecuán" for other activities: canoeing, bicycle riding, beach hiking, and bird watching.

HOTEL RANCHO EL TECUÁN

183 km from P.V. on the Manzanillo Highway. (Km marker 33)
73 km north of the Manzanillo Airport
10 km from the highway
down a narrow, winding, paved road

Rancho El Tecuán is a vast expanse of land combining a working ranch (mango and coconut plantations, cattle breeding, etc.), a land development section, and a beach resort hotel.

As a beach resort hotel, despite the expensive-sounding connotation, it is perhaps the best deal for the money of all the hotels between P.V. and Manzanillo at $35 double. Built on a slope, the view encompasses the ocean, a lagoon, the mountains, and, as it's above our heads, the often overlooked sky. All of the hotel's 36 rooms have phones, air conditioning, and a view. On the grounds there's a pool, a large lagoon, restaurant-bar, tennis court, and a 2,500-foot asphalt landing field (radio unicom 122.8). To explore the area, horses, bicycles, and canoes are available to rent.

For reservations, call or write: Desarrollos Turísticos Tecuán, Garibaldi 1676, Guadalajara, Jal. 44100. Tel.: 16-00-85 and 16-01-83.

BEACHES AND ACTIVITIES

El Tecuán's beach is another of the long, wide, desolate beaches typical of this area. It stretches south for about 7 miles connecting with Tenacatita Beach.

Exploring can be done on foot or you can rent a horse. If you're keen on horseback riding, you could spend a couple of days exploring the ranches, hills, and trails. Ask for a discount if you plan to ride several times.

Another good way to explore the grounds is by bicycle. There is plenty of hard ground to ride on. The ride up the paved road that connects with the main highway is fairly flat for about a mile and a half before it starts to climb sharply up the mountain.

El Tecuán also boasts of its own lagoon, which covers several square acres. Canoes are available for rent to explore the many hidden coves.

As you paddle along, a variety of water birds can be spotted. Wading in the bathtublike calm waters are grebes and cormorants, and hidden among the mangrove vegetation along the lagoon's edge, you can see egrets, herons, and ibises. Calmly, you may approach them to get a closer look or to take a picture before they take off in graceful flight.

Besides the water birds found in the lagoon and along the beach, serious bird watchers can find dozens of other bird species to identify in the low brush areas, mountain slopes, and along the banks of the Purificación River, a couple miles south of El Tecuán.

For additional beach activities, snorkeling, scuba diving, windsurfing, and deep-sea fishing, see "Hotel Plaza Careyes."

PLAYA TENACATITA

186 km from P.V. (Km marker 29)
68 km north of the Manzanillo Airport

This is the location of the bridge over the Río Purificación (well marked). At the southern end of the bridge is the beginning of the 9-km (5.5-mile) dirt road to Tenacatita Beach (not marked). It's a bumpy road, full of deep potholes. As you reach the last kilometer, the road branches to the right and left. Stay to the left to get to Tenacatita Beach and village. The branch to the right comes to a dead end about a mile down at the Purificación River. A couple of isolated camping spots can be found along this branch of the road.

The tiny village of Tenacatita consists of about fifteen *palapa* houses where fifty or so locals make a living from fishing and tourism. There is no running water, sewage system, or electricity. About the only things you can buy are warm soft drinks and beer and a couple of brands of cigarettes.

BEACHES AND ACTIVITIES

Playa Tenacatita One of the many crescent-shaped beaches found along the coast of this region. It's a wide beach of fine, golden sand edged by a 15-foot sandy ridge covered with crawling vines and stiff, pointed grass. The water is clear and shallow with waves about a foot high. You can walk a good distance into the ocean but it's advisable not to go much beyond the point where the waves break to avoid stepping on sting rays who often inhabit shallow, calm water.

Playa La Mora Located a couple hundred yards over the small hill behind Tenacatita village. This tiny beach faces the open sea and has strong, tricky waves and currents as it's located on a point.

Playa Sola Stretches from Playa La Mora to Rancho El Tecuán about 4 kilometers down the coast. The farther you go from the northern point of Tenacatita Bay, the milder the waves. The beach is wide and has an area of hard-packed sand good for walking, and higher up the ridge, a soft sand area for beachcombing and collecting firewood for campfires.

CAMPING

Tenacatita is an unofficial rustic campground for North American campers. In the high season, the 1.5-mile dirt road that stretches along the beach's low, sandy ridge looks like a camping exposition. There, lined up one after another, are campers and tents of all types and sizes, some equipped with latrines, solar panels, wind generators, and other accessories.

To camp here, it's necessary to bring all your own equipment and to stock up with food at Puerto Vallarta or San Patricio. As there are no sanitary facilities, make sure to bury degradable waste and to remove plastic, glass, and other nondegradable refuse.

SNORKELING

The rocky point at the northern end of the beach has a shallow, protected area for underwater sightseeing. The visibility is around 30 to 40 feet but deceiving even on a calm day. Visibility is usually better before noon. When snorkeling around rocks, always stay 3 feet or more away from them as a few moray eels inhabit rock crevices along this area. If they feel cornered they may bite and inflict a painful wound with their thin, sharp teeth.

A TO Z

BUGS

The lagoon located behind the beach is a wildlife refuge for mosquitoes and no-see-ums. Although their populations are greatly reduced in the dry season, they can still be a problem to some of us sweet-blooded people. When buying a tent, if possible, get one with no-see-um netting and have a stock of mosquito repellent at hand.

BUSES

To get to Tenacatita or to leave, it's necessary to go to the town of Agua Caliente, 1 km north of the bridge over the Purificación River.

FOOD

Groceries, produce, and meats can be bought at the village of El Rebalsito, 2.5 km from Tenacatita Beach. As you drive from the beach into the village take the first street to the left. The two grocery stores are located on the first two blocks. Between the two, you might get what you need, otherwise try the town of San Patricio on the main highway, 30 km south of the Purificación River bridge.

GAS STATION

There is a *gasolina* stand at the town of Agua Caliente. Also a Pemex gas station is located 29 km south of the Purificación River.

RESTAURANTS

During the day **El Puerquillo** (The Little Pig), in the village, serves the day's fish catch ($2) and shrimp dishes ($4). Coldish beer and soft drinks available. At night, the most popular eatery is **El Gringo**, a four-table, family-run operation. Depending on the availability, the menu consists of fried fish and chicken served with french fries.

WATER

Purified water may be bought by the 5-gallon jug at El Rebalsito Village, 2.5 km from Tenacatita Beach. For drinking, however, it may still be wise to add water purification tablets just in case it comes straight from the Purificación River.

HOTEL FIESTA AMERICANA AT LOS ANGELES LOCOS DE TENACATITA

195 km south of P.V. (Km marker 20)
54 km north of the Manzanillo Airport
4 km from the highway over a cobblestone road

Originally, the name of this place was Los Angeles Locos de Tenacatita, meaning "Tenacatita's crazy angels," as the first owners used to land here in their private plane. The locals thought they were crazy to come to such an isolated, undeveloped spot and thus the reason for the name.

A deluxe, brand-new hotel operated by Fiesta Americana now sits on this crazily idyllic beach. But being new and unknown, its 240 rooms are practically empty. So, if you get the crazy notion of taking a vacation in the midst of high season, it's a sure bet you can get a room here. The rates are $60 for a double.

The hotel is a self-contained village with restaurants, bars, tennis courts, shops, medical services, travel agency, and other deluxe accommodation services. For reservations: Contact your travel agency or call (800) 223-2332.

HOTEL BAHÍA DE TENACATITA

199 km from P.V. (Km marker 17)
47 km north of the Manzanillo Airport
1 km from the highway over a dirt road

The region's jungle is full of interesting animals, armadillos, wild boar, deer, etc., but no one would dream of finding a "white elephant" standing among the coconut trees right next to the beach. It's named Hotel Bahía de Tenacatita and has 140 rooms with ocean view, a large swimming pool, and a restaurant (open at mealtimes only). The lobby is an impressive structure about three stories high resembling a church nave that would hold three or four hundred people. But lo and behold, the hotel is empty right in the height of the season.

This is the spot for thinkers, loners, fugitives, and busloads of tourists who cannot get a room in busy Puerto Vallarta. Rates are approximately $10 for a double, depending on the length of your stay and your bargaining ability. Ask to see the room first to check that all systems work—water, lights, fan, sliding door, etc.

BEACHES AND ACTIVITIES

This desolate beach is the longest of several found within Tenacatita Bay. It's wider than an L.A. freeway, but without the rush-hour traffic jams. What's more, there are no minimum-speed-limit signs so that you can take your time hiking to the town of La Manzanilla, about 3 miles south.

CAMPING

Campground Boca de Iguanas has the same access as Hotel Bahía de Tenacatita and is 2 km from the highway at the north end of the dirt road. Boca de Iguanas is a small, well-kept campground with about 18 shaded spaces that accommodate mid-size R.V.s plus spaces for tents. It has full hook-ups, showers, clothes- and dishwashing areas, a mini-store with a limited selection of canned goods, soft drinks, beer, and jugs of purified water.

Rates: R.V.s with two occupants, $6; camping space, $2 per person. There are also two rustic bungalows renting for $10 per unit for up to four occupants.

Boca de Iguanas is right on the beach, not to be confused with Las Palmeras behind it. Mosquito repellent is a must.

LA MANZANILLA

202 km south of P.V. (Km marker 14)
44 km north of the Manzanillo Airport
1.5 km (1 mile) from the main highway
over a narrow paved road

The tiny beach town of La Manzanilla is the spot for budget travelers who think that even the slow pace of Barra de Navidad 16 km (10 miles) south is too touristy for them. La Manzanilla has a population of about three hundred people and has a couple of inexpensive hotels, restaurants, and stores.

BEACH

La Manzanilla Beach is the southern end of the longest, widest beach stretch within the large Bay of Tenacatita. It is the same beach stretch where Hotel Bahía de Tenacatita and Campground Boca de Iguanas are located. The water along the town's beachfront is choppy due to a strong persistent ocean breeze that keeps mosquitoes and no-see-ums safely away. As you hike about a mile north along the hard-packed sand, the breeze subsides and in the afternoon no-see-ums make a bloody dive for your ankles and other soft-skin parts.

WHERE TO STAY

Posada Del Cazador, along the main street parallel to the beach, has double-occupancy rooms for $10.

Posada La Manzanilla, in the same vicinity, has double rooms for a bit less. A long-distance phone booth operates at Posada La Manzanilla from 8:00 A.M. to 2:00 P.M. and 4:00 to 8:00 P.M. Closed Sundays and the second Wednesday of every month. Strange but true.

RESTAURANTS

Restaurant María, right on the beach, serves one of the best deviled shrimp dishes I have ever eaten. Other patrons raved about the red snapper in garlic and shrimp in garlic. Sometimes the best places to eat are the little restaurants like this one because their very existence depends on keeping and attracting customers with their delicious home cooking. The pleasure of this little restaurant is not only in the food but in the service. At María's, the whole family takes part in the cooking and serving of food. I had three different waiters, aged 8 to about 14, bringing duplicate orders of tortillas, beer, and even plates that belonged at other tables. Their eagerness and big smiles are the sweetest dessert you could have. When the bill comes, check for errors as all three "waiters" may add the one beer going to your table on their individual tabs. It may be a good idea to keep all the empty plates and bottles on your table for clarification. María's is open from 9 A.M. to 5:00 P.M. At night, a couple of other eateries open along the town's main street.

BARRA DE NAVIDAD—SAN PATRICIO-MELAQUE

219 km south of P.V.
28 km north of the Manzanillo Airport

Barra de Navidad has the look of a town that is merely 50 years old but the fact is that 420 years ago, on November 21, 1564, an expedition of Spanish galleons set off from here to start the exploration of the Philippine Islands. When carpenters, blacksmiths, and other craftsmen were needed for the construction of the galleons, the settlement became a lively one.

The settlement got its name when an important Spanish official arrived on Christmas Day, to report on the progress of the shipbuilding, and baptized it Barra de Navidad. The word *barra* refers to the sand bar at the southern end of town that separates the lagoon from the bay.

In time, Manzanillo and Acapulco became the major trade ports between the Philippines and Mexico, then Nueva España (New Spain) and the out-of-the-way Barra de Navidad became a ghost town for centuries.

With the opening of the coastal highway in 1970 between Puerto Vallarta and Manzanillo, Barra de Navidad, San Patricio-Melaque, and other sleepy towns in the area were brought back to life.

GETTING THERE

Airplane The Manzanillo Airport is the closest one for Barra de Navidad and the neighboring towns of San Patricio-Melaque. From the airport, communal VW vans commute the 28 km to these towns.

Bus Barra de Navidad—San Patricio-Melaque are the main stopping points between Manzanillo and Puerto Vallarta and all buses stop here. Riding time from Manzanillo is 1 hour and 4 to 5 hours from P.V.

Car Barra de Navidad—San Patricio-Melaque are easily accessible from P.V. on the Manzanillo Highway (Route 200). From Manzanillo, Barra de Navidad is 61 km (38 miles) north. As this is a main highway, Pemex gas stations are plentiful.

GETTING AROUND

Barra de Navidad and San Patricio-Melaque are small towns about 4 km from each other. San Patricio and Melaque are the same town even though you may hear separate references and see separate signs. To better explain, references to San Patricio generally mean the greater part of town, including downtown, while references to Melaque indicate the beach area north of town.

In Barra, the main streets are Avenida Veracruz and, parallel to it, Avenida López de Legaspi (referred to by the locals as only "Legaspi") which runs one block from and parallel to the beach.

Most of the hotels, restaurants, and stores are located on the six blocks of these two streets.

The main streets of San Patricio-Melaque are López Mateos, running for about six blocks from the main highway to the beach, and Gómez Farías, running north to south one block parallel to the beach and crossing López Mateos at the trailer park.

Most of the hotels in San Patricio-Melaque are located on Gómez Farías.

There are no city buses connecting the two towns. Taxis are the only means of transportation between the two.

WHERE TO STAY

Barra's accommodations are mostly for budget-minded travelers.

CHEAP

Beach Palapa Rooms *North end of Calle Legaspi.* For the price you can't complain about a clean room with a cement floor, a double bed, shower, and toilet. Best of all, they're right on the beach and only a couple of blocks from the center of town.

Hotel Jalisco *Calle Jalisco 81.* Bathroom in rooms. No fans.

Hotel Delfin *Calle Morelos 23.* Very clean and comfortable. Ample rooms, pool, social *palapa.* Linda, the manager, is extremely helpful. A great place to meet other travelers.

Hotel El Marquez *Calle Filipas.* New, small, and clean. Some parking available.

Hotel Sands *Calle Morelos 24.* Fans, large pool, parking lot. On the beach. A classy old hotel with a touch of Caribbean French Colonial architecture (if such a thing exists). Also has six bungalows.

Hotel and Bungalows Karelia *Calle Legaspi.* Bungalows with kitchen and fridge. Dark, small, and unventilated but right on the beach. The hotel was under construction but looked much better than the bungalows.

BUDGET

Hotel Barra de Navidad *Calle Legaspi 250.* Fans, pool, restaurant, bar, on the beach. Tel. 70122.

Hotel Tropical *Calle Legaspi 96.* Fans, restaurant, bar, on the beach.

MODERATE

Hotel Cabo Blanco This is Barra's four-star hotel with accompanying comforts: air conditioning plus fans in rooms, pool, restaurant-bar, and its own marina and airstrip. The Cabo Blanco is not on the beach but they provide a shuttle bus to their beach club, Club de Playa Mar y Tierra, five blocks away. For reservations call Mister Mexico: in California (800) 452-4521; outside California (800) 824-4234.

There are about fifteen hotels/bungalows in San Patricio-Melaque.

CHEAP

Posada Clemens and **Posada San Patricio** *Calle Gómez Farías.* Both offer simple, clean rooms with fans and bath.

Posada Las Gaviotas *Calle Gómez Farías.* New, clean, fans, pool, on the beach.

Hotel Vista Hermosa *Calle Gómez Farías.* Fans, pool, nice, on the beach. Also offers bungalows with sea view.

Posada Pable de Tarso *Calle Gomez Farías 408.* Fans, pool, on the beach. One of the more attractive hotels in town. Tel. 70117.

Hotel Club Nautico *Melaque, Calle Madero 1.* New, fans, restaurant-bar, on the beach. Tel. 70239.

Hotel Melaque *Paseo Primavera.* Fans, pool, restaurant-bar, parking lot, on the beach. Large and new but unattractive. Tel. 70001.

RESTAURANTS

Tiny Barra de Navidad has some thirty restaurants and eateries. Some are open all day, while the seafood restaurants operating on the beach open only for lunch. The eateries are small, family-run places open only at night. Most offer a small selection of good, inexpensive dishes.

Y Todo Por No Estudiar *Next to the church.* The name of this

great little eatery refers to the Mexican saying that roughly translates as "If I had only gone to school, I wouldn't be working this
hard." Serves tacos, enchiladas, *carne en su jugo*.

El Tambo *On the sea-side street of the church.* Lupe, the pleasant
lady who runs this small eatery, is aided by her two children. The
menu consists mainly of charcoal-broiled chicken and beef served
with tortillas and a large pot of beans.

Restaurant El Mariscal *Calle Legaspi.* Built in authentic ware-
house style, including an asbestos roof, this restaurant is open for
breakfast, lunch, and dinner and offers a varied menu.

Restaurant Guadalajara *Ave. Veracruz almost at Plaza Principal.*
Great Mexican dishes for less than $3. Try Milanesa de Puerco
(breaded pork steak), it's delicious. Open all day.

Restaurant Mozoka *At the end of Ave. Veracruz, at the edge of the
lagoon.* Open all day but quieter in the evening when the day
tourists are gone. Good seafood dishes for approximately $2.

Restaurant-Bar Club de Playa Mar y Tierra *Calle Legaspi.* This
beachside restaurant with its tall *palapa* roof is Barra's nicest spot
for a fancy yet reasonably priced dinner. Also open for breakfast
8:00 to 11:00 A.M.

Many of the hotels in San Patricio-Melaque have their own restaurant. In and around town, a number of eateries open at night and
offer tacos, tostadas, enchiladas, and other inexpensive choices.

Restaurant Rincón Tropical *Ave. L. Mateos 34 (in front of Banamex).*
The fanciest restaurant in town but prices are quite reasonable.
Shrimp, octopus, and other seafood entrées as well as Mexican
food. Open all day.

B.B.Q. Chicken *L. Mateos at Plaza Principal.* The specialty here is
charcoal-broiled chicken marinated in the delicious Yucatecan spice
called achiote. This is where "finger-licking good" takes on its
true meaning. Eat it there or order it to go. Open all day.

BEACHES AND ACTIVITIES

Playa Bahía de Navidad The crescent-shaped beach of the Barra
de Navidad Bay runs roughly south to north for about 2 miles
from the mouth of the lagoon at Barra to the foot of El Mirador
hill at San Patricio-Melaque.

Most of the beach faces the open sea and has a steep grade that at its highest point resembles a sand dune (an indication of how high the waves reach during a storm). Throughout most of the year, the waves are small and the water is calm and blue. The golden sand is perfect; not too fine or sticky and not too coarse or gritty.

The southern end of the beach is protected by a rocky point and thus has the calmest waves in the bay.

Playa Cuastecomate For directions, see "Beach Hikes." Cuastecomate is a tiny village with a beach about a third of a mile long. The beach is very protected, with waves about a foot high. Life here is peaceful and despite its proximity to Barra-San Patricio, the village gets very few visitors. There are a couple of *palapa* restaurants on the beach selling the day's catch. If you ask around, there are a couple of rooms for rent in private homes, such as in the two-story house up the dirt road from the restaurants on the beach. On the north end of the beach, there are a few spots to accommodate pickup-size campers. These are private lots so ask for their owners to get permission to camp. A small fee may be charged.

BEACH HIKES

A pleasant stretch of sandy beach connects the towns of Barra and San Patricio-Melaque. From the water's edge to the vegetation line, the beach has about a 30-degree incline. The highest point of the beach is usually cluttered with driftwood, thorny branches, and various refuse of Mexico's plastic age—one-of-a-kind thongs that never match the one you lost; bald, maimed dolls; empty bleach containers, and, strangely enough, real seashells.

Although mid-way down the incline there are no ground-level sightseeing objects, the sand is too soft for easy walking and you will sink up to your ankles every step of the way. The best beach-hiking ground is somewhere between the soft, dry sand and the waterline. You may have to dodge a few fast waves that will lick at your feet, but the salty spray is refreshing.

Colimita to Playa La Culebra Plan a day trip for this 4-kilometer hike, as you could combine it with a delicious seafood lunch at

Colimita (across the lagoon from Barra) and a 2- to 3-hour stay at La Culebra Beach. Or, if you prefer, pack your own lunch. Mosquito repellent, and shoes or sandals are advisable. Although the ground on the road is soft, the black sand areas of the beach are burning hot.

To begin your adventure, hire a *panga* (outboard motorboat) at Barra's lagoon ($5 for up to eight people) to take you to Colimita. Establish the time and place that you want to be picked up from for the return trip. Once in Colimita, Restaurant Mary is the best departure point for your hike. From the restaurant go up a few steps to the dirt road directly behind the restaurant and take the road that goes away from the lagoon. A couple hundred steps away, over a small hump of a hill, the road comes to a "Y" junction. Stay on the right.

From here, the road goes through a tunnel of jungle vegetation. If you want to see or hear the jungle life, sharp eyes and ears are necessary. A slight rustle in the dried-up leaves could be a purple land crab, whereas a louder thrashing might be a green iguana. To spot them, look for a roundish purple form or a long, green shape in the mass of brown dried leaves.

By now, the mosquitoes most certainly will have spotted you, and at that time the most important thing to know about the jungle is who has the mosquito repellent—especially on very cloudy days, in the rainy season, and late afternoon.

La Culebra Beach An empty expanse of sand dunes stretching south toward Manzanillo. It's great for beachcombing, tanning, and camping but its rough waves make it dangerous for swimming.

To get to Playa La Culebra by car drive 7.4 km (4.5 miles) to the south from the Barra de Navidad junction on the main highway. Take the dirt road on your right and follow it for 7.2 km (4.4 miles) till you see the beach. The road then runs parallel to the beach for an additional 4 km (2.5 miles).

Cerro El Mirador and **Playa Cuastecomate** El Mirador (the lookout) is the hill overlooking the bay at the north end of Barra de Navidad beach. Playa Cuastecomate is a tiny beach located behind El Mirador.

Both hikes are about a mile long. Wear comfortable walking shoes as the road to these spots has sharp gravel. For the hike to El Mirador, bring your own food and beverage. And, if you wish, a field guide to Mexican birds and binoculars. In the late afternoon, particularly in the rainy season, mosquito repellent may come in handy.

The following directions are for driving or hiking to El Mirador and Playa Cuastecomate.

At San Patricio, take Ave. López Mateos to the main highway; turn left and go about half a kilometer to where the highway splits to the right (to Guadalajara-P.V.) and to the left (to Melaque). At this junction, continue straight on the dirt road. There's a pond on your right. Four hundred meters (a quarter mile) ahead the road splits as follows: straight, to Cuastecomate Beach; lower left, to Melaque; and upper left to the top of El Mirador.

To El Mirador: The hike from here to El Mirador is enjoyable as there are no houses, no traffic, and usually no people except for a boy or two tending a herd of goats. The road climbs gently on the edge of the hill, and most of it is shaded by thick vegetation. Shortly, you'll see glimpses of the sea and even before you reach the top you will be able to see the beach stretching all the way to Barra, the valley behind it, with its thick mat of coconut and banana trees, and ultimately the blue Pacific ocean sinking into the horizon.

The hike's end is a large, flat area ideal for camping, picnicking, tanning, and contemplating. Be careful not to get too close to the edge of the hill—it's a dangerous one-way ticket to the beach.

To Playa Cuastecomate: Where the dirt road separates (see above), continue straight. The road is wide and has very light vehicle traffic. There's a hill you will climb, and as you start down the hill toward the beach, you will get a good view of the scenic bay and village. At the town's entrance, take one of the two lower branches of the road to get to the beach.

BOATING

The Barra de Navidad lagoon covers a couple hundred square acres and offers a number of activities (lagoon fishing, bird watching, etc.) to those who bring their own boats.

DAY TRIP TO COLIMITA

Colimita is a tiny village located about a mile across the lagoon from Barra. It is popular with Mexican tourists because of its *palapa* seafood restaurants on the waterfront.

The restaurants' main specialty is *pescado sarandeado*, a whole pan-sized fish that has been marinated in a mild chile sauce and then cooked over charcoal. The price of your order depends on the size of your hunger as the fish is sold by the kilo. Other entrées include shrimp and octopus.

The *pangas* to Colimita can be hired beside the lagoon. They will take you to Colimita, drop you at the restaurant of your choice, and pick you up at the time you request.

DEEP-SEA FISHING

Barra de Navidad doesn't have a deep-sea fishing fleet per se. However, the large fleet of outboard motorboats that carry tourists across the lagoon to Colimita are run by experienced fishermen supplementing their income with the tourist trade. You may not be able to get a twin-engine cruiser here, but you can certainly get experienced fishermen who can really land the fish with their 18-foot outboard *pangas*. Compared to the prices charged in Puerto Vallarta by similar-size *pangas*, the rates here are a real deal. A 3-hour trip (minimum duration) costs approximately $25. Share the cost with a couple of fishing partners, and it's a steal of a deal.

Dorado, yellow fin tuna, jack, sierra, and other deep-water, mid-size fish are abundant just a few minutes off the coast. Marlin and sailfish are also not far off as Barra's waters are practically an extension of Manzanillo's bill fish corridor. But *pangas* can better handle smaller species, and during the 3-hour minimum rental you should be able to catch more than enough fish for you and your fishing party to have a dinner party.

Contact the fishermen by the Embarcadero (boat landing point) at the lagoon. Check their prices and, if possible, ask other people who have gone fishing for their opinion.

SHORE FISHING

The north end of the Barra de Navidad lagoon is a good spot for casting as it has lots of fish traveling in and out. For additional shore-fishing information, check the "Puerto Vallarta" section.

SNORKELING

The mouth of the Barra de Navidad lagoon is located at the southern end of the beach. Opposite the sandy side of the lagoon's mouth is a protected rocky shoreline with fairly good visibility for snorkeling. The lagoon's mouth is only about 30 yards wide. When swimming across to the rocky side, watch out for small-boat traffic. With a little luck, you should be able to spot schools of jack and mullet as they travel in and out of the lagoon. By the rocks are several species of angel fish, surgeon fish, and other rock dwellers.

A TO Z

AIRPORT

The Manzanillo Airport is the closest one to Barra de Navidad and San Patricio-Melaque.

BANKS

Barra de Navidad: **Banco Somex** *Ave. Veracruz.* Hours: Monday to Friday, 9:00 A.M. to 1:30 P.M. Does not change Canadian currency.

San Patricio: **Banamex** *Ave. L. Mateos.* Hours: Monday to Friday, 9:00 A.M. to 1:30 P.M. Changes both American and Canadian currency.

BUSES

There is no city bus service connecting Barra de Navidad to San Patricio-Melaque and no central bus station. Buses serving Manzanillo, Puerto Vallarta, and Guadalajara stop in Barra de Navidad and San Patricio.

In Barra de Navidad, buses stop at Ave. Veracruz in front of the Plaza Principal. In San Patricio, buses stop at the corner of Gómez Farías and Lopez Mateos.

GAS STATIONS

Main highway at the Barra de Navidad junction and 3 km north down the highway at Puerto Vallarta junction.

HORSE RENTAL

Don Ruben, known locally as "El Molacho," is a semiretired rancher in search of a part-time hobby. When I visited him, he hadn't rented a single horse. The next day I sent him four Canadian "Mounties" and a "Texas Ranger," all of whom had had too much sun and were in need of adventure. They were delighted with the man and the ride. They claimed Don Ruben probably spent more on the tequila he offered them than they spent on the horse rental. So tell Don Ruben *"Memo nos mando"* (Memo sent us) and you might get the royal treatment. He is located on the Barra de Navidad highway, almost at the main highway junction.

LONG DISTANCE

Barra de Navidad: Calle Legaspi. Hours: Monday to Saturday, 9:00 A.M. to 9:00 P.M.; Sunday, 9:00 A.M. to 2:00 P.M.

San Patricio: Calle Gómez Farías #203. Hours: Monday to Saturday, 8:00 A.M. to 10:00 P.M.; Sunday, 8:00 A.M. to 2:00 P.M.

MEDICAL SERVICES

Dr. Roberto Pimienta Woo *Ramon Corona #401, San Patricio.* Office hours: 9:00 A.M. to 2:00 P.M. and 4:00 to 8:00 P.M. Tel. 70077.

POST OFFICES

Barra de Navidad: Calle Guanajuato #100.

San Patricio: Plaza Principal. Hours: Monday to Saturday, 9:00 A.M. to 1:00 P.M. and 4:00 to 6:00 P.M.

TELEGRAPH OFFICES

Barra de Navidad: Veracruz #222.

San Patricio: Clemente Orozco #62. Hours: Monday to Friday, 9:00 A.M. to 1:00 P.M. and 3:00 to 6:00 P.M. Saturday, Sunday, and holidays, 9:00 A.M. to noon.

TIRE REPAIR (LLANTERA)

Directly at the entrance to San Patricio (Calle López Mateos).

TRAILER PARK PLAYA

Gómez Farías #249. Rather than a trailer park, this looks more like a parking lot. It has 45 unshaded, cramped spaces located at the intersection of the town's two main streets just across from the bus terminals. But it's on the beach and is the only one on the Barra de Navidad Bay. Vehicle with two occupants is $2.

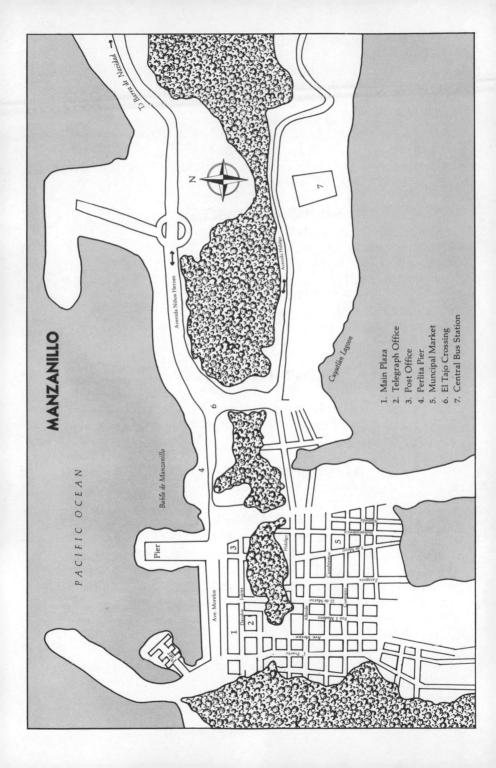

MANZANILLO

PACIFIC OCEAN

Bahía de Manzanillo

Coyutlán Lagoon

1. Main Plaza
2. Telegraph Office
3. Post Office
4. Perlita Pier
5. Muncipal Market
6. El Tajo Crossing
7. Central Bus Station

MANZANILLO

The Bay of Santiago, where Manzanillo is located, was discovered by Alvaro de Saavedra in 1527. The settlement that was established on the southern end of the bay was named Manzanillo after the manzanilla trees that are so common in this region. (Manzanilla trees bear fruit resembling small apples.)

Since its early days, Manzanillo has been an important port. Numerous expeditions set off from here to establish settlements along Baja and Alta California. It is also from here that galleons departed to join those built in Barra de Navidad for the expedition to explore the Philippines in 1564.

At present, Manzanillo is the most important port on Mexico's Pacific coast. The city's economy relies mostly on its port and industrial activities and, to a lesser extent, on tourism. There is no conflict, however, between the two. The southern end of town is predominantly industrial, while the northern end is where the hotels and beaches are located.

GETTING THERE

Airplane Direct flights serve Manzanillo from Los Angeles. From other cities connections must be made via Guadalajara or Mexico City.

Bus Second-class Autotransportes Cihuatlán offers the largest number of runs from Puerto Vallarta. Tres Estrellas, a first-class line, leaves once a day. From Guadalajara, bus service is continuous throughout the day.

Car It's an easy 4-hour drive from Puerto Vallarta to Manzanillo. The highway is in good condition and lightly traveled as far as Barra de Navidad, where it becomes quite busy. There are plenty of Pemex gas stations along the way.

GETTING AROUND

The core of the old city is centered around Jardín Alvaro Obregón, the Plaza Principal. As in most Mexican towns and cities, the city hall (Presidencia Municipal), post and telegraph offices, banks, and many stores are located on the streets edging the plaza.

Traveling four short blocks east from the Plaza Principal, Avenida Morelos meets with Avenida Niños Heroes at Crucero El Tajo (El Tajo Junction), recognizable by the Pemex gas station. East of El Tajo Junction, Avenida Niños Heroes becomes the highway to Puerto Vallarta and Guadalajara. Most of Manzanillo's main hotels, restaurants, supermarkets, and junctions to other hotels, etc., are located between Km 8 Crucero Las Brisas (marked by a monument of a stylized concrete sailship) and Km 19, the entrance to Club Santiago. The addresses of establishments on this highway are given by the kilometer distance from Manzanillo.

Las Brisas Junction (Km 8) is the beginning of the 3-kilometer highway that serves the residential area of Las Brisas. This highway runs two blocks parallel to the beach and is lined with a dozen bungalow-hotels, several inexpensive restaurants, and a couple of stores.

Continuing down the main highway, you will drive through the tiny town of Salahua (Km 12.5) and the town of Santiago (Km. 14–15) where you'll find a shopping mall, Plaza Santiago, with a bank, movie house, a couple of restaurants, and some souvenir shops.

WHERE TO STAY

Manzanillo's accommodations consist mostly of a good selection of hotels and bungalows in the cheap and budget ranges. In the Las Brisas section of town alone, there are bungalow-hotels on or near the beach with many more to be found between Kms 8 and 19 along the main highway. Rates are often the same for one to four persons. Bungalows do not normally take reservations. Except at peak vacation periods (Christmas and Easter Week), there is no problem getting budget accommodations in Manzanillo even in the winter season (December to April).

As there are only a handful of accommodations above the budget range, it is advisable to make reservations for the winter season well ahead of time.

Groups of four or more are advised to check out the rental houses or condominiums available at Club Santiago (Km 10). They are fully furnished, provide maid service, and may well be cheaper than renting hotel rooms. Likewise, inquire into the villas at Club Maeva (Km 16.5).

Newlyweds may want to profit from the honeymoon package offered by the deluxe Las Hadas. Depending on how many days of honeymooning you can take, the prices range from $500 (4 days/3 nights) to $900 (7 days/6 nights).

CHEAP

The first four hotels on this list are the cheapest available to low-budget travelers. They have fans and hot water—sometimes.

Casa de Huespedes Ibarra *Calle Galeana 46, near the central bus station.* Recommended for travelers leaving or arriving by bus in the wee hours of the night.

Hotel Emperador *West end of Plaza Principal.* Fairly new and clean and a better deal for your money than the Savoy or Miramar.

Hotel Savoy *West end of Plaza Principal.*

Hotel Miramar *East end of Plaza Principal.*

Hotel Colonial *Ave. Mexico 100, near Plaza Principal.* Restaurant-bar, fans, phones in rooms. The only "fancy" hotel downtown.

Hotel Las Brisas *Km 1, Las Brisas Highway.* New, clean; fans. One block from the beach. The best deal on the beach.

Motel and Suites "Star" *Km 1, Las Brisas Highway.* Rooms, bungalows, suites. New, clean; fans, tiny pool, restaurant, right on the beach. Near grocery stores, restaurants, and pharmacy.

Bungalows San Francisco *KM 9.5, main highway.* Roomy bungalows, clean, pool, fans. About four blocks from the beach. Tel. 30429.

Hotel Anita *Km 14, Bahía de Santiago.* This may be Manzanillo's oldest beach hotel and with some repairs and redecorating it could become one of its nicest. Fans and pool. No restaurant, but there is one at the Marlyn Hotel next door. Tel. 30161.

Hotel-Bungalows Marlyn *Km 14, Bahía de Santiago.* Fans, pool, restaurant, clean, quiet, fairly new but unappealing, on the beach. Six bungalows also available. Res.: Hotel-Bungalows Marlyn, Apartado Postal 288, Manzanillo, Colima 28200. Tel. 30107.

BUDGET

Suites-Bungalows Orduña *Playa de Audiencia.* Fifty steps from the nicest beach in Manzanillo. New pool, mini-store, restaurant-bar.

Rancho Playa Condo-Hotel *Km 9.5, main highway.* Pool, fans, on the beach. Tel. 30925.

Hotel Playa de Santiago *Km 14, Bahía de Santiago.* Fans, pool, telephones in rooms, restaurant-bar, tennis court, clean, view, friendly service, on the beach. Suites and bungalows are also available. Res.: Hotel Playa de Santiago, Apartado Postal 90, Manzanillo, Colima 28200. Tel. 30055 or 30270.

Hotel La Posada *Km 3, Las Brisas Highway.* Without a doubt La Posada is the most charming, cozy, and pleasant hotel in Manzanillo, and considering it's a three-star establishment, it's also the most reasonably priced. With only 23 rooms and an established clientele, reservations are a must. Res.: Hotel La Posada, Apartado Postal 135, Manzanillo, Colima 28200. Tel. 22404.

Condominios Roca del Mar *Km 3, Las Brisas Highway.* Inquire about rates. New, on the beach. Twenty-six condos with fully equipped kitchenettes, air conditioning. Res.: Condominios Roca del Mar, Apartado Postal 7, Manzanillo, Colima. Tel. 21990.

Tenisol Hotel Club Santiago *Km 19, main highway.* Tenisol is the exclusive land-development complex of private homes and condominiums known as Club Santiago. Pool, bar, mini-supermarket, restaurant, two blocks from the beach, six lit tennis courts. Access to Club Santiago's 9-hole golf course. Golf fees not included in the price of rooms. Two- and three-room condos and houses arc also available through Tenisol. For information and reservations call toll-free 1 (800) 525-1987, Denver, Colorado.

PLUSH

Club Maeva *Km 16.5, main highway.* Doubles are $50. In addition, the club has one-bedroom villas (1–4 persons) for $75 and two-bedroom villas (2–6 persons) for $98 (prices without tax). Villas have fully equipped kitchenettes. More than a hotel resort, Maeva resembles a Greek village snuggled in the emerald green vegetation of the hills of Santiago Bay. The Maeva Village spreads over 90 acres allowing plenty of space and privacy for the resort's 500 units.

Offers an array of activities such as a splash in the gigantic swimming pool (the largest in Latin America), tennis (12 courts), volleyball (2 courts), and even football. For reservations call toll-free in the U.S. (800) 223-0888; in Canada (800) 268-7106.

Las Hadas This is the hotel where Dudley Moore fell madly in love with Bo Derek in the movie *"10."* It is the ultimate beach resort. No expense was spared in building this Moorish fantasy of 200 rooms, suites, and villas. Eighteen-hole golf course, ten tennis courts, four restaurants, marina, and every water sport imaginable. Call Westin Hotels toll-free for reservations. Tel. 30000.

RESTAURANTS

Compared to a beach resort town, such as Puerto Vallarta, where restaurants are geared predominantly to tourists, Manzanillo's restaurants cater to the local population, offering a choice of very good food at reasonable prices.

Being an important fishing port on Mexico's Pacific coast, Manzanillo also offers a fresh and varied supply of seafood. Depending on the season, oysters, shrimp, langostino, octopus, conch, scallops, and lobster may be available.

Even in the splurge range, Manzanillo's finer dining spots are reasonably priced. Dinner plates consisting of filet mignon or shrimp in garlic sauce cost less than $8 at most of these restaurants. What's funny is that they classify their food as international cuisine, when, in fact, most of them serve American-cut meats (rib-eye, New York, and T-bone steaks), and various shrimp and lobster dishes. But when it comes to house specialties and atmosphere, there are some pleasant surprises awaiting you.

Los Agachados Food Market *Calle Cuauhtémoc, near the corner of Ave. Mexico.* A conglomeration of about twenty tiny restaurants, which in other Mexican cities would normally be located at the same site as the city's market. Dishes include beef, chicken, or pork stews (*cocidos*) in red or green sauces, *chiles rellenos, bistec con* *papas, milanesas, pollo frito,* etc. Price per dish is around $1. Open daily 6:00 A.M. to 10:00 P.M.

Restaurant Chantilly *Main square.* You can always have a good, inexpensive meal in this popular restaurant. If there is no table when you arrive, stick around until one is vacant. The menu is large. To top it off, the Chantilly serves real, fresh coffee, cappucino, and espresso. Open 8:00 A.M. to 11:00 P.M. Closed Saturdays.

Restaurant Savoy *Main square.* Offers a menu, food quality, and prices similar to Chantilly, but less crowded. Open 24 hours.

Restaurant Ly Chee *Niños Heroes 397, three blocks east of main square.* The only Chinese restaurant in Manzanillo and serves about twenty different dishes. It's on the waterfront with a good view of the port and the bay. Open for lunch and dinner.

Restaurant Rey Coliman *Niños Heroes 411, three blocks east of main square.* This is the most popular seafood restaurant in downtown Manzanillo. It's located on the waterfront and has a good view of the bay and port. Open daily 11:00 A.M. to 11:00 P.M.

Restaurant Las Cazuelas *At the beginning of Las Brisas Highway.* A family-run restaurant serving good Mexican food at very reasonable prices. A dinner of *carne asada* with french fries, salad, and a couple of beers is less than $2. Open 8:00 P.M. to midnight.

Restaurant El Sombrero *Km 2.5, Las Brisas Highway, across from Club Vacacional.* Mexican-born Otto Meyer, 70 years young, and his wife, Carmen, are your charming hosts in this simple and very hospitable little restaurant. Between the two of them, they speak Spanish, English, French, German, and Czech. They both cook and wait on tables and offer the fastest service in Manzanillo. Their menu consists of Mexican specialties such as a combination plate of quesadilla, enchilada, and tacos for $1, or *pozole*, a pork and hominy corn stew. Beer only. Hours: 7:30 P.M. to 11:00 P.M. Closed Sundays.

Restaurant-Bar El Vaquero *Las Brisas Junction.* El Vaquero (the cowboy) serves charcoal-broiled Hereford steaks by the kilo. So weigh your appetite and order a quarter-kilo of T-bone (6.5 ounces) or a half-kilo (13 ounces). Also available are rib-eye steaks, baby goat, and quail, all grilled. The décor is much like that of an old western saloon. Open for lunch and dinner.

Restaurant-Bar Osteria Bugatti *Las Brisas Junction.* When you enter the narrow stairway of Osteria Bugatti you will feel as though you are walking through a time tunnel, leaving the hot Mexican tropics and entering a medieval dining hall. With its solid masonry archways, pillars, and dome ceilings, Osteria Bugatti bills itself as the oldest, newest spot in town and in a very short time it has become Manzanillo's prime spot for dining, wining, and dancing.

The menu is unoriginal (T-bone, filet mignon, fish fillet, lobster) but the atmosphere is elegant and romantic. Live music alternates with tapes until 2:00 A.M. so you can burn off calories on the spacious dance floor. Hours: 1:00 P.M. to 2:00 A.M.

Restaurant-Bar Pajaritos *Km 6.5, main highway.* When I visited this restaurant it had just opened. The menu consists of the standard seafood plates common at most restaurants, but the prices are reasonable. A definite plus for Pajaritos is that it's on the beach, and that's rare in Manzanillo. Hours: 1:00 P.M. to midnight.

Carlos 'n Charlie's Restaurant-Bar *Km 9, main highway.* One of Manzanillo's most popular and lively restaurants, a good place to meet people and socialize.

Aldea Bruja *Km 9, main highway.* Aldea Bruja (Witch Village) is a large seafood restaurant with a mess hall atmosphere. Very popular with the locals, it offers a large selection of reasonably priced seafood dishes. Open daily, noon to 10:00 P.M.

Restaurant-Bar Money Pancho *Km 10, main highway.* Despite its elegant, candlelit atmosphere, Money Pancho is reasonably priced. Hours: 1:00 P.M. to 1:00 A.M. Closed Mondays. Reservations: Tel. 30489.

Restaurant-Bar Manolo's *Km 10.5, main highway.* Offers great daily house specials such as frog legs in brandy batter and pork loin in ginger sauce plus seafood and beef dishes. Manolo prides himself on his "salad boat" and the fact that "my vegetables have taken the pill," as he likes to put it. If you haven't guessed, this means his salads are safe to eat. Manolo's dining area is set under a large, airy candlelit *palapa*. Hours: 6:00 to 11:00 P.M. Closed Sundays.

El Pollo Norteño *Across the highway from Plaza Santiago.* Charcoal-broiled chicken is the specialty of this simple to-eat-here-or-to-go restaurant. Half chicken served with steaming tortillas, mild hot sauce, and pickled onions only $2. Hours: 11:00 A.M. to 11:00 P.M. Closed Tuesday.

Restaurant Los Carrizos *Across the highway from Plaza Santiago.* The menu in this modest restaurant consists of only eight items, but there isn't a better deal in Manzanillo than the small order of *carne en su jugo* for only $2. All dishes served with plenty of tortillas and three different hot sauces. Beer only. Hours: 1:00 P.M. to 11:00 P.M.

Restaurant-Bar El Dorado *Km 16, main highway.* House specialties include Dorado Cadiz, red snapper in mushroom and white sauce, El Dorado Chateaubriand for two, and yes, they also have New York and rib-eye steaks. Decorated with nautical objects. Very cozy atmosphere. Hours: 2:00 P.M. to 2:00 A.M. Res.: Tel. 30102.

Restaurant-Bar El Oasis *At Club Santiago, straight after checkpoint to Calle Delfines, turn left and go two blocks.* One of the few beach restaurants in Manzanillo with some kind of a life-is-a-beach social scene. But this scene varies greatly with the seasons, and it goes from booooring in the summer to lively in the winter with activities such as water skiing, live and taped disco music, and beginning, intermediate, and advanced tanning. For information on wintertime shows and dinner reservations, Tel. 30937.

Tangaroa Restaurant-Bar *Km 17.5, main highway.* The on-the-beach restaurant for Club Maeva Hotel, but it's open to nonguests also. An ample menu of seafood, meat, and chicken. The dinner menu consists mostly of Oriental-Hawaiian–inspired dishes: shrimp tempura, Cantonese lobster, Hawaiian fish fillet, etc. The Tangaroa features special events—Hawaiian luaus, Friday at 8:00 P.M.; Parrillada (barbecue cookout), Sunday from noon to 5:00 P.M. Tel. 30596, ask for the Tangaroa extension.

Restaurant-Bar L'Recif *Km 21.5, main highway.* Located atop a cliff with a spectacular view of the ocean. It has a bar you can swim up to and a sunbathing area. The menu has a little of everything: bouillabaisse, garlicky black bean soup, seafood combination large enough for two. The pool bar opens at 10:00 A.M. Lunch is served from 1:00 to 5:00 P.M. Dinner from 7:00 to 11:30 P.M. Tel. 30624.

NIGHTLIFE

No matter how hard I look for some nightlife in Manzanillo, I can't find any. I set out one hot, Friday night assuming that the bars and the discos would be jumping.

I started out at **Joe's and Jaws**, one of the more popular hot

spots in town. As I walked toward the entrance I saw a crowd of
people standing there and thought to myself, Well, at least something seems to be cooking here. But, crushing disappointment,
the crowd by the door were waiters. The few patrons inside
stared at me, hoping I was the master of ceremonies of a flashy
cabaret show that was waiting in the wings for my order, "Let's
start the show!" I turned to one of the waiters and asked, "Why is
this place so dead? I thought it was supposed to be the hottest
spot in town." He gave a wide, toothy smile and replied, "It is,
that's why we're standing by the door catching the ocean breeze."

Manzanillo's nightlife gets livelier in the winter months, when
North American sun-seekers put a badly needed transfusion of
life into the town's nightspots.

For fancy dining and dancing to live and taped music, try
Osteria Bugatti at Las Brisas Junction. **Restaurant-Bar El Oasis at
Club Santiago** offers dining, dancing, and Mexican fiesta nights
in its informal beach *palapa* setting. **Club Maeva** offers a well-
organized Mexican fiesta night Saturdays at 8:00 P.M. The admission price includes a cocktail, buffet dinner, and show. They also
offer a Hawaiian Night at their beach restaurant **Tangaroa**. Reservations recommended. Tel. 30389 for reservations and information on both shows. For dancing into the late hours of the night,
try Maeva's disco or **Caligula Disco** at Km 14 on the main highway.

BEACHES AND ACTIVITIES

Manzanillo's vast beaches offer plenty of privacy, sea, sun, and
sand. They are easily accessible, located one or two blocks from
the Las Brisas Highway and the main highway. City buses run
on these highways and stop about every four blocks.

During the rainy season (June to September) the water can be a
bit brackish and the waves can reach 6 feet as they break on the
beach. Use the utmost caution and, when in doubt, stay out.

In the winter months, the water is calmer, bluer, and clearer,
but even then remember that there are no lifeguards in Manzanillo, except at a couple of the big hotels.

Playa Azul (Blue Beach) The longest stretch of beach on the
Manzanillo Bay, starting at the rock jetty (south end of Las Brisas
residential area) and curving northwest for about 6 kilometers,

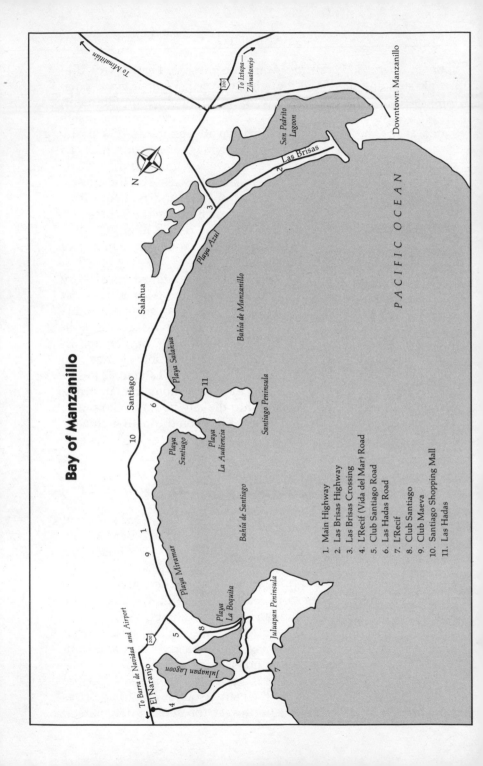

Bay of Manzanillo

To Minatitlán

To Ixtapa–Zihuatanejo

200

Downtown Manzanillo

San Pedrito Lagoon

Las Brisas

2

N

3

Playa Azul

PACIFIC OCEAN

Bahía de Manzanillo

Salahua

Playa Salahua

11

Santiago

6

Santiago Peninsula

10

Playa Santiago

Playa La Audiencia

1

9

Playa Miramar

Bahía de Santiago

1. Main Highway
2. Las Brisas Highway
3. Las Brisas Crossing
4. L'Recif (Vida del Mar) Road
5. Club Santiago Road
6. Las Hadas Road
7. L'Recif
8. Club Santiago
9. Club Maeva
10. Santiago Shopping Mall
11. Las Hadas

To Barra de Navidad and Airport

200

El Naranjo

Playa La Boquita

5

8

4

Juluapan Lagoon

Juluapan Peninsula

7

ending around the area of the Rancho Playa Condo-Hotel. The beach has a steep grade and is safe when the sea is calm. However, when a storm hits, the waves can crest at more than 6 feet, literally taking your pants off as you stand in waist-high water. Numerous accommodations (bungalows, hotels, and two trailer parks) are located on or near the beach. Despite this, Playa Azul is a quiet, empty beach, except on weekends when a few locals drop by. There are no beach restaurants on Playa Azul, not even a refreshment stand.

Playa Salahua Access at Km 10, main highway at Lavandería Toni's. Go one block toward the beach, turn right, and go two blocks to the end of the dirt road past Restaurant El Mariscal. Playa Salahua is a magical combination of soft sand dunes and a beautiful grassy meadow (actually a part of the Las Hadas golf course). At the stone bridge there is a small shady oasis adjacent to the sunny beach. Choose a spot for your nap and when you're ready for some exercise walk up some 50 steps to the top of the sea cliff for a spectacular view of the Manzanillo Bay and Las Hadas Hotel.

Playa La Audiencia Follow the cobblestone street at Las Hadas entrance, Km 13, main highway, for 1.3 km to the end. Here, you'll find a tiny bay within the Bay of Santiago, with soft, golden sand and gentle waves. The grade drops rapidly but is not as steep as most of Manzanillo's beaches. There is a small *palapa* restaurant with inexpensive seafood dishes and beverages available. Park on the edge of the beach.

Playa de Santiago Entrance at Km 14, main highway. Go 1 km to the beach, which is only about a mile long and is located on the northeast corner of Santiago Bay. It's a shallow, protected beach with a gentle grade and small waves. Although there are three hotels, it's not crowded. For food and beverages, try the restaurants at either Hotel Marlyn (reasonably priced) or Hotel Playa de Santiago (a bit more expensive).

Playas Olas Altas and *Miramar* Parallel to the main highway from Km 14 (town of Santiago) to Km 19 (Club Santiago). Playa Olas Altas is at the town of Santiago and, despite its name, meaning high waves, is not as turbulent as Playa Miramar. Although at both beaches there are plenty of calm days when the waves are gentle and safe, stormy days produce waves that are high and mean, resembling the inside of a giant washing machine as they break. The most popular beach spot is at Club Maeva's beach where the overhead pedestrian bridge crosses the highway. Here you can rent windsurfing boards, snorkeling gear, and other beach accessories. Maeva's Tangaroa Restaurant offers good food and tropical cocktails at reasonable prices.

Playa Club Santiago Entrance at Km 19, main highway. Although Club Santiago is a private development, there is a restaurant open to the public, so to gain access use the password "El Oasis Restaurant" at the security checkpoint. El Oasis is the only food-and-beverage supply depot on this beach. The beach runs north and south from the main highway to the Juluapan Peninsula and is about 2 kilometers in length. The sand is very soft, mostly grayish with patches of very black, hot sand. On sunny days, walking on this black sand is like walking on hot coals. The water is shallow with small waves, but in some areas the bottom is very rocky.

Playa La Boquita Km 21.5 (El Naranjo) on the main highway. Watch for the sign "El Naranjo" and follow the narrow paved road for 5.3 km until you reach a tiny wooden bridge. (The bridge has a height limit of 6 feet.) Here, you'll find La Boquita (the little mouth), referring to the narrow mouth of the Juluapan Lagoon, which empties into the Santiago Bay. It's a wonderful, usually empty beach that offers snorkeling, fishing, bird watching, hiking, and camping. The ocean on the bay side is shallow but somewhat rocky and subject to currents. The lagoon side is sandy, shallow, and calm. Bring your own picnic supplies. Note: There is a checkpoint about 1 km from the main highway. To gain access say you're going to L'Recif Restaurant.

BEACH HIKE

Salahua Beach to Las Hadas Hotel Adventurous guests at the maximum-security Las Hadas Hotel take this hike in reverse and when they return, proudly tell their friends, "I just came back from that village over there and paid only 20 cents for a Coke."

If Las Hadas's security doesn't intercept you, you should be able to tell your grandchildren, "Once upon a time, down in Manzanillo, I walked into Las Hadas Hotel, swam in their pool, sat in their lounge chairs, and drank a Coca-Cola right out of my backpack."

DEEP-SEA FISHING

Manzanillo bills itself as the world's bill fish capital, and with a record catch of 336 bill fish in a single tournament, it just might have a right to that title. According to local fishermen, blue, black, and striped marlin and sailfish can often be caught right at the entrance of the Manzanillo Bay. "One hour after leaving the dock you could have a 300-pound black marlin on the boat," explains one of the boat owners of the local fishing co-op. That's quite different from other ports where bill fish are caught after 2 or 3 hours of motoring into the open sea. So, pack your fishing cap and come fish in Manzanillo, where the big fish come to you!

To make fishing arrangements for bill fish or smaller species (rooster fish, skip jack, mackerel, yellow fin tuna) contact: **Sociedad Cooperativa de Pesca**, *Niños Heroes 597 (downtown), Manzanillo, Colima. Tel. 21031.*

The co-op, also known as Flota Amarilla (yellow fleet), has about ten Mexican-made diesel-powered boats, all with four lines, and offers half- (5 hours) and full-day outings. Sample full-day rates: 36-foot boat, $70; 30-foot boat, $60; and 27-foot boat, $50.

For information about Manzanillo's Deep-Sea Fish Rodeo, held twice a year around November 20 and February 5, contact: **Deep-Sea Fish Rodeo,** *Ave. Mexico 251, Manzanillo, Colima.* The first three prizes are late-model Datsun and VW cars.

SHORE FISHING
A couple of good spots for casting are the rock jetty and channel at the end of Las Brisas Highway and by the wooden bridge at Playa La Boquita. The long beach stretches, such as Playa Azul, have fast drop-offs and fishing conditions similar to those described in the Puerto Vallarta shore-fishing section.

SNORKELING
Aside from the fancy Las Hadas Hotel, the only other spot in town to rent snorkeling equipment is at Club Maeva's beach.

Playa La Boquita The area under the wooden bridge is good for spotting angel fish and sergeant majors. Inside the lagoon, you can see schools of silvery mullets and long-beaked ballyhoo skimming the surface. If the beach is calm and the visibility good, you may spot a variety of species, among them toothy, long-snouted needlefish. Although fierce looking, they are harmless to humans.

With good visibility, the area around the two half-sunken shipwrecks down the beach from La Boquita offer good snorkeling, provided that you are an experienced swimmer.

Playa La Audiencia The rocks on either end of this tiny bay provide good underwater sightseeing of several species of rock-fish and occasional schools of jack and mullet. The calmer and bluer the water is, the better the visibility.

WATER SKIING

For the smoothest water and year-round service, try the Aqua Mundo shop at Las Hadas Hotel.

WINDSURFING

There are three places where you can rent equipment in Manzanillo:

Hotel Roca del Mar *Km 3, Las Brisas Highway*. If not open, check next door at La Posada with Bart Varelman, Manzanillo's veteran windsurfer. He has a couple of boards he might be willing to rent out.

Tangaroa Restaurant *Km 17.5, Manzanillo-Santiago Highway*. Look for the Aqua Mundo stand on the beach.

Las Hadas Hotel. Look for the Aqua Mundo stand on the beach. Accessible to hotel guests only.

TOURS

LAND TOURS

Two companies, Bahías Gemelas Tours and Recorridos Turísticos de Manzanillo, offer tours of Manzanillo, Barra de Navidad, and the state's capital city, Colima. Both companies conduct their tours in VW vans and the itinerary and duration of the tours are almost identical, only the prices differ. Bahías Gemelas Tours are less expensive (Tel. 30000 and 21818) but Recorridos Turísticos de Manzanillo (RTM) tours to Barra de Navidad and Colima include lunch. Tel. 30055 and 30270.

BAY BOAT TOUR

Every day at 5:00 P.M. the catamaran *Argos* leaves from La Perlita Pier downtown for a 2-hour sunset cruise of the bay. The cost is approximately $3 per person and includes two soft drinks. Tel. 22262 for information and reservations.

SPECIAL TOURS

Gaby Sevilla of Bahías Gemelas Tours will be glad to make arrangements for special tours to places such as Guadalajara for groups of six or more. She is very personable, speaks excellent English, and is a very professional tour guide.

A TO Z
AIRPORT

The Manzanillo International Airport is located 43 km from downtown Manzanillo. At the terminal there is a restaurant-bar, Avis car rental, and a couple of souvenir shops but no bank or money-exchange booth. So, make sure you have small-denomination dollar bills to pay for transportation until you can get to a bank. Transportation into town is provided by white and yellow communal VW vans.

From Manzanillo to the airport, the vans leave from Crucero El Tajo at Ave. Niños Heroes 638, downtown. Departures are at 6:45 A.M., 1:00, 3:00, and 6:00 P.M. and coincide with airplane departures. The vans will also pick up groups of six to eight by special arrangement. For additional information call Transportes Turísticos Benito Juarez, Tel. 21086, between 9:00 A.M. and 2:00 P.M., or inquire at the front desk of major hotels.

For groups of three to four people it is more practical to take a taxi from the hotel and the cost is comparable to the vans.

BANKS

Downtown Manzanillo: **Banco Internacional** and **Banamex,** *Ave. Mexico.* One short block from the main square.

Comermex *West end of main square.*

Serfin *One block east of main square.*

Santiago: **Banco Somex** *Plaza Santiago.*

Banco Internacional *Two blocks north of Plaza Santiago.*

BUS STATION

The central bus station is located on Ave. Hidalgo about ten blocks from downtown Manzanillo. Direct buses may be taken from here to Puerto Vallarta (5–6 hours), Guadalajara (6 hours), Mexico City (16–18 hours), Mazatlán, and Tijuana on Tres Estrellas first-class buses. The latter two travel via Puerto Vallarta. Colima, the state of Colima's capital, can be reached in an hour with frequent departures.

CAR RENTALS

AMMSA *Km 9, main highway.* Car makes: VW Beetle, Fairmont, Grand Marquis. Tel. 30418 and 30419.

Avis *Km 9, main highway.* Car makes: VW Beetle, Rabbit, Jeeps Ford Topaz, VW vans. Also has an airport office. Tel. 30194.

Thrifty *Km 8, Las Brisas Junction.* Car makes: all Ramblers. Tel. 21495.

CITY BUSES

Buses are the cheapest way to get around town, although not usually the most comfortable. Ruta 1 runs from the railroad station downtown to Las Brisas Junction through Salahua, Santiago, and ends at Miramar. Ruta 2 same as Ruta 1, but goes only as far as the entrance to Club Santiago. Ruta 3 leaves from the main market downtown to Las Brisas Junction and through the 3-km length of the Las Brisas Highway.

CONSULATE

Volunteer U.S. Consular Representative Bill Le Coq can be contacted at the Club Santiago between the hours of 9:00 A.M. and 1:30 P.M. Tel. 30413.

FISHING GEAR

It's cheaper to bring your own equipment but if you need fishing or snorkeling gear, **Pesca y Deportes Marinos** at Niños Heroes 638 has a good selection.

FOOD TO GO

If you are planning a picnic, try one of the following suggestions, all located at Plaza Santiago.

Pollo Norteno Restaurant Charcoal-broiled chicken. Opens at 11:00 A.M. Closed Tuesdays.

Restaurant Los Carrizos Beef and beans (*carne en su jugo*). Opens at 1:00 P.M.

Hamburgesa Juanitos Hamburgers, hot dogs, fried chicken. Opens at 9:00 A.M.

GOLF

Las Hadas has a spectacular seaside championship 18-hole course named La Mantarraya and designed by Roy Dye. But as best as I could find out, it's exclusively for guests. **Club Santiago** has a beautiful 9-hole course designed by Larry Hughes and it's open to the general public. Tel. 30413.

IMMIGRATION OFFICE

Oficina de Migración *Edificio Federal, 2nd Floor, Playa San Pedrito.*

LAUNDROMATS

There is no self-service *lavandería* here, but the following give one-day service.

Lavandería Gissy *Km 9.5, Manzanillo-Santiago Highway.*
Lavandería Toni's *Km 10, Manzanillo-Santiago Highway.*

LONG DISTANCE

Downtown: **Caseta Telefonica de Larga Distancia at Muelle (Pier)**
La Perlita *Two blocks east of main square.* Hours: 8:00 A.M. to 11:00 P.M.

Santiago: **Larga Distancia at Hamburgesas Juanito** *Two blocks north of Plaza Santiago.* Hours: 8:00 A.M. to 11:00 P.M.

MARKET

Mercado Cinco de Mayo *Calles Cuauhtémoc and Cinco de Mayo.* Hours: 7:00 A.M. to 1:00 P.M. A surprisingly small market for a city the size of Manzanillo, but it nevertheless has most of the basics, vegetables, fruits, groceries, and meat shops.

MEDICAL SERVICES

Dr. Roberto Gaytan Farias *Centro Medico, Ave. México and Calle Torres Quintero.* Office hours: 5:00 P.M. to 8:00 P.M. At other hours, call his home, Tel. 20660.

POST OFFICES

Downtown: **Oficina de Correos** *Juarez y 5 de Mayo, Manzanillo, Colima.* One block east of the main square. Open Monday to Friday: 8:00 A.M. to 7:00 P.M.; Saturday and Sunday: 9:00 A.M. to 1:00 P.M. Tel. 28200.

Santiago: **Oficina de Correos,** *V. Carranza #2, Santiago, Colima.* Open: 9:00 A.M. to 1:00 P.M. and 3:00 to 6:00 P.M. Closed Saturday and Sunday. Tel. 28860.

RAILROAD STATION

Two blocks east of main square. For a mere 50¢ in the first-class coach you can take a day trip to the capital city of Colima, leaving Manzanillo at 6:00 A.M. and returning from your independent tour at 4:00 P.M. from Colima. The trip takes 2 hours each way. If the first-class fare seems steep, try your return trip in second class for only 40¢. Departures daily.

SUPERMARKETS

Manzanillo doesn't have a large, well-stocked supermarket, but, depending on the area where you are staying, you may shop for groceries, vegetables, fruits, liquor, etc., in one of the following supermarkets:

Downtown Manzanillo: **Tienda Azul** and **Supermercado Cuauh-témoc** *Ave. México.* Four and six blocks respectively south of the main square.

Las Brisas Junction: **Super Mercado Sedena** This supermarket is for Mexican Army personnel, but it's open to the general public.

Super 10 Mostly canned goods and liquor.

Salahua: **Servi Super** *On the highway, next to the town square.*

Santiago: **Super Camacho** *Calle Juárez, two blocks east of Pollo Norteño.*

TAXIS

Taxis in Manzanillo are not uniformly painted and except for the downtown areas, they don't cruise the streets much. Ask your hotel clerk to call one for you or ask the location of a *sitio de taxis* (taxi stand), which abound throughout the city.

TELEGRAPH OFFICES

Downtown: **Oficina de Telegrafos** *Presidencia Municipal, Manzanillo, Colima.* Located at the main square. Hours: Monday to Saturday, 8:00 A.M. to 9:00 P.M.; Sunday, 9:00 A.M. to 1:00 P.M.

Santiago: **Oficina de Telegrafos** *V. Carranza #2, Santiago, Colima.* Hours: Monday to Friday, 9:00 A.M. to 1:00 P.M. and 3:00 to 6:30 P.M.; Saturday and Sunday, 9:00 A.M. to noon.

TENNIS

Tenisol Hotel at Club Santiago has the best setup in Manzanillo with six Lay-Kold courts with very reasonable fees. The swimming pool is right next to the courts for a dip after the match. Tel. 30413.

TRAILER PARKS

Trailer Park El Cid *Km 9 main highway.* El Cid has 15 crowded, shaded spaces suitable for pickups and cars. It's right on the beach and has separate restroom and shower facilities for men and women (the men's has no hot water). It's about $3 per vehicle with two people.

Trailer Park Sunset Gardens *Km 9.5, main highway.* This is the largest trailer park in Manzanillo, with 75 shaded spaces. All have water, lights, and sewage hook-ups and can accommodate trailers of any size. For vehicles without cooking facilities, there's a section with a cooking area. Other facilities include a pool, a *palapa*, and very clean restrooms, showers, and grounds. One block from the beach. Vehicle space with two persons is $3.

Trailer Park Don Felipe *Playa La Audiencia.* Twenty crowded, shaded spaces with concrete floors. A few steps from the beach. Rates not available.

TRAVEL AGENCY

Agencia de Viajes Bahías Gemelas *Niños Heroes 652 (downtown).* Tel. 21818.

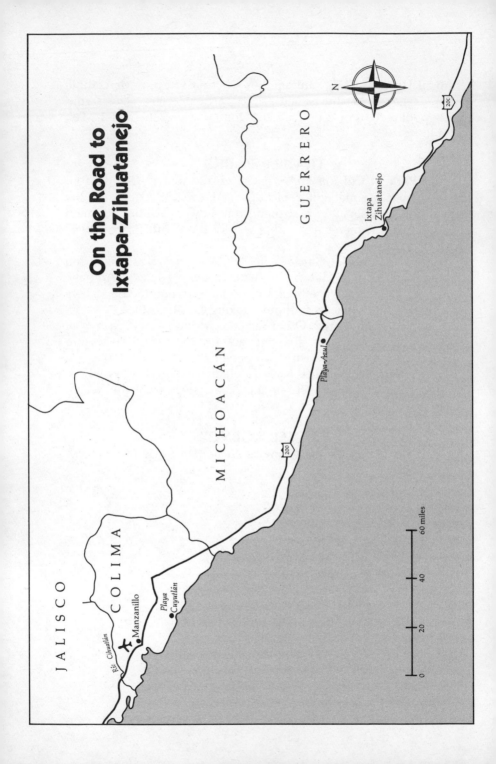

On the Road to
Ixtapa-Zihuatanejo

N

JALISCO

COLIMA

MICHOACÁN

GUERRERO

Río Cihuatlán

Manzanillo

Playa Cuyutlán

Playa-Azul

Ixtapa Zihuatanejo

200

200

0   20   40   60 miles

ON THE ROAD TO IXTAPA-ZIHUATANEJO

The paved road connecting Manzanillo with Ixtapa-Zihuatanejo has been in operation for about 3 years. It is very lightly traveled and scenic; however, there is a stretch on this road where you had better forget about the view and keep your eyes on the road. Between the town of La Placita, 64 km (40 miles) south of Tecoman, and Playa Azul, the road becomes a roller-coaster going up and down several successive mountain ranges. You'll see here more hairpin curves than you ever did in previous hair-raising driving experiences. Every curve in this stretch should be considered dangerous, but they are not marked as such. There are no gas stations between Tecoman and Lázaro Cárdenas, a distance of 210 km (131 miles). Make sure to fill up at both points.

The coastline between Manzanillo and Ixtapa-Zihuatanejo consists of rocky stretches alternating with sandy beaches. Some of these beaches are so-so, some are nice, and a few are great, but this area does not have any tourist amenities (hotels, restaurants, campgrounds, etc.). The only two beach towns located in the area, Playa Azul and Caleta de Campos, are on beaches that could only be classified as great in Siberia or Antarctica.

The only regular visitors to this area's beaches are surfers, who are always in search of the big wave, and campers, who are always in search of that lonely, desolate beach. If you are a cross-breed of the two, pack your surfboard and toothbrush into your pickup camper and head straight for this area.

The best camping beaches and surfing spots between Manzanillo and Ixtapa-Zihuatanejo are found between the towns of La Placita, 115 km (72 miles) south of Manzanillo, and Caleta de Campos, about 160 km (100 miles) south. La Tilla, Colola, and

Maroata bear the trademark golden sand and clear blue waters of other well-known Pacific beaches and are waiting to be discovered.

Remember, when camping on these beaches, you are totally on your own. Make sure you have sufficient water, food, and fuel. The area is not known to be unsafe, but for peace of mind camp next to or nearby local settlements, even if it's just a lone fisherman's family *palapa*. Mexicans, unlike Americans, are not preoccupied with ideas of privacy and private property. On the contrary, they are curious, and sometimes can be too hospitable and friendly, particularly in the case of country folk. It's a good idea to have on hand small gifts (toy trucks, dolls, balls, etc., that you can buy in Puerto Vallarta or Manzanillo) to make friends with kids and to reward them for services rendered.

PLAYA CUYUTLÁN

34 km south of Manzanillo on the Tecoman Highway

Playa Cuyutlán is the most southern of the Manzanillo area beaches. The beach town has a population of about 600 and as a tourist attraction is only a shadow of what it once used to be. Around the turn of the century, this was a popular beach resort for the cities of Colima and Guadalajara when it could be comfortably reached by train. At present, Cuyutlán resembles a ghost town. Out of about ten hotels, only two are open year-round. The other eight are open only during peak vacation periods, such as Christmas and Easter holidays.

GETTING THERE

Bus A few direct buses leave daily from the Manzanillo Central Bus Station.

Car Cuyutlán is about half an hour from Manzanillo on the Armeria-Colima Highway. On the return trip, take the back road, the paved highway heading north at the Cuyutlán main square, which leads right into downtown Manzanillo. The highway is wide and deserted, running right next to the beach, the top of which is the continuous sand ridge on your left. Beware of the rest stops along the way, as I think they were designed by mosquitoes from the Cuyutlán lagoon to catch unsuspecting tourists off guard. To get on this back road from downtown Manzanillo, start at the Savoy Restaurant and ask for CFE (ceh-efeh-eh). From there ask for *camino a Cuyutlán* (road to Cuyutlán).

Train Take the early morning train from Manzanillo to Guadalajara and get off at the Cuyutlán station. Walk or take a taxi into town. Catch the afternoon train back to Manzanillo or take the bus from the main square.

WHERE TO STAY

The only two hotels open year-round are in the cheap category and are located one block from the beach. They are both simple but clean and quiet and have fans.

Hotel Colima.

Hotel Morelos This hotel has the only year-round restaurant. Fish fillet in garlic is only $2.

THE BEACH

With the coming of the wide-gauge railroad tracks around 1910, Cuyutlán became a popular beach resort, but then was overshadowed by beaches closer to Manzanillo. One of its main attractions, then and now, is the *ola verde* (green wave). The green-colored waves are attributed to plankton or algae and can best be appreciated in the afternoon between the months of April and June, when the sun casts its rays from behind the cresting waves.

The beach is a long, wide stretch of fine, dark sand. So fine, in fact, that it's sticky and hard to brush off your skin, and so dark it can be very hot. The water is shallow for the first few feet and as it gets deeper it has a few tricky currents. There is a lifeguard on duty (rare on Mexican beaches). Ask him how safe the water is before going in.

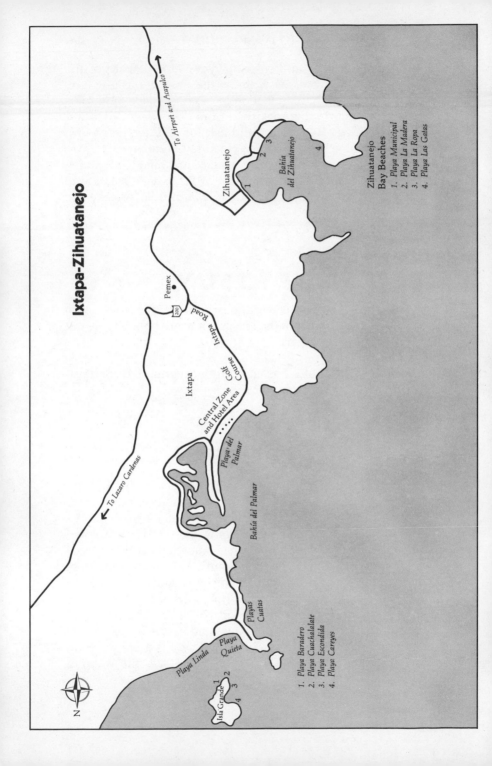

Ixtapa-Zihuatanejo

Over the years many Mexican beach resorts, like Puerto Vallarta, have evolved slowly from sleepy fishing villages to sleepless towns where locals and tourists dine, dance, and have fun while the sun takes a siesta. Zihuatanejo was born as a sleepy fishing village and slowly has awakened to become a tourist town.

On the other hand, Ixtapa was designed as a full-service tourist town, where tourists can relax and be pampered 24 hours a day or play a little golf, a few sets of tennis, or embark on a deep-sea fishing outing.

Zihua is a quaint old Mexican town, while Ixta is an up-and-coming modern tourist resort, but their proximity to each other (a mere 5 miles separates them) blends the two into a unique tourist destination unlike any other found in Mexico.

GETTING THERE

Airplane Aeromexico flies to Ixta-Zihua's international airport from New York and Houston, while Mexicana flies from Los Angeles, Denver, and Dallas. Western Airlines has a couple of weekly flights from Los Angeles.

Bus There are numerous daily bus runs from Mexico City and Acapulco to Zihua. For a few pennies more, take Estrella De Oro first-class buses for faster, more comfortable service. There are no direct buses from Manzanillo to Ixta-Zihua. You must transfer at Lázaro Cárdenas.

Car From Mexico City to Zihuatanejo, the shortest route is the

169

new highway via Toluca and Ciudad Altamirano, a total of 300 miles. The old highway goes via Acapulco to Ixtapa-Zihuatanejo, a total of 400 miles. On both of these roads you will find plenty of Pemex gas stations.

A new road connects Ixta-Zihua with Manzanillo. (Please read "On the Road to Ixtapa-Zihuatanejo.")

GETTING AROUND

You should encounter little or no difficulty in getting around in either Ixtapa or Zihua, or between the two.

In Ixtapa the big hotels, shopping centers, restaurants, bank and exchange house, and discos are located along the first 2 miles of Paseo del Palmar, Ixtapa's main avenue.

In Zihuatanejo the downtown area is a compact, mall-like grid of streets, where you will find Zihua's largest concentration of shops, restaurants, banks, the Plaza Principal, etc. Paseo Cocotal is the main downtown avenue running north to south, with the market and a number of shops located here. The ocean end of Paseo Cocotal as it turns left becomes Paseo La Boquita and in a couple of blocks, at the Japanese Temple Gate turn-around, it becomes a paved road to Playas La Madera and La Ropa.

Zihua's street names are poorly marked, not so much in the downtown area as in its outer perimeters. The main avenue into town, for example, Paseo Zihuatanejo, is unmarked, and forget about street numbers—they simply don't exist.

Buses Regular bus service connects Zihua, from Paseo Cocotal, to Ixtapa's Paseo del Palmar about every half-hour until the early evening.

Taxis For a small town, taxis abound day and night in Zihua. They cruise the main streets during the day, and the main tourist restaurants and bars at night. In Ixtapa there are always a couple of taxis stationed by the lobby of the big hotels.

To visit the beaches north of Ixtapa there is a special bus that you can catch in front of the Dorado Pacifico Hotel.

WHERE TO STAY

The accommodations in Ixta-Zihua are concentrated in four main zones.

Downtown Zihua consists mostly of hotels in the cheap category. La Madera Beach offers about half a dozen hotels in the budget category, all within two blocks of La Madera beach. La Ropa Beach also has about half a dozen hotels and bungalow complexes, all located on the beach, and priced in the top of the budget range and lower end of the moderate category. Ixtapa houses the cream of the crop of the area's hotels. Most hotel rooms are priced in the moderate and deluxe categories.

CHEAP

The hotels in this category are models of cleanliness and are located in downtown Zihua within a block of the town's beach.

Hotel Susy *Corner of Juan Alvarez and Guerrero.* Small, family-run hotel with fans and hot water.

Hotel Citlali *Calle Guerrero.* Among the cleanest, most comfortable little hotels I have ever seen. Hot water, fans, ample patio.

Hotel Avila *Juan Alvarez.* The priciest of the three and only a little bit better than the two above.

BUDGET

Hotel Irma *La Madera Beach.* Terraced into the hillside and offers a good view of the bay from most rooms. Restaurant-bar, pool, fans or air conditioning. Res.: P.O. Box 4. Tel. 42025.

Hotel Posada Caracol *La Madera Beach.* Superclean, friendly, and efficient. With 60 rooms, it's one of the largest hotels in this category. Two pools, air-conditioned rooms, some with sea view. Res.: P.O. Box 20. Tel. 42035.

Villas Miramar *La Madera Beach.* A tiny new place with 12 units. If you think of it as a hotel, it's very comfortable and cozy, but as villas it's a bit cramped. Its rooms would put to shame many of the more expensive hotels in Ixta-Zihua. Pool, restaurant, air conditioning, no ocean view. The best deal for your money. Res.: P.O. Box 211. Tel. 42106.

Hotel Catalina-Sotavento *La Ropa Beach.* Offers a choice of rooms, bungalows, and suites with prices depending on their location. Esthetically, it is an unattractive concrete mass, terraced into the hillside, but is comfortable, friendly, and has a great social atmosphere, particularly in high season. If you think nothing of the fabulous bay views from your room here, it's probably because you found the climb from the beach to your room rather breathtaking Res.: P.O. Box 2. Tel. 42032 or Telex 16208 HOSOME.

Hotel Calpulli *La Ropa Beach.* A simple hotel with about a third of its rooms located right smack along the center of Zihua's best beach and prime beach scene. Ample open space between rooms, shaded grounds with a swimming pool and restaurant-bar. Fans, no air conditioning. Res.: P.O. Box 110.

Hotel Fiesta Mexicana *La Ropa Beach.* A modern, cozy hotel, like Villas Miramar, but right on the beach and with bay view rooms. Restaurant-bar, pool, air-conditioned rooms. Res.: P.O. Box 4, Tel. 43776 or Telex 16219 IRMAME.

Bungalows Palacio *La Ropa Beach.* About 15 bungalows ideally located in the middle of La Ropa. Reservations not reliable.

Hotel Playa Linda *Located at Playa Linda.* Ixtapa's nothernmost hotel and the only one on this long, desolate beach. It has 250 air-conditioned rooms, pool, restaurant-bar, tennis, and basketball courts. Res.: P.O. Box 179. Tel. 43381.

MODERATE

Hotel Villa del Sol *Playa La Ropa.* This jewel of a little hotel is one of the finest in Ixtapa-Zihua with 17 very attractive rooms, each one accompanied by a terrace and hammock. The layout of Villa del Sol resembles a tiny village with a Polynesian flavor. Pool, restaurant-bar, and tennis courts. Modified American Plan, which means breakfast and dinner are included. The food is excellent. Res.: P.O. Box 84 or Tel. 42239.

PLUSH

The hotels in this category are located along Ixtapa's beautiful Bahía del Palmar. All of them are high-rise buildings with several hundred rooms each. Most hotels offer rooms with superb ocean views and less-expensive rooms, but still superb, with mountain views. They offer two or more restaurants and bars, car rental, travel agency, boutiques, large swimming pool(s), tennis courts (usually), game rooms, convention facilities, some kind of night life, satellite TV in some cases, and other services.

Holiday Inn Tel. 42396. Telex 16207.

Hotel El Presidente Tel. 42788. Telex 16205.

Hotel Riviera del Sol U.S. representative: Utell International, New York. Tel. (212) 757-2981 or (800) 223-9868. Telex 424716.
Dorado Pacifico Hotel P.O. Box 15. Tel. 43060. Telex 16215.
Hotel Krystal Ixtapa Tel. 42618. Telex 0016201.
Ixtapa Sheraton Hotel Tel. 43184. Telex 16210 TUIXME.
Hotel Camino Real Tel. 43300. Telex 016203.

RESTAURANTS

I last visited Ixtapa-Zihuatanejo during the summer, or off season. At the time, many of the restaurants catering to tourists were closed for the season and several that were open should have also been closed (preferably year-round). With the help of friends who live there, I was able to compile a list of what are considered to be the town's better restaurants, including those that close during slow season.

Paseo del Pescador *Zihua's waterfront.* A number of small restaurants serving lunch only are located along this shady walkway. They serve the best and freshest seafoods in town and for a couple of bucks you can have live oysters and clams, or seafood cocktails: oyster, shrimp, octopus, or combinations. Seafood soups and many other seafood plates are also available.

KapiKofi *Cuauhtémoc.* A small cafeteria right in the heart of downtown serving sandwiches, hamburgers, cakes, and pies. Serves a good lunch special and the best coffee in town (including espresso and capuccino). Air-conditioned. Open all day. Serves beer.

Mi Casita *Ejido 7.* Superclean and efficient little restaurant that caters to Mexicans craving *picante* hamburgers as well as Americans craving mild enchiladas. Serves mostly Mexican food, including combination plates. Daily lunch special (*comida corrida*) is a real bargain. Open breakfast, lunch, and dinner. Serves beer.

Las Cazuelas *Ejido and Galeana.* Very Mexican décor and Mexican food are the distinguishing characteristics of this popular restaurant and bar. The menu includes traditional *chiles rellenos,* beef Tampiquena, enchiladas, and, for a taste of everything, combination plates. Open breakfast, lunch, and dinner. Tel. 42797.

La Bocana *Juan Alvarez.* One of the most popular restaurants with the locals. In addition to seafood, Mexican specialties such as

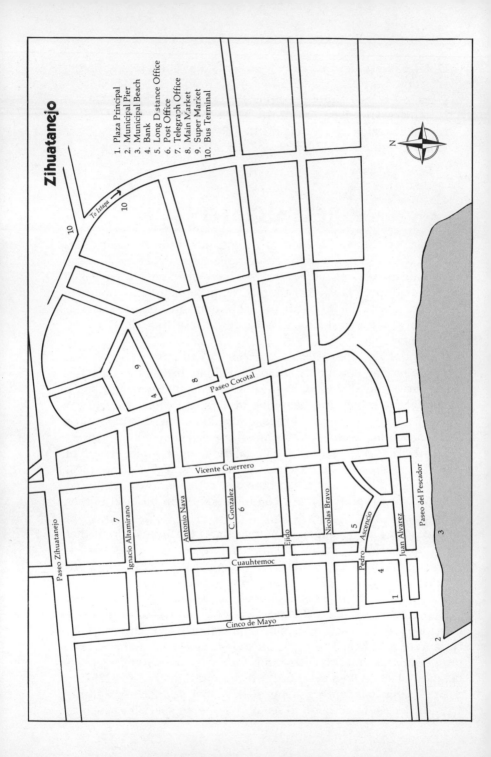

Zihuatanejo

1. Plaza Principal
2. Municipal Pier
3. Municipal Beach
4. Bank
5. Long Distance Office
6. Post Office
7. Telegraph Office
8. Main Market
9. Super Market
10. Bus Terminal

To Ixtapa

Paseo Zihuatanejo
Ignacio Altamirano
Antonio Nava
Vicente Guerrero
C. Gonzalez
Ejido
Nicolas Bravo
Pedro Ascencio
Juan Alvarez
Paseo del Pescador
Cuauhtemoc
Cinco de Mayo
Paseo Cocotal

tacos, tostadas, enchiladas, and *pozole* are served. Open breakfast, lunch, and dinner.

Garrobos *Juan Alvarez near Aeromexico.* Another of the locals' favorite restaurants. Specializes in seafood and features a great paella Garrobo-style. Open all day.

Tacos y Cosas *Pedro Ascencio, behind Aeromexico.* The Mexican's Mexican restaurant. Here just about every plate is a delicious treat, whether you are Mexican or not. Open for dinner only.

Las Brasas *Cuauhtémoc.* Small menu offers grilled pork, beef, chicken, or fish, and a few other dishes. No special décor, no atmosphere, but serves a good meal. Serves beer. Open for dinner only.

Canaima *Paseo del Pescador.* One of the classier restaurants in Zihua. It has large, open windows facing the waterfront. Unfortunately, the place is so bright that you get the feeling that you are going to be interrogated rather than served a fine meal. Menu includes a variety of Mexican and American dishes. Two house specialties are Chicken Pio Pio and Octopus à la Mexicana. Open breakfast, lunch, and dinner. Tel. 42003.

Don Juan *Ejido and V. Guerrero.* A small, pleasant restaurant with a touch of class. Large menu of international dishes such as chicken cacciatore, filet mignon béarnaise, and shrimp pernod. Open lunch and dinner. Tel. 43210.

Hacienda del Sol *Located at Riviera del Sol Hotel, Ixtapa.* Traditional Mexican cuisine served amid Mexican décor and topped with saucy Mexican music. Open for dinner only. Closed Tuesdays. Res.: 42406.

Ville del Sol Hotel *Playa La Ropa.* The restaurant of this posh little hotel caters mostly to its guests but accepts a few outside diners by reservation only. Excellent international cuisine. Tel. 42239.

Villa Sakura *Centro Comercial, Ixtapa.* Tempura, sashimi, and other traditional Japanese dishes prepared at the table. Res.: Tel. 43706.

Coconuts *On V. Guerrero, Zihua.* International menu, patio dining. Very popular in high season.

Los Mandiles *Ixtapa shopping center.* Mexican and international dishes. Open for dinner only.

Montmartre *Ixtapa shopping center.* French cuisine. Open for dinner only.

Pepperoni *Cinco de Mayo and Ascencio.* Italian dishes, wood-fired-oven pizzas.

SHOPPING

Gift and souvenir shopping in Ixta-Zihua is pretty much limited to the standard handicrafts found throughout Mexico. Cuauhtémoc, Galeana, and J. Alvarez streets in downtown Zihua house a large number of shops selling onyx, wood, glass, and ceramic handicrafts and clothing articles from various regions of Mexico. A large and well-stocked arts-and-crafts store is the Guerrero State *Casa de Artesanias* located on Paseo Cocotal in downtown Zihua. Most silver shops are located on Cuauhtémoc, about five blocks from the Plaza Principal.

Shoppers looking for high-quality boutiques will be disappointed to find only a handful of them. They are:

Aramara Women's clothing. One-of-a-kind, hand-made exclusive designs by Beatriz Russek.

El Embarcadero *Cinco de Mayo and J. Alvarez.* Women's clothing. Specializes mostly in hand-made, Indian clothing—Guatemalan *huipiles,* San Antonio, Oaxaca dresses, and smaller items such as belts and bags.

La Zapoteca *Cinco de Mayo and Paseo del Pescador.* Beautiful pure wool rugs and hangings with exquisite designs in soft, pastel colors. Also Yucatán hammocks.

Boutique La Fuente *Cuauhtémoc and Ejido.* Women's clothing. Stylized folkloric clothing.

Once you have exhausted these shopping possibilities, you may consider exploring the boutiques and shops in Ixta's big hotels.

Across Paseo del Palmar from the Dorado Pacifico Hotel is Ixta's shopping center, where, besides a number of restaurants, mini-supermarkets, and exchange houses, you will also find a few arts-and-crafts stores.

NIGHTLIFE

In low season the nightlife can put you to sleep (particularly in Zihua), but the rest of the year there's plenty happening at night. In Zihua the nightlife consists mostly of dinner and drinks, or drinks, dinner, and drinks.

Coconuts, on *V. Guerrero,* is perhaps the town's most popular spot for mingling, meeting, and people watching. It has an outdoorsy atmosphere with lots of greenery and also serves good food. A few blocks away is **La Tortuga** on *Juan Alvarez and Cinco de Mayo*, featuring loud taped rock music. For the best live music and atmosphere, head for **Gitanos**, at *Cinco de Mayo and Bravo*. Here you can shake your anatomy and rattle your bones to the tropical rhythms of Latin music. The bar has a friendly, informal atmosphere and the dance floor is right next to it, so that you can turn into a tropical storm whenever the mood strikes you.

In Ixtapa, every hotel has one or more nightspots ranging from guitar or piano bars to nightclubs with live music or floor shows. Of course, no big hotel would be truly big without a disco. The hotels are so close to each other that you can easily walk from hotel to hotel to check out which nightspot appeals to you the most.

Ixtapa has a number of stylish, well-designed discotheques that surpass most of the discos in the more popular beach resorts such as Puerto Vallarta and Mazatlán. As in discos throughout Mexico, the music played is often dated, so don't expect to hear the top forty.

The most popular discos in Ixtapa are **Christine**, which immodestly bills itself as "the most beautiful disco in the world," and **Joy**, which inaccurately calls itself a concert club. They are both located within steps of the Dorado Pacifico Hotel.

Hotel discos usually attract a slightly older crowd, but the music is still the same. The most popular of the big hotel discos is **La Esfera**, at the Camino Real. The cover charge at most discos is around $4.

At beach resorts, discos are among the most perishable of nightspots. Some open with a fresh new look and atmosphere and become nightlife staples. Others are rotten from day one and disappear within weeks. Ask the younger desk clerks, bellboys, waiters, and taxi drivers which are the "in" discos and other hot nightspots in town. (*¿Cuales son las discotecas, clubes nocturnos, y bares mas populares?*)

BEACHES AND ACTIVITIES

Visitors to Ixta-Zihua are sure to get their money's worth from the quality, quantity, and beauty of the area's beaches.

Playa Zihuatanejo, also known as *Playa Municipal* This popular beach is located right downtown in Zihua, parallel to Calle Juan Alvarez. It is the most protected of the bay's beaches with small waves and waist-deep water for the first 20 to 30 feet. The water is not very clear. On weekends, this beach is packed, hardly the place for peace and quiet. There is plenty of shade and several restaurants serve some of the best seafood in town.

Playa La Madera La Madera starts around the rocky point at the northern end of the municipal beach; however, it is best reached by car or on foot via the same road that leads to Playa La Ropa. Lumber (*madera*) was loaded on to ships from this beach in the distant past. It's a small beach only about 300 yards long, edged by a rocky hillside with calm, fairly clear water and a gradual drop. There are a couple of restaurants on this beach.

Playa La Ropa Of all the beaches covered in this guide, La Ropa ranks high among my favorites. It's over a mile long and has a wide strip of golden, toasty, fine sand. Sheltered by the Zihuatanejo bay, the ocean here is a delight of clear, blue water with curling waves that are a pleasure to duck, jump over, and get splashed by. The grade drops gently, with water coming up to waist level about 20 feet from the edge. La Ropa has several good restaurants scattered along its length. Around the middle of the beach are a couple of beach clubs frequented by the locals. From what I have noticed, topless sunbathing can be done on this part of the beach without any hassling from onlookers. According to its name (*la ropa* means clothing) clothes have always been dropped on this beach. The story goes that in the distant past a ship sank off the coast and the sea washed onto the shore its cargo of clothing and fabrics.

Playa Las Gatas This small, pleasant beach by the southern point of the Zihuatanejo bay can be reached via the shuttle *pangas* that leave from the municipal pier about every 15 minutes. Las Gatas is a fairly shallow, well-protected beach with small waves and possibly the clearest water in the Zihua bay. The bottom is somewhat rocky on both ends, so watch your step. The beach proper is a very narrow strip of fine, whitish sand. For its tiny size, Las Gatas has an unusually high number of restaurants. On Saturdays and Sundays this beach is as crowded as Coney Island.

Beaches in Ixtapa and north of it include:

Playa del Palmar This long, wide, beautiful beach is the soft, warm cradle of Ixtapa's big hotels. It's about 3 miles long and topped with fine, golden sand. Swimming conditions can vary greatly on this beach. Even on the calmest of days the waves can reach a height of 4 to 5 feet before they curl over and break. Nonswimmers should be very careful not to get caught at the breaking point of these waves. The beach does have a wide area where the water is shallow and safe. If in doubt as to the ocean's swimming conditions, look for the warning flags posted by the big hotels. Around the middle of Playa del Palmar, next to Hotel Castel Palmar, is Carlos and Charlie's Restaurant-Bar and Beach Club. Besides food, fun, and drinks, there's a swimming pool and backgammon tables.

The following beaches are reached via the paved road that starts in front of the Dorado Pacifico Hotel in Ixtapa. The farthest of them is Playa Linda, located at the end of this 5-mile-long road. To get to these beaches you may either hire a taxi, take a city bus (in front of the Dorado Pacifico), or rent a motor bike (see "A to Z"). A couple of tiny, hidden beaches along this road are not described here. It's up to you to find and explore them.

Playa Quieta The name of this beach means quiet or still beach. The water is in fact very calm on the southern end of Playa Quieta as it is protected by a land point (Punta Ixtapa) and by Ixtapa Island, directly in front. Here, hardly a ripple disturbs the water's surface and it's shallow for a distance. The beach is about a mile long and from around its middle to its northern end the water becomes livelier with waves reaching a couple of feet in height. Club Med is located along this beach. Its private installations are off limits to nonguests, but the beach itself is public property.

Playa Quieta is the boarding point for *pangas* to Ixtapa Island. There is plenty of parking space right by the beach and a restaurant in nearby Playas Cuatas.

Playas Cuatas The entrance and parking lot for Playa Quieta is the same as for Playas Cuatas, or twin beaches. Except for a beauty mark more or less, these tiny twins are almost identical. They are located at the base of a slope and are lined with a narrow strip of golden sand. They are safe for swimming when the ocean is very calm. On rough days the waves reach up high on the sand and have a strong pull when retreating. A pleasant restaurant sits on a height between the twin beaches. It serves good seafood, drinks, and large portions of ocean view.

Playa Linda Playa Linda means pretty beach and is the northernmost of the beaches in the Ixta-Zihua area. It is indeed a pretty beach, with a long and wide expanse of powdery brownish sand.

That is exactly what stops Playa Linda short of being "Playa Hermosa" (beautiful beach), as the sand gives the water a brackish color. The part of Playa Linda directly in front of Ixtapa Island is safe for swimming as it is fairly shallow and has small waves. A *palapa* restaurant on the beach here serves good seafood, including charbroiled fish, and offers plenty of shady parking.

Ixtapa Island has four tiny beaches within easy walking distance from each other. As you arrive at the island from the 10-minute boat ride from Playa Quieta, you will land on *Playa Cuachalalate*. This beach faces the mainland and is the shallowest and most protected of the island's beaches. It's ideal for children and shy swimmers, but a bit boring for surfers. There are three large restaurants.

Playa El Baradero Take the path behind the restaurants at Cuachalalate and go right to its end. It's a matter of steps before you are at El Baradero beach. It's a small, curving beach with fine, gold sand, nice, clear water waves, and a fairly fast drop. It also has a couple of restaurants.

Playa Careyes, also known as *Playa El Coral* Take the path behind the restaurants at Playa Cuachalalate and follow it to the left. Zoom, you are there. Playa Careyes faces the ocean and has a steep grade and undertow. It's only recommended for sun tanning in its relative privacy, as it is the quietest of these first three beaches.

Playa Escondida As you arrive at Cuachalalate, go left to the end of the beach, then hike over the rocky shoreline till you reach La Escondida (the hidden) beach. It's only about a 10-minute walk, but it's worth it for the greatest amount of privacy that you can get on this popular island. This beach also faces the mainland and has calm waters, but it's a bit rocky. There is no restaurant or shade here.

Playa Barra de Potosi This is the southernmost beach you could visit within the Ixta-Zihua area. It can be reached on a rented vehicle or by taxi (negotiate the best rate). The beach at Barra is 17.5 miles south of Zihua on the Acapulco highway. The first 11 miles (18 km) to Puente (bridge) Los Achiotes is an easy drive. The remaining 6.5 miles (10 km) is a bit confusing, as the dirt road leading there splits into several unmarked branches. Once you are on the dirt road, take the following road branches: first one to the right, second to the left, third to the right, and from there follow the dirt road with the most tire tracks. Don't

take any road with grass growing on it. It sounds more compli-
cated than it is. If confused, just follow other vehicles. The advantage of this personal side trip is that you get a close look at the
area's countryside, with its coconut plantations, cattle ranches,
and the fishing village of Barra de Potosi, with its long, desolate,
unspoiled beach.

Once at Barra de Potosi, you can either relax and sip a beer or
soda in one of the *palapa* restaurants there, have a fresh fish in
garlic, go bottom fishing in the lagoon, or hire a *panga* for a ride in
the lagoon's mangrove vegetation.

Playa Majahua To get to this ignored little beach from downtown Zihua, take Paseo Zihuatanejo up and over the hills in the
northern point of the Zihua bay. The beach is 2 miles away and
unmarked. The reason this beach is not more popular may be its
strong waves and undertow. But for tanning and solitude it's a
great spot.

CAMPING
Hotel-Trailer Park Playa Linda Located 5 miles north of Ixtapa at
Playa Linda, it has 50 unshaded, paved trailer spaces with full
hook-ups, showers, swimming pool, game courts, and other facil-
ities. For reservations and additional information, see "Hotel Playa
Linda."

La Ropa Campground This small campground at Playa La Ropa
is actually nameless. Located at the first entrance, it has grass
grounds, a few trees for shade, showers, and restrooms. It's right
on the beach and within easy walking distance of several good
beach restaurants.

DEEP-SEA FISHING
Since the days when Zihuatanejo was a sleepy little town, it has
been known as a fishing paradise. Back then, a local fisherman
recalls catching practically as many rooster fish as he wanted.
That was about 15 years ago and the fishing then was fantastic.
Nowadays the fishing is just good, but that's good enough for me
and most sports fishermen. There still are, however, some fantastic fishing days to be had. Recent reports tell of sailfish, rooster
fish, and dorado caught right inside the small bay of Zihuatanejo.
The open sea is only about 10 minutes from the municipal pier,
the departure point of fishing boats. Sailfish is available year-
round and the fishing boat captains, most of whom are experi-

enced commercial fishermen, know what to do and where to go
to give you your money's worth of fishing. When visiting Mexico,
there is a tendency on the part of North American fishermen to
set their minds on catching a sailfish, regardless of the time of the
year, which is a little like insisting on skiing in Colorado in
August. To see how good the fishing is, find out what time of day
the sport-fishing boats return. Wait for their arrival, see what they
are bringing in and talk to the fishermen and captains.

Check the municipal pier for the selection of sport-fishing boats
available. They range from fancy fitted outboards to cruiser-type
craft.

A very valuable source of fishing information, fishing equipment, and reservations for fishing trips is Señor Luis Villasenor.
He is the owner of what I consider the Pacific coast's best-equipped
fishing store, La Rapala, located at Juan Alvarez in downtown
Zihua.

SHORE FISHING

Come equipped with a casting rod and reel and an assortment of
1- to 2-ounce saltwater lures. Hopkins and Kastmasters lures
generally work well here. For bait fishing bring an assortment of
hooks and lead weights. In general, try casting with lures from
rocky shorelines, always being careful not to cast in very shallow
rocky bottoms where lurking rocks may catch your lure, never to
let it go. Sandy beaches make for good fishing as long as you cast
your baited hook (or hooks) beyond the surf line (the point where
waves crest and break). On some local beaches, such as Playa del
Palmar, you will need a surf-casting rod, as the surf line is at least
50 yards from your casting point. On other beaches, such as Playa
Linda, the surf is almost nonexistent, but the catch is more often
than not blowfish due to this beach's brackish waters. The cleaner
a beach's waters, the more interesting the catch is. Then you can
hope for surf perch and other exciting catches.

Playa La Ropa During the winter months the surf along this
shallow beach is not too rough and it allows for bait fishing. Make
sure to add enough weight to your line to allow you to cast
beyond the breaking point of waves. On the rocky southern end
of La Ropa, there is a spot that protrudes a bit into the sea and is
ideal for casting with lures. Use 1-ounce lures and retrieve quickly
so they won't get caught in the shallow rocky bottom.

Playa Quieta Try bait fishing along the beach's sandy bottom and casting from the rocky point where boats leave for Ixtapa Island.

SAILING

There are very few Hobiecats or windsurfers for rent in Ixta-Zihua, so you'll probably turn green with envy when you see the Club Med guests sailing around in the tranquil waters of Playa Quieta. Unfortunately, the windsurfers and Hobiecats are there for the exclusive use of guests. Directly across from Playa Quieta, on Ixtapa Island, a Hobiecat can be rented at Oliverio's Dive Shop.

SCUBA DIVING

Scuba diving in the Ixta-Zihua area is best left to experienced, certified divers. In my opinion, the resort courses for first-time divers are totally inadequate and unprofessional. Out of three dive shops, one was manned by very young people (16 or under), another one by a pompous "dive master" whose shoptalk I was unable to understand even in my own language. For one thing, he kept using the Spanish word *inversion* (investment) instead of *imersion* (immersion or dive). I sincerely hope this young man finds a new career in banking or linguistics.

The only shop where I found an acceptable level of professionalism is Oliverio's Dive Shop on Ixtapa Island. Oliverio, the owner and operator of this shop, is around 50, personable, and interesting. With his dark skin, long, graying beard and mustache, and patriarchal looks, he seems like a mythical Mexican sea god who has just emerged from his ocean kingdom. In fact, he might as well have, as Oliverio is Ixta-Zihua's most experienced diver. He knows every diving spot in the area like the palm of his hand and, naturally, the diving conditions and sea life that can be found in any individual spot. Even in the rainy season, when diving conditions are not at their best, Oliverio can take you to the best diving spots available.

Oliverio's shop is located on Ixtapa Island. To make diving arrangements, take the shuttle boats that leave frequently from Playa Quieta. The shop is located at the right end of the beach as you land. Two-tank, one-tank, and snorkeling trips often go on the same boat and last around three hours. Costs are as follows: two-tank $40, one-tank $25, snorkeling $10. All costs include equipment.

The rocky shorelines, bays, points, and small islands that are a treat to the eye of most visitors to the Ixta-Zihua area are a banquet to behold to divers, who are never content to look from afar. A diver has twice the pleasure of looking at the ocean view—once from outside and once from within.

SNORKELING

During the dry season (October through May), snorkeling can be great along the rocky areas of Zihua's and Ixta's beaches. But good snorkeling visibility is never the same from day to day and varies even within the same 24-hour period. In the rainy season (June through mid-October), due to silt and plain mud from heavy downpours, avoid snorkeling along the shoreline. At this time of the year, the best snorkeling is out around the many tiny islands found in the vicinity of Zihua's bay. Snorkeling tours may be arranged through dive shops. See "Scuba Diving."

Playa Las Gatas To get there, see "Boat Tours" for Las Gatas. The best snorkeling area here is the rocky shoreline to the left of the concrete pier where you get off the shuttle boats from Zihua. The visibility is in the 20- to 40-foot range on calm, dry-season days, and somewhere around zilch in the rainy season. From the pier you could snorkel along the rocks toward the south end of Playa La Ropa for around 300 yards.

Beginning snorkelers may start out from the sandy edges of Las Gatas and swim out a bit to catch a glimpse of a school of mullet or jacks. The name of this beach, Las Gatas (the cats), refers to the long-whiskered plankton-feeding nurse sharks that at one time were abundant here. They lie still a ways off the beach's sandy bottom and are as harmless as goldfish. They are, however, a very rare sight and fortunately the only sharks to be found in the area. Snorkeling equipment can be rented on the beach here.

La Ropa Beach Both rocky ends of the beach are good for snorkeling. The south end is an extension of Las Gatas. The north end of La Ropa, at the foot of Hotel Catalina-Sotavento, has a tiny rocky point where snorkeling is good even during the rainy season. A short snorkel around this point and you'll land on Playa La Madera.

Playa del Palmar At the south end of this beach, the shoreline turns rocky and offers good snorkeling on calm days. On rough days the waves may push you against the rocks and hurt you. Around the point from here is the Camino Real Hotel beach. It also offers good snorkeling on its rocky ends. Use your best judgment before snorkeling along the rocks here in bad weather.

Playa Cuachalalate (on Ixtapa Island) This shallow, protected beach is ideal for beginning snorkelers. The rocky ends of the beach house a number of common rock fish such as sergeant majors, a couple of species of angel and surgeon fish. Visibility is around 20 feet.

Playa Baradero Located behind and to the right of Cuachalalate, Playa Baradero is recommended to the more experienced snorkeler. At both of its ends the sandy beach turns into a rocky shoreline with abundant sea life. The water depth here drops quickly and the visibility is in the 20- to 30-foot range. At both ends, you can snorkel for quite a ways. Snorkeling equipment can be rented at Oliverio's Dive Shop on Playa Cuachalalate.

WATER SKIING

Arrangements for water skiing can be made through hotel travel agencies in Ixtapa. In Zihua, inquire at the hotels on La Ropa beach, or at the beach clubs there.

TOURS

Zihuatanejo is an old town, but it lacks the impressive churches and venerable old buildings that can be seen in countless other Mexican towns. For lack of these, the sights visited on the city tour organized by travel agencies include downtown Zihua, its Plaza Principal, the *malecón* (Paseo del Pescador), and a couple of the bay's beaches. The duration of this tour is 3 hours and the cost is around $5. Departures are at 4:00 P.M. For the most part, anyone visiting for a week or so will see the sights anyway in their goings around town.

GUIDED BOAT TOURS

Las Gatas Beach and Ixtapa Island can also be visited on guided tours. Tours for both destinations leave daily from the Ixtapa hotels at 10:00 A.M. and return by 3:00 P.M. The price for either one is around $7 and includes a light lunch.

BOAT TOURS ON YOUR OWN

It's nice to organize your own tour and have the pleasure of discovering places on your own.

Las Gatas Beach *Pangas* for this popular beach leave every few minutes from the municipal pier (Muelle Municipal) in downtown Zihua between 8:00 A.M. and 5:00 P.M. The ride is only about 10 minutes long. Buy your ticket at the base of the pier. The clerk will ask you how many people in your party and will write the number on the ticket. You will show the ticket on the way down but you won't hand it to the boat driver until your return trip. It is best to return around 4:30 P.M. The price of the round-trip ticket is around 25¢ per person.

Ixtapa Island The ticket purchase prices and departures are the same as for Las Gatas Beach, but the departure point for Ixtapa Island is Playa Quieta (4 miles north of Dorado Pacifico Hotel at Ixtapa). If you are really interested in a longer boat ride, you may hire a boat at the municipal pier to take you to Ixtapa Island. The rate runs around $7 per hour for six or so passengers.

A TO Z

AIRPORT

The Ixtapa-Zihuatanejo airport, located 12 km (7 miles) south of Zihua on the Acapulco highway, has an exchange house, restaurant-bar, car rentals, and a few small souvenir and liquor shops. Communal cars and vans offer transportation into town for about $1 per person. To arrange for the transportation back to the airport, call Tel. 42170 or ask for a taxi at your hotel's lobby.

AIRLINES

Aeromexico *Corner of Juan Alvarez and Cinco de Mayo* (Zihua). Tel. 42018.

Mexicana *Corner of Vicente Guerrero and Nicolas Bravo* (Zihua). Tel. 42208.

Western Airlines Office only at airport, open only during departures and arrivals. For reservations or changes call collect Tel. 40716 in Acapulco.

Continental Airlines Same as Western, except call collect Tel. 46900 in Acapulco. Flies here irregularly.

BANKS

Banamex *Corner of Cuauhtémoc and Juan Alvarez (Zihua).* Exchange open until noon.

Banco Somex *Paseo Cocotal, next to the market (Zihua).* Check before exchanging as rates here may be the lowest in town.

Bancomer *La Puerta shopping center in Ixtapa.* The bank's exchange section has walk-in type windows and is supposedly open till 9:00 P.M.

BUS TERMINALS

Zihuatanejo does not have a central bus station, but the bus lines that service it have their terminals around the corner of Pase Paseo Zihuatanejo and Paseo Cocotal. "Estrella de Oro," first-class buses, service Acapulco and Mexico City and are the best for only a few pennies more. "Flecha Roja" second-class buses offer numerous departures to Acapulco and Mexico and fewer to Lázaro Cárdenas and Puerto Escondido.

CAR RENTALS

Car rental offices can be found at the airport, in the lobbies of the higher priced hotels, and in Zihua.

Avis *J. Alvarez 12.* Tel. 42275.

Fast *Sheraton Hotel.* Tel. 43184.

Hertz *Paseo Cocotal, Zihua.* Tel. 42255.

EXCHANGE HOUSES

Zihua's exchange houses are open daily from 8:00 A.M. to around 9:00 P.M. They are located near the corners of Juan Alvarez and Cuauhtémoc and Galena and Nicolas Bravo. Bancomer's exchange house at Ixtapa's La Puerta shopping center has similar hours.

FISHING GEAR

La Rapala *Juan Alvarez, by the Aeromexico office.* Probably the best-equipped fishing gear store on the west coast of Mexico. Gear is no less expensive than in the United States or Canada but at least it is a relief to be able to get it here. Custom fishing rods are made here to your specifications.

GOLF

Ixtapa's **Palma Real** 18-hole golf course was designed by Robert Trent Jones. It is open to the public and has also a spacious swimming pool, tennis courts, and a restaurant-bar. For reservations go directly to the course or ask at your hotel's desk.

HORSE RENTALS

In Ixtapa, arrangements for horseback riding can be made at your hotel's travel agency. On Zihuatanejo's La Ropa Beach, horses can be rented at **El Bandido** at the entrance to Hotel Calpuli.

IMMIGRATION OFFICE

The **Oficina de Migración** is located at Paseo del Pescador, in downtown Zihua. It has standard office hours.

LONG DISTANCE

Long-distance calls can be easily made from the better hotels or from the *larga distancia* office in downtown Zihua. It's located at the corner of Pedro Ascencio and Galeana. Open daily from 8:00 A.M. to 9:00 P.M. (closed for lunch, 2:00 to 4:00 P.M.). Open Sunday from 8:00 A.M. to noon.

MARKET

Mercado Municipal *Paseo Cocotal.* This market has a good selection of vegetables and fruits by the front entrance and numerous butcher shops in the back. Surprisingly for a sea town, there are only a couple of small fish shops. On a side street between the market and Banco Somex is located the town's best-stocked supermarket, open till about 8:00 P.M.

MEDICAL SERVICES

Inquire at your hotel's desk for the house doctor. In town, look in the phone book for English-speaking Doctor Rogelio Grayeb's new address and phone number.

MOTOR BIKE RENTALS

One-passenger 60cc motor bikes can be rented in the parking lot of Dorado Pacifico Hotel, Ixtapa, daily between 9:00 A.M. and 7:00 P.M. The safest recommended area to ride motor bikes is the paved road from Ixtapa to Playa Linda, as it's lightly traveled. The highway to Zihuatanejo is much too busy for carefree motor bike riding.

POST OFFICE

Oficina de Correos *Catalina Gonzalez near the corner of Vicente Guerrero.* Zihua's post office is so tiny and inconspicuous that it is easily missed. You can also buy stamps and mail your letters at the better hotels.

SUPERMARKETS

A couple of small supermarkets can be found at Ixtapa's La Puerta shopping center. They are stocked with toiletries, snacks, canned goods, liquors, beer, and soft drinks. See also "Market."

TAXIS

There is an abundance of taxis in both Ixtapa and Zihua. All major hotels always have a number of taxis parked outside the lobby. In Zihua, taxis can be found all over town cruising the streets. As always, get the rate before you board.

TELEGRAPH OFFICE

Oficina de Telegrafos *Calle Ignacio Altamirano.* The tiny local office is open Monday through Friday, 9:00 A.M. to 1:00 P.M. and 6:00 to 8:00 P.M.; Saturday and Sunday from 9:00 A.M. to noon.

TENNIS

Most of the better hotels in Ixtapa have one or more tennis courts. Some charge for their use while others let their guests use them free of charge. The **Palma Real Golf Club** has several Lay-Kold tennis courts for day and night playing.

TOURIST OFFICE

State Tourist Office is located at *Paseo del Pescador*, by the Municipal Pier.

FOOD GUIDE

As many well-seasoned travelers know, all Mexican cooking is not spicy and does not consist solely of enchiladas and tacos. There are innumerable local, regional, and national dishes found in every corner of the country. In order to make it easier to discover these, here is a guide to help you "digest" the language found on menus.

Adobo A sauce made with *chile ancho,* one of the mildest of dry chiles. Other ingredients are tomatoes, garlic, onion, white pepper, cumin, cloves, oregano, and cinnamon. *Adobo* is usually added to pork dishes, but it can also be used with beef or chicken. If you would like a spicy dish that won't kill all your taste buds, try *adobo.*

Antojitos The word literally means a little craving and refers to a specific category of foods that includes tacos, enchiladas, tostadas, and *quesadillas.*

Chiles Rellenos Many people are acquainted with these stuffed peppers. North of the border, *chiles rellenos* are made with bell peppers; in Mexico, they are made with the mildly *picante* (hot) *chile poblano.* Cheese or ground meat is the most common stuffing, but tuna fish or sardines are often used.

BEBIDAS (BEVERAGES)

Café negro	black coffee
Café con crema	coffee with cream
Café con leche	instant coffee with milk
Té de manzanilla	camomile tea
Té de yerba buena	mint tea

Té negro	black tea
Té helado	iced tea
Té de azar	orange-blossom tea
Refresco	soft drink

Aguas de Frutas Fruit drinks are very common in Mexico. They are sold at street stands and restaurants.

Agua de limón	lemonade
Agua de Jamaica	hibiscus-flower water
Agua de horchata, de arroz	rice water
Agua de tamarindo	tamarind water
Naranjada	orangeade

Cerveza (beer) *Superiór, XX (Dos Equis) lager, XXX (Tres Equis) clara, Corona, Carta Blanca, Bohemia,* and *Tecate* are standard beers. *Brisa, Sol, Pacífico,* and *Chihuahua* are comparable to the light, low-alcohol "dietetic" beers popular in Canada and the U.S. *XX (Dos Equis), XXX (Tres Equis) obscura,* and *Negra Modelo* are dark beers. *Noche Buena* is a special heavy, dark beer available only during the Christmas season.

Jugos y Licuados Juices and fruit drinks are sold throughout Mexico at street stands or formal juice bars with rows, piles, and pyramids of papayas, oranges, pineapples, watermelons, and so on.

HOW IS IT?

Bueno, muy bueno: Good, very good
Delicioso: Delicious
Sabroso, muy sabroso: Tasty, very tasty
Rico, muy rico: Also means tasty or very tasty
Picante, muy picante: Spicy hot, very hot
Picoso: Same as *picante*
Pica poco: A bit *picante*
Pica mucho: Very *picante*
No pica: It's not *picante*
Picante pero sabroso: Picante but tasty
Para chupase los dedos: Finger-licking good

Licuados are made in a blender (*licuadora*) with fresh fruit slices, purified or filtered water, or milk and sugar.

Vino There are many brands of Mexican wine as well as imported wines available throughout the region.

Vino tinto	red wine
Vino blanco	white wine
Vino rosado	rosé wine
Champaña	champagne
Sidra or champaña	apple cider

ENSALADAS (SALADS)

Many visitors avoid salads for fear of catching *turista* or other stomach disorders as a result of the water in which the vegetables are washed. Personally, when a salad is served with the main dish, I ask to have it brought to me on a separate plate. I then drain the liquid from the salad and squeeze the juice of a lime onto it. In Mexico, we believe that lime kills the bacteria in the salad. While eating the rest of the meal, I occasionally stir the salad, eating it at the end of the meal in order to allow time for the lime to do its work.

The most common vegetables used in salads are *lechuga* (lettuce), *col* (cabbage), *jitomate* (tomato), *pepino* (cucumber), *cebolla* (onion), and *pimiento verde* (green pepper).

FRUTAS (FRUITS)

Mexico is fresh-fruit country and most in this region are available year-round.

cereza	cherry	*manzana*	apple
chabacano	apricot	*melón*	cantaloupe
ciruela	plum	*naranja*	orange
coco	coconut	*papaya*	papaya
durazno	peach	*pasa*	raisin
fresa	strawberry	*pera*	pear
guanábana	guanabana	*piña*	pineapple
granada	pomegranate	*plátano*	banana
guayaba	guava	*sandía*	watermelon
jicama	jicama	*tamarind*	tamarind
lima	lime	*toronja*	grapefruit

GO BANANAS

Bananas are usually called *plátanos* in Mexico. But in certain regions of Mexico and other Latin American countries they are also *bananas*.

The type of banana sold in the United States and Canadian markets is known in Mexico as *tabasco* or *porta*. A slightly shorter and chubbier variety is known as *manzano*, while a tiny banana about 3 inches long is known as *dominico*. The largest banana of them all is about a foot long and is known as *macho* in Mexico, while in North America it's called plantain. This banana is usually eaten fried or baked.

Although most bananas are yellow, the exception is a chubby purple banana known as *morado*. This is the tastiest of them all. Try it and go bananas.

limón	lemon	*uva*	grape
mamey	mamey	*uva pasa*	prune
mandarina	tangerine	*zapote blanco*	white zapote
mango	mango	*zapote negro*	black zapote

HUEVOS (EGGS)

Huevos (pronouced "waybose") are cooked in a variety of styles in Mexico. Breakfast (*desayuno*) dishes are often served with a portion of refried beans and tortillas or bread.

Huevos poché	poached eggs
Huevos revueltos	scrambled eggs
Huevos con jamón	ham and eggs
Huevos con chorizo	sausage and eggs
Huevos con frijoles	refried beans and eggs
Huevos cocidos (duros)	hard-boiled eggs
Omelet de jamón	ham omelet
Omelet de hongos	mushroom omelet
Omelet de queso	cheese omelet
Omelet surtido	mixed omelet
Huevos fritos	sunny-side-up eggs

MEALTIMES

Desayuno (breakfast). *Café con leche*, which is milk with instant coffee or milk with coffee concentrate, and *pan dulce* (sweet rolls) is the most common breakfast throughout Mexico. Eggs served various styles, meat, or pancakes are also standard breakfast foods.

Comida (lunch). Just like the sun, Mexican appetites are at their zenith during this part of the day. Ironically, while the sun is burning up a few calories, Mexicans are storing them up for use in the cooler parts of the day. *Comida*, the Mexican's main meal, is served somewhere between 2:00 and 4:00 P.M., except on workdays when it is served about 1:00 P.M.

Cena (supper or dinner). *Cena* can be a full-course meal, like dinner in North America, or a light meal of *café con leche* and *pan dulce*. Usually, Mexicans have *cena* after 8:00 P.M.

Huevos a la Mexicana Two eggs scrambled with chopped tomatoes, onion, and *serrano*.

Huevos rancheros Two fried eggs served on a lightly fried tortilla topped with tomato sauce.

MARISCOS (SEAFOOD)

Seafood restaurants abound in the coastal towns and cities of this region.

Camarones	shrimp
Ceviche de camarón	shrimp ceviche
Camarón empanizado	breaded shrimp
Camarón al natural	boiled shrimp
Brocheta de camarón	shrimp brochette
Camarón a la parrilla	grilled shrimp
Camarón al mojo de ajo	garlic-fried shrimp
Camarón a la gabardina	breaded shrimp
Langosta al natural	boiled lobster
Langosta a la parrilla	grilled lobster
Filete de pescado empanizado	breaded fish fillet
Filete de pescado al mojo de ajo	garlic-fried fish fillet
Filete de pescado a la parrilla	grilled fish fillet

Ceviche A very popular seafood dish, made with boned fillets of red snapper cut into small chunks. The raw fish is then marinated for a couple of hours in enough lime juice to cover it. Black pepper, thyme, rosemary, and salt are added to the fish as it marinates. The acid in the lime juice "cooks" the fish, and at the end of two hours, it's ready. Serve with crackers or fried tortilla chips. This is the commercial recipe. A good homemade ceviche should also have chopped tomatoes, onions, parsley, garlic, and avocado. Then it's really mmmm! Ceviche can also be made with cooked shrimp, squid (*calamar*), and octopus (*pulpo*).

Cocteles Seafood cocktails are made with raw oysters, cooked shrimp, octopus, lobster, or squid, and are served with cocktail sauce, lime juice, and usually a touch of hot sauce.

Langosta Lobsters found in this region are spiny ones without claws.

Langostino Crayfish is mostly served sautéed in garlic.

Pescado frito Whole fried fish is one of the most popular seafood dishes. It's usually made with pan-size fish such as grunts and small snappers, and served with a mixed salad, cabbage, or french fries.

Filete de pescado The best fish fillets are from red snapper (*huachinango*) or grouper (*cabrilla*), but many other fish are also used.

Filete a la Veracruzana This dish originated in the state of Veracruz and is one of Mexico's favorites. It consists of red snapper (*huachinango*) fillets cooked with chopped tomatoes, onion, garlic, olives, olive oil, and fragrant spices.

MOLES

Mole Poblano Originally from Puebla State in central Mexico, mole is the traditional dish for birthday parties and weddings. It's an elaborate dish containing some twenty different ingredients such as chocolate, sesame seeds, raisins, fried and ground bread and tortillas, four different kinds of dried chilies, garlic, onions, and much more. All the ingredients are ground into a sauce, which is served over chicken or turkey.

Mole rojo or chile rojo A simple, quick red *mole* made with chiles (*ancho* and *cascabel*), tomatoes, garlic, and any meat. This dish can turn you into a flamethrower.

Mole verde or chile verde Green tomatoes (*tomates*), used in this dish, are a common ingredient in Mexican cooking. They are smaller than a regular tomato (*jitomate*), but when ripe they turn yellow-green instead of red. Green tomatoes are never eaten raw, as they are quite acid. Besides green tomatoes, *mole verde* is made with fresh *chile serrano*, garlic, onion, and cilantro (a type of parsley). Pork, beef, or chicken is used in this dish. It is another "highly flammable" dish.

Plátano frito Fried bananas are slices of *plátano macho* (*plantain*) fried or baked, and topped with sour cream. If they are fried in butter they are even better.

PUERCO (PORK)

Pork is used in many home-cooked dishes, but in restaurants only a few pork plates are available.

Carnitas	deep-fried pork in tacos
Chuletas de puerco	fried pork chops
Milaneza de puerco	breaded thin pork strips
Pierna de puerco	sliced roast pork in tortas

RES (BEEF)

Albóndigas Meatballs are cooked in many stocks and sauces. The most common are *albóndigas en jitomate* (meatballs in tomato sauce) and *albóndigas al chipotle* (meatballs in *chipotle chile* and tomato sauce).

Biftec Some restaurants in the larger cities specialize in American steak cuts such as T-bone (*tibón*) and sirloin (*sirlón*). Mexican steaks have the thickness of a shoe sole, and, at times, its consistency. The better the restaurant, the more tender the steak.

Biftec frito Pan-fried steak is also known as *carne asada*.

Filete de res A better quality, more tender steak.

Filete de res Tampiqueña Tampico-style filet is a pan-fried steak served with an enchilada, refried beans, and rice.

Filete de res à la Mexicana Steak cooked in tomato sauce with garlic and onions.

Picadillo Ground beef served with tomatoes, onions, garlic, and spices; diced zucchini is sometimes added.

POLLO (CHICKEN)

Pollo frito	fried chicken
Pollo con arroz	chicken with rice
Pollo rostizado	roasted chicken

Pollo a las brazas   coal-roasted chicken
Pollo en mole poblano   See "Moles"

POSTRES (DESSERTS)

Flan Custard with caramelized sauce. One of the most popular Mexican desserts.

Arroz con leche Rice pudding cooked in milk with raisins, cinnamon, and vanilla.

Nieve In Spanish, *nieve* means both "ice cream" and "snow," but in sunny Mexico there is little chance you'll ever be served strawberry snow. Sherbet is called *nieve de agua*, while ice cream is called *nieve de leche*. The most popular ice cream flavors are *coco*, *chocolate*, *nuez* (walnut), *piñon* (pine nut), *vainilla*, *café*, and *pistache*.

Pay The spelling of the English word "pie" happens to mean "foot" in Spanish. Since no one in Mexico would have a foot for dessert, the spelling of the word becomes p-a-y, pronounced just like pie.

Pastel Cake comes in many shapes and flavors, and with a variety of icings.

SOPAS (SOUPS)

A Mexican meal always starts with soup. Broths (*caldos*), consommés, rice (*arroz*) similar to Spanish rice and pasta in broth are considered soups and first courses.

Caldo de pollo   chicken broth
Consomé de pollo   chicken consommé
Consomé de res   beef consommé
Consomé de camarón   shrimp consommé
Sopa de lentejas   lentil soup
Sopa Juliana or de verduras   vegetable soup

Sopa de ajo Fried garlic and bread chunks cooked in chicken broth; a good *sopa de ajo* should also have *chorizo* (sausage).

Sopa de arroz The rice is cooked in tomato sauce until all liquid is absorbed. Without tomato sauce, it's called *sopa de arroz de natural*.

Sopa de pasta There are about two dozen shapes of pasta used for soups; some of the most common are *fideo* (vermicelli), *tallarín* (pasta-shaped egg noodles), *letras* (alphabet soup), and *codo* (elbow macaroni). The most common way to make pasta soup is to fry the pasta lightly, add tomato sauce with garlic and onion and chicken consommé.

Sopa de pescado There are many recipes for fish soup, but it is most often made with tomato sauce, potatoes, carrots, and spices such as thyme and rosemary.

Sopa de mariscos Seafood soup is a variation of *sopa de pescado* with shrimp and octopus added.

Sopa de tortilla Fried tortilla chips are added to a tomato-based broth and are topped with grated cheese. However, there are many variations of this soup, some of which include a clear broth. In some restaurants, tortilla soup may be called *sopa azteca*.

TAMALES

In Mexico, real *tamales* are made with coarsely ground corn dough and pork lard (*manteca*) and wrapped in corn husks or banana leaves. Pork, chicken, or raisins and cinnamon are also added to *tamales* before they are steam-cooked for a couple of hours. If your *tamales* are not served in corn husks or banana leaves, you could very well sue the restaurant for ta-mal practice. The singular of *tamales* is *tamal*, and not *tamale*.

TORTAS

Tortas are the Mexican cousins of submarine sandwiches. They are made with small bread loaves, and like sandwiches, they have just about any filler. Sour cream, onion, and tomato slices, avocado (*aguacate*) and a couple slices of *chile jalapeño* are the usual fixings.

TORTILLAS

Tortillas are made from a dough of boiled, ground corn, shaped like a thin pancake and cooked on a hot iron skillet. Tortillas made with wheat flour are called *tortillas de harina*. Flour-tortilla tacos are called *burritos*.

Tortillas change their name when they are combined with other foods, just as a piece of bread becomes a sandwich when you put ham, mayonnaise, and other goodies on it. Here are some of the most common dishes that use tortillas as a base.

Chilaquiles Made with crumbled, dried tortillas, lightly browned in oil. Tomato, garlic, onion, and *chile serrano* sauce are then added. The sauce is cooked on a low flame until the liquid evaporates and then served with shredded cabbage and sour cream.

IS IT CHILI DOWN SOUTH?

When it's chilly up north, it's "chili" down south, and just like Eskimos have two dozen or so names for different types of snow and ice, Mexicans have at least that many different types of chiles.

To begin with, the Mexican name of this high explosive is *chile* (pronounced "cheeleh"), and the Spanish words used to describe its potency are *picante* or *picoso*. They translate literally into English as "stingy" or "prickly." The English word "hot" translates into Spanish as *caliente* and is used only to indicate temperature.

Many Mexican dishes are traditionally made with one or more types of chiles, and without them, they would be something entirely different. *Mole poblano*, for example, is one such dish. Many other dishes can be made with or without chile. In tourist areas, such as P.V., restaurants often modify their *picante* plates to suit the palates of foreign visitors. To be on the safe side, however, always ask how *picante* a particular dish is.

Enchiladas Made with a lightly fried tortilla, which is dipped in a red or green chile sauce and filled with meat or chicken. The *enchilada* is then folded or rolled and usually topped with cheese and sour cream.

Flautas Rolled, deep-fried tortillas filled with shredded meat; their shape resembles a flute, therefore the Spanish name. *Flautas* are topped with sour cream and shredded cheese.

Quesadillas The word *quesadilla* comes from the combination of the words *queso* (cheese) and tortilla. The best *quesadillas* are made by melting Oaxaca cheese with an herb called *epazote*.

Tacos Take a tortilla, put a couple of spoonfuls of any food in it, fold it, and presto! You have a taco.

Tostadas Crisp, fried tortillas with layers of refried beans, shredded pork, beef or chicken, lettuce, tomato slices, avocado, and sour cream. It's easy to know when you are eating a tostada because it always crumbles to pieces on the first bite.

HEALTH CARE AND FIRST AID

INTRODUCTION BY DR. JOHN H. MABREY

To maintain good health in foreign countries, be informed. When medical attention is needed, get it promptly. An adequate awareness of the culture and the environment is the first step toward maintaining good health. Traveling to and from a tropical climate subjects the human body to environmental changes which may precipitate an illness in the unprepared traveler. Prior to arrival, investigate the weather conditions as well as the time of year most favorable for traveling in Mexico.

Acclimatizing to the new surroundings is the immediate goal upon your arrival. Give yourself 24 to 48 hours to adjust. From November to March, the weather is optimal with slight humidity, good sunshine, and cool evenings. Should you visit mid-June through October, expect showers. Colds, bronchitis, and viral infections are not uncommon during the rainy season. Vitamin C, abundant liquids, and proper dress with rain gear is the ounce of prevention that's worth the pound of cure.

A little sun sense will ensure a safe suntan. Keep in mind the sun's rays are more intensive near water. Come equipped with a good sunscreen and do not overexpose yourself the first few days. A gradual tan is preferable to a fast fry.

Gastrointestinal disorders are the most common ailments among travelers, but with precautions, they can be avoided. Do not drink tap water. Purified water or bottled water is safe to drink. When in restaurant-bars make sure the ice is cube or cone shaped. Irregular-shaped ice has been chipped from ice blocks and is not safe to drink.

Accidents are unexpected but they can ruin your vacation through carelessness. The streets of Puerto Vallarta are made of cobblestone and slippery when wet, plus the curbs are high and, if you're not paying attention to where you're going, could result in an injury. So, watch your step.

Turista What is it?

Bacteria are really the major culprit in *turista*, or "Montezuma's revenge." Bacteria, particularly one type, *E. coli*, are a normal part of any person's digestive tract, no matter where in the world he or she resides. However, some enteric or intestinal bacteria differ slightly from others. These different bacteria enjoy the digestive tracts of people new to their particular region; and the worst of these toxic bacteria often live in tropical zones.

The major reason most people get *turista* or diarrhea is that their systems have not had time to adjust to the new bacteria. When your body initially fights new bacteria, it needs plenty of fluids, i.e., water. Too much heat, alcohol, and sunburn can cause dehydration and a breakdown of the body's built-in defenses. This results in *turista*, which in turn results in further fluid loss. This loss further weakens the body's resistance to illness, and so a cycle is formed. The trick, of course, is to prevent this cycle from starting in the first place. To avoid getting *turista*, follow this advice:

1. During your visit, stick to bottled drinks, distilled and boiled water. *Never drink tap water!*

2. Don't drink alcoholic beverages in excess; they dehydrate you.

3. Do not spend too much time out in the sun; this, too, will dehydrate you.

4. Take a siesta, or relax in the shade during the hottest part of the day (usually between noon and three in the afternoon).

5. Take acidophilus tablets at least 5 days before you arrive in Mexico and continue taking them throughout your stay.

If you do become ill, *turista* will usually manifest itself in the form of diarrhea, but in some cases it will also be accompanied by nausea and/or vomiting, colic pains, and fever and/or chills.

For diarrhea, mash a couple of fairly green bananas mixed with a couple of tablespoons of Donnamycina P.G. or, if bananas are not available, take Donnamycina P.G. or Bentimycin—2 teaspoons every 6 hours. These medicines are available over the counter without prescription in just about every *farmacía* in Mexico. They serve to cut down the colony count of the *E. coli* bacteria in your afflicted intestinal tract and will allow your natural immune system to adapt to the new bacteria (toxic *coli*). Drink plenty of purified water or mineral water with lime. Eat bananas and plain yogurt to re-establish the intestinal flora.

If you are nauseated and vomiting, take Tigon in capsule form (*capsoulas*); one every 6 to 8 hours should help. If this or Alka-Seltzer doesn't work, and if the nausea lasts more than 24 hours, a doctor or clinic should be sought.

If symptoms consist of alternating diarrhea and constipation, flatulence and colic pain, do not attempt to treat yourself, consult a physician.

Too Much Sun With mild sunburn there is redness and the skin feels hot to the touch, but no fever, nausea, vomiting, or blistering.

One folk remedy is to soak the sunburned areas with vinegar or olive oil; let it stay on for a half-hour, then rinse off. Aside from smelling like a tossed green salad, the mild sunburn will quickly become a tan.

For moderate and severe sunburn, there are a number of medications available over the counter in *farmacías* in Mexico. Solarcaine is by far the most popular remedy. Relief is immediate due to the benzocaine that this preparation contains. For ultimate results, apply the healing *crema con savila* (aloe vera cream) between applications of Solarcaine.

Another folk remedy for moderate sunburn is lime juice, followed by a paste made with equal amounts of papaya and well-mashed papaya seeds. Now you will feel like a fruit salad, but the *papaina* from the papaya seeds, which is used in commercial meat tenderizers, may give you relief. After an hour or so, wash off the papaya paste and apply a moisturizing cream, such as *crema con savila*. Most important, remember to stay out of the sun, drink plenty of liquids, and wear a hat.

For the severest burns, see a physician.

Sea-Urchin Spines First remove the spine slowly and carefully with pointed tweezers and/or a sharp, sturdy needle; then get the puncture to bleed. Next, apply *trofodermin* over the afflicted area every 8 to 12 hours.

Coral Scratches First wash off the afflicted area with warm salt water; then apply *trofodermin*. The pain will go away in a short while. This remedy also applies to scratches caused by underwater rocks.

Jellyfish Stings Wash the afflicted area with warm salt water and then apply a paste of papaya seeds and/or *ablandador de carne* (meat tenderizer containing *papaina*, not to be confused with plain MSG). Buy the meat tenderizer in the spice section at supermarkets. Leave the paste on for one hour; then wash it off. Repeat the treatment if the stinging persists.

Scorpion Stings Scorpion stings are very seldom a problem to visitors in this region. In general, the severity of a scorpion sting depends on the size and species of scorpion, the size of the person stung, and the degree of his or her allergic reaction to the sting. The species of scorpions found in this region, however, are not considered particularly dangerous.

Just to be safe, the following precautions are advisable, especially for campers. Scorpions are nocturnal creatures. They like dry, woody areas. They love to hide in cracks, gaps, under tents, inside shoes, etc. So don't walk barefoot in the darkness around *palapa* or wood buildings or dry brush, and shine a flashlight before reaching into dark places.

If stung by a scorpion, stay calm. To inhibit the spread of the poison, apply ice to the affected area and take an antihistamine. If symptoms such as pain, numbness, difficulty in breathing, and stiffness of the jaw persist or seem severe, then seek medical attention as soon as possible.

Campfire Burns Most light burns can be treated with ice to numb the pain and keep down the swelling. Be careful not to apply the ice for too long. Apply *furacin* over the burned area.

Tick Bites Occasionally when exploring the jungle areas, you may pick up a tick or two. The most common type of tick found in this region are about the size of an "o" in this book.

After a hike through heavy vegetation, check yourself for ticks. They love the body's soft areas: scalp, armpits, groin, back of the knees, and between the toes. The most effective way to remove a tick is to touch it with the tip of a lit cigarette causing it to dislodge itself. Do not attempt to pull out the tick, as part of its head may remain in your skin. The treatment for tick bites is the same as for insect bites.

Insect Bites For relief of mosquito, gnat (or no-see-um), and other, unidentified insect bites, apply Caladryl lotion on the afflicted area as often as necessary. Calamine lotion, available in the U.S. and Canada, can be brought for the same purpose. When the bites are numerous, it is advisable to take one antihistamine such as Chlor-Trimeton or Benadryl every 8 hours.

Cuts In general, all cuts should be cleaned well with either Betadine solution, alcohol, *agua oxigenada* (peroxide), lime juice, or, if none of these is available, resort to tequila or another type of alcohol. Remove all sand and/or dirt and apply *trofodermin*.

USEFUL SPANISH EXPRESSIONS

IN THE BANK *En el Banco*

I wish to change _____.
Deseo cambiar _____.
Do you change _____?
¿Cambia _____?
  American dollars
  Dólares Americanos
  Canadian dollars
  Dólares Canadienses
  Dollar bills
  Dólares en billetes
  Traveler's checks
  Cheques de viajero
Do you charge a commission?
¿Cobran una comisión?

How much is the commission?
¿Cuánto es la comisión?
What is the exchange rate?
¿Cuál es la taza de cambio?
Exchange
Cambio
Exchange hours
Horas de cambio
What are the exchange hours?
¿Cuáles son las horas de cambio?
Where is another bank?
¿Dónde hay otro banco?

ON THE BEACH *En la Playa*

The sand
La arena
The water
El agua
The wave
La ola
The sun
El sol
Shade
Sombra

Beach chair
Silla
The coconut
El coco
The coconut tree
El cocotero, la palmera
The shell
La concha
The tide
La marea

High tide
Marea alta
Low tide
Marea baja
Is there a current?
¿Hay corriente?
Is there an undertow?
¿Hay resaca?
Heat
Calor
It's hot.
Hace calor.

Gee, it's hot!
¡Qué calor!
It's cloudy.
Está nublado.
Is it going to rain?
¿Va a llover?
It's raining.
Está lloviendo.
Wind
El viento
It's windy.
Hace viento.

ON THE BUS *En el Camión*

Bus
Autobús or *camión*
Direct
Directo
The driver
El chofer
Does the bus go to _____?
¿Pasa por _____?
I'd like a ticket for _____ at
_____ (time).
Quiero un boleto para _____
a las _____.
First class
Primera clase
Second class
Segunda clase
I'd like a seat by the window.
Quisiera un asiento junto a la
ventanilla.

What time does the bus leave
for _____?
¿A qué hora hay camiones a
_____?
How many hours to _____?
¿Cuánta horas hace a _____?
How much is the fare to
_____?
¿Cuánto cuesta el pasaje a
_____?
Is there a toilet on the bus?
¿Hay baño en el camión?
How long is the stop here?
¿Cuánto tiempo para aquí?

DIRECTIONS *Direcciones*

To the right
A la derecha
To the left
A la izquierda
Straight ahead
Derecho

How many blocks?
¿A cuantas cuadras?
One block from here
A una cuadra de aquí
On the corner
En la esquina

In front
  En frente
Behind
  Atrás de

Near
  Cerca
Far
  Lejos

ON THE FERRY   *En el Ferry*

The pier or the marina
  El embarcadero
What time does the boat leave
  for _____?
  ¿A qué hora sale el barco a
  _____?
How long does it take from
  _____ to _____?
  ¿Cuánto tiempo toma de
  _____ *a* _____?

How much is the fare to
  _____?
  ¿Cuánto cuesta el pasaje a
  _____?
Is there a toilet on the boat?
  ¿Hay un baño en la lancha?

GREETINGS AND FAREWELLS   *Saludos y Despedidas*

Hi
  Hola
How goes it?
  ¿Qué tal?
How are you?
  ¿Cómo está? (singular)
  ¿Cómo están? (plural)
Good morning
  Buenos días
Good afternoon
  Buenas tardes

Good evening
  Buenas noches
Good night
  Buenas noches
Until tomorrow
  Hasta mañana
See you, so long
  Hasta luego or *Hasta la vista*

ON THE HIGHWAY   *En la Carretera*

Paved road
  Camino pavimentado
Dirt road
  Camino de terracería
Hole
  Bache
Curve
  Curva
Speed
  Velocidad

Slow
  Despacio
Stop
  Alto
Danger
  Peligro
Traffic bumps
  Topes
Narrow bridge
  Puente angosto

Cattle
  Ganado
Gas station
  Gasolinera
Gasoline
  Gasolina
Regular
  Nova
Super
  Extra
Fill it up, please.
  Lleno, por favor.
How far is _____?
  ¿Cuántos kilómetros a _____?
Where is the highway for _____?
  ¿Dónde está el camino para _____?
Where is _____?
  ¿Dónde hay _____?

a gas station
  una gasolinera
a tire repair shop
  una llantera
a mechanic
  un mechanico
a spare parts shop
  una refaccionaria
I need _____.
  Necesito _____.
oil
  aceite
air
  aire
water
  agua
a tire
  una llanta
an inner tube
  una cámara

AT THE HOTEL   *En el Hotel*

I would like _____.
  Deseo _____.
  a single room
  un cuarto sencillo
  a double room
  un cuarto doble
  a triple room
  un cuarto para tres
  a quiet room
  un cuarto tranquilo
  kitchen utensils
  untensilio de cocina
I would like a room _____.
  Deseo un cuarto _____.
  with a view
  con vista
  without a view
  sin vista

with a ceiling fan
  con ventilador
without a ceiling fan
  sin ventilador
with air conditioning
  con aire acondicionado
with a bathroom
  con baño
with a shower
  con regadera
with a bathtub
  con una tina
downstairs
  abajo
upstairs
  arriba
in the back
  atrás

with a double bed
con cama doble
with a single bed
con cama sincilla
Do you have _____?
¿Tiene _____?
  toilet paper
  papel sanitario
  soap
  jabón
  hot water
  agua caliente
  cold water
  agua fría
  a towel
  una toalla
How much is a _____
  room?
  ¿Cuánto cuesta un cuarto
  _____?
Are there cheaper rooms?
¿Hay cuartos más baratos?

Does it include tax?
¿Incluye el empuesto?
Do you have weekly or monthly
  rates?
  ¿Tiene descuentos por semana o
  mes?
Do you have rooms with
  kitchens?
  ¿Tiene cuartos con cocina?
I would like to change rooms.
  Deseo cambiar cuarto.
My room is too _____.
  Mi cuarto es demasiado
  _____.
  noisy
  ruidoso
  dark
  obscuro
  hot
  caliente

IN THE RESTAURANT *En el Restaurant*

May I have _____.
  _____ por favor.
  the menu
  el menú or *la carta*
  a table
  una mesa
  food plate
  platillo
  ceramic plate
  plato
  a fork
  un tenedor
  a spoon
  una cuchara
  a knife
  un cuchillo

  a napkin
  una servilleta
  a glass of water
  un vaso de agua
  salt
  sal
  pepper
  pimienta
  waitress
  mesera
  waiter
  mesero
  lunch special
  comida corrida
  house specialty
  especialidad de la casa

hot sauce
salsa picante
a beer
una serveza
a piña colada
piña colada
with ice
con hielo

without ice
sin hielo
Tip
Propina
The bill is wrong.
La cuenta está mal.
Separate bills, please.
Cuenta separada, por favor.

SHOPPING *Compras*

How much does it cost?
¿Cuánto cuesta?
size
talla
small
chico
medium
mediano
large
grande
I want _____.
Quiero _____.
  a blouse
  una blusa
  a skirt
  una falda
  a dress
  un vestido

jeans
unas pantalones de mezclilla
pants
unos pantalones
a sweater
un sueter
a jacket
una chamarra
a shirt
una camisa
a purse
una bolsa
a belt
un cinturón
shoes
unos zapatos
boots
unas botas

TAXIS

How much to _____?
¿Cuánto cuesta a _____?
How many passengers will you take?
¿Cuántos pasajeros puede llevar?
Do you have change for _____?
¿Tiene cambio de _____?

Will you wait _____ minutes?
¿Puede esperar _____ minutos?
I will be back in _____ minutes.
Regreso en _____ minutos.

IN THE LONG-DISTANCE OFFICE
En la Caseta de Larga Distancia

I wish to call _____ (place).
Quiero hacer una llamada a

_____.

collect
por cobrar
person to person
persona a persona
to phone number _____
al número _____
I wish to talk to _____.
Quiero hablar con _____.
With anyone answering
Con quien conteste

I'll pay here.
Pago aquí.
Charge it to my credit card.
Quiero pagar con mi tarjeta de crédito.
The number of my card is

_____.

El numero de mi tarjeta es

_____.

Person calling _____
(name).
De parte de _____.

POLITE EXPRESSIONS *Expresiones de Cortesía*

Excuse me
Disculpe (Use when you ask a question or when you excuse yourself to leave the room or the company of other people.)
Excuse me
Discúlpeme or *Dispénseme* (Use when you step on someone's toe, etc.)
Thank you
Gracias
Thank you very much
Muchas gracias or *muchísimas gracias* (Use the latter expression for emphasis.)
You're welcome
De nada
I'm sorry
Lo siento
Repeat please
Repita por favor
I'm sorry, I don't understand
Lo siento, no entiendo
Pardon me
Con permiso (When you wish to pass someone who is blocking your way.)
Go right ahead
Pase por favor (When you wish to allow someone to pass you.)

ACKNOWLEDGMENTS

The invaluable help of my editors/typists, Laura Patricia Drake and Petrine Burke, was essential in producing this book. *Muchas gracias* in a hundred languages. My sincerest thanks to Harriet Bell, my editor at Harmony Books. My very special gratitude to Toni Valley's public relations firm in Beverly Hills, California, for promoting Mexico and this guide in particular. I am forever grateful to my alma mater, Eastern Oregon State College, and to my friends there: Ted and Mary Brown, Bud Cocknell and family, Bob Sheehy and family and to my advisor, Anne Helm. Last here, but first in my heart are my dearest friends: Laurie Norton, Anna and Helen Billings, Jean Williams, Jan Martin, Stella Johnson and Cindy Hamburger.

POSTSCRIPT

I would very much like to hear your praise, criticism, and comments about the entries in this book. Please address your letters to: Memo Barroso c/o Harmony Books, 225 Park Avenue South, New York, New York 10003.

When in Puerto Vallarta drop by for a chat at The Toucan at Ignacio Vallarta 332.